THE COMPLETE **IDIOT'S** GUIDE® TO

Getting Out of Debt

Getting Out
of Debt

by Ken Clark, CFP

ALPHA

A member of Penguin Group (USA) Inc.

To everyone overwhelmed by debt—I've been there! Don't give up ...
so much can change in just a matter of months!

ALPHA BOOKS

Published by the Penguin Group

Penguin Group (USA) Inc., 375 Hudson Street, New York, New York 10014, USA

Penguin Group (Canada), 90 Eglinton Avenue East, Suite 700, Toronto, Ontario M4P 2Y3, Canada (a division of Pearson Penguin Canada Inc.)

Penguin Books Ltd., 80 Strand, London WC2R 0RL, England

Penguin Ireland, 25 St. Stephen's Green, Dublin 2, Ireland (a division of Penguin Books Ltd.)

Penguin Group (Australia), 250 Camberwell Road, Camberwell, Victoria 3124, Australia (a division of Pearson Australia Group Pty. Ltd.)

Penguin Books India Pvt. Ltd., 11 Community Centre, Panchsheel Park, New Delhi—110 017, India

Penguin Group (NZ), 67 Apollo Drive, Rosedale, North Shore, Auckland 1311, New Zealand (a division of Pearson New Zealand Ltd.)

Penguin Books (South Africa) (Pty.) Ltd., 24 Sturdee Avenue, Rosebank, Johannesburg 2196, South Africa

Penguin Books Ltd., Registered Offices: 80 Strand, London WC2R 0RL, England

International Standard Book Number: 978-1-59257-847-4
Library of Congress Catalog Card Number: 2008933150

13   12   11   8   7   6   5   4

Interpretation of the printing code: The rightmost number of the first series of numbers is the year of the book's printing; the rightmost number of the second series of numbers is the number of the book's printing. For example, a printing code of 09-1 shows that the first printing occurred in 2009.

Printed in the United States of America

Note: This publication contains the opinions and ideas of its author. It is intended to provide helpful and informative material on the subject matter covered. It is sold with the understanding that the author and publisher are not engaged in rendering professional services in the book. If the reader requires personal assistance or advice, a competent professional should be consulted.

The author and publisher specifically disclaim any responsibility for any liability, loss, or risk, personal or otherwise, which is incurred as a consequence, directly or indirectly, of the use and application of any of the contents of this book.

Most Alpha books are available at special quantity discounts for bulk purchases for sales promotions, premiums, fundraising, or educational use. Special books, or book excerpts, can also be created to fit specific needs.

For details, write: Special Markets, Alpha Books, 375 Hudson Street, New York, NY 10014.

Publisher: *Marie Butler-Knight*
Editorial Director: *Mike Sanders*
Senior Managing Editor: *Billy Fields*
Executive Editor: *Randy Ladenheim-Gil*
Development Editor: *Lynn Northrup*
Production Editor: *Kayla Dugger*
Copy Editor: *Catherine Schwenk*

Cover Designer: *Bill Thomas*
Cartoonist: *Steve Barr*
Book Designer: *Trina Wurst*
Indexer: *Tonya Heard*
Layout: *Ayanna Lacey*
Proofreader: *John Etchison*

Contents at a Glance

Part 1:   **How Debt Works**   1

   1   Where Debt Comes From   3
A look at how and why you get into debt problems in America. Includes statistics on debt as well as a brief look at the psychology that may have contributed to you having a debt problem.

   2   Long-Term Debt   13
An overview of the various types of home mortgages and student loans, including warnings about riskier options.

   3   Short-Term Debt   21
A guide to understanding the various types of short-term consumer loans, as well as their unique features that lead you to the edge of financial disaster.

   4   The Math of Debt   29
Everything you need to know about how interest rates and fees turn borrowed money into a weight around your neck.

   5   Denial, Acceptance, and Action   37
A step-by-step guide to understanding the extent of your debt problem and where to begin setting goals for positive change.

   6   Sticking to Your Plan   53
A motivational look at the cost of not sticking to your plan to get out of debt once and for all!

Part 2:   **Your Debt Reduction Plan**   63

   7   Controlling Your Cash Flow   65
One of the most important steps in eliminating your debt will be controlling the money that flows in and out of your household. Includes tips for increasing your income and decreasing your expenses.

   8   How to Make a Budget   75
Everything you need to know about how to build an effective budget without having to get a degree in accounting.

   9   Spending Plans: The Key to Beating Debt   85
Because budgets by themselves rarely work, a spending plan is the most essential ingredient in your debt reduction plan.

10 Expect the Unexpected 95

It's not a matter of if, but when, a large unexpected expense will attempt to send your debt reduction plan back to square one. Learn how to be prepared as well as how to take advantage of surprising influxes of cash.

11 Getting Your Debt Organized 107

Tips, tricks, and techniques for taming the paperwork monster.

12 Creating a Payment Strategy 117

A breakdown of how to decide which creditors you should work to pay off first.

Part 3: Debt-Specific Strategies 129

13 Credit Card Strategies 131

Special tactics for dealing with the biggest source of most people's debt problems.

14 Mortgage Strategies 143

Mortgages are a necessary part of life, but they can turn into an unnecessary evil. Tips for regaining control of an out-of-control mortgage.

15 Student Loan Strategies 157

A deeper look at the primary types of college loans and the most common repayment options.

16 Strategies for Other Types of Debt 169

Strategies for reducing balances and monthly payments on balances owed to the IRS, medical institutions, legal bills, alimony, and child support.

17 Strategies That Can Backfire 183

While these methods can cut your balances significantly, they can also backfire in a big way.

18 Bankruptcy 191

A look at a taboo topic that can provide big relief for the most exhausted households.

Part 4: Protecting Yourself 205

19 Getting Your Creditors Off Your Back 207

Taking a stand against the harassing letters, phone calls, and collection actions.

20   Salvaging Your Credit Score   219
*How to take your credit score from lousy to lovely in a
relatively short period of time.*

21   Guarding Against Identity Theft   231
*Identity theft is the fastest-growing crime in America.
Learn how to guard your credit and your good name, so
you don't waste years of your life trying to prove certain
debts aren't yours.*

22   Avoiding Scams and Rip-Offs   243
*The stress that comes from debt leaves people vulnerable
to scam artists offering extreme solutions. Knowing the
warning signs of debt relief scams and rip-offs will save you
time, money, and heartache.*

Part 5:   Life After Debt   253

23   You and Debt: Is It Really Over?   255
*While we've spent most of the book viewing debt as an
enemy, there are still certain times when it will pay to
make it your ally. Know the limits and rules of thumb
before you get in over your head again.*

24   Tools and Tips for Staying Out of Debt   267
*Staying out of debt isn't just about keeping credit cards out
of your wallet, but also about planning for life's big events.
Spend some time reviewing the big financial goals we all
have in common and how to prepare for them so your use of
debt is minimized.*

25   Passing Along Good Debt Skills   279
*Besides the fact that you'd hate to see your loved ones not
learn from your own lessons with debt, their bad habits can
also affect you as you're forced to come to the rescue. Learn
how to set your loved ones up for success and pass on the
lessons of your war with debt, not the experience itself.*

Appendixes

A   Glossary   291

B   Sample Letters   299

C   Resources   305

D   Student Loan Forgiveness Programs   313

Index   317

Contents

Part 1:   **How Debt Works**   **1**

  1   **Where Debt Comes From**   **3**

      Learn from My Story 4

      A Tale of Two Frogs 5

      Stats to Make You Feel Better (and Worse)! 6

      Businesses and You: Partners in Crime 7

      Not All Debt Is Bad 8

        Good Debt vs. Bad Debt 8

        Identifying Your Needs and Wants 9

        Appreciating vs. Depreciating Assets 10

      Avoiding the Unavoidable 10

      You Bought This Book for a Reason … 11

      … So Read It with Purpose! 12

  2   **Long-Term Debt**   **13**

      Risks of Long-Term Debt 14

      Mortgage and Real Estate Debts 14

        Fixed-Rate Mortgages 15

        Adjustable-Rate Mortgages (ARMs) 16

        Interest-Only Loans 17

        Payment-Optional or "NegAm" Loans 17

      Student Loans 18

        Government Programs 19

        Private Loans 19

  3   **Short-Term Debt**   **21**

      Credit Card Debt 22

        The Major Credit Card Companies 22

        Retail Credit Cards 22

        Installment Purchases 23

      Other Types of Debt 23

        Auto Loans 24

        401(k) and Retirement Plan Loans 24

        Payday Loans 25

        Medical Bills 25

        Legal Bills 26

Child Support and Alimony 27
The IRS and Other Government Agencies 27

4 The Math of Debt **29**

How Interest Rates Work 30
Simple Interest Loans 30
Compound Interest 31
The Minimum Payment Trap 32
Minimum Payment—Maximum Time 33
Fees, Fees, and More Fees 33
The Fine Print Isn't So Fine 34

5 Denial, Acceptance, and Action **37**

Debt and Denial 38
How Bad Is It? 39
What Is Your Monthly Debt Service? 40
Could You Get a Loan If You Needed It? 40
Tracking Your Progress 42
What's Your Credit Score? 43
Credit Scores and Monthly Payments 44
Is Someone Making It Worse? 45
The In's and Out's of Change 46
Change Your Lifestyle and Your Spending Habits 46
Reward Yourself Along the Way 47
Start Today 47
Set Realistic Goals 48
The Need for Accountability 48
Should I Get Professional Help? 50

6 Sticking to Your Plan **53**

Opportunity Costs: Understanding What You Are Missing 54
Opportunity Cost #1: Your Future Goals 55
Retirement: The Mother of All Financial Goals 55
Four Immediate Retirement Strategies 57
College Costs 58
Opportunity Cost #2: Paying Less Interest 59
Opportunity Cost #3: Your Health and Sanity 60

Part 2: **Your Debt Reduction Plan** **63**

7 Controlling Your Cash Flow **65**

Discretionary Income Is the Key..66
The Formula for Discretionary Income............................*66*
Fixed vs. Variable Expenses..*67*
Ways to Increase Discretionary Income.................................68
Twelve Ideas for Increasing Income...............................*69*
Twelve Ideas for Decreasing Fixed Expenses....................*70*
Twelve Ideas for Decreasing Variable Expenses..................*72*

8 How to Make a Budget **75**

The Purpose of a Budget...76
What a Budget Is—and Isn't..76
The Basic Ingredients of Any Budget....................................77
The Three Types of Budgets..77
The Ideal Budget...*77*
The Actual Budget..*78*
The Compromise Budget..*79*
Time to Do Your Budget!..80
Avoiding Budgeting Pitfalls...83

9 Spending Plans: The Key to Beating Debt **85**

Why Do Budgets Fail?..86
There's Too Much to Remember *86*
No Barriers to Impulsive Spending...................................*87*
Spending Plans to the Rescue!...88
Using Your Compromise Budget to Create a Spending Plan....89
The Envelope System...90
The Two-Account System..90
Step 1: Open Two Bank Accounts....................................*91*
Step 2: Use the Fixed Account for All Your Fixed Expenses..........*91*
Step 3: Transfer Your Variable Expenses to the Second Account....*91*
Step 4: Keep Your Eye on the Bottom Line..........................*91*
Step 5: Decide What to Do with Your Discretionary Income.........*92*
The Three-Account System for People Sharing Finances.........92
Adjusting Your Spending Plan...93

10 Expect the Unexpected **95**

The Problem with the Unexpected 96
   The Top Five Expenses That Catch Us Off Guard 96
   The Five Biggest Windfalls We Tend to Waste 97
Was It Really Unexpected? 98
Strategies for Dealing with Unexpected Expenses 98
   Pay It All Now 99
   Request a Payment Plan 99
   If You Have to Borrow … 100
   Learn from the Experience 101
Strategies for Dealing with Unexpected Windfalls 102
   Think About How Much You'd Save 102
   Eliminate Debt Once and for All 103
   Decide on a Formula in Advance 104
   Talk About It and Sleep on It 105

11 Getting Your Debt Organized **107**

Taming the Paperwork Monster 108
   Open Your Bills Immediately 109
   Review the Details 110
   Transfer the Balances to Your Chart 110
   Write Next Month's Payment Now 110
   File Your Essential Paperwork 111
   Shred the Rest 112
Using Technology to Simplify 112
   Get Your Paycheck Direct Deposited 112
   Pay Your Bills Online and Automatically 113
   Use Online Account View and E-Lerts 114
   Personal Accounting Software 114
When to Avoid Technology 115
   Don't Rely on Online Statements 115
   Avoid E-Mailing Your Creditors 115
   Avoid Shopping Online 116

12 Creating a Payment Strategy **117**

As Much as You Can, as Soon as You Can 118
Use the Roll-Down Method 118
Debt Elimination: The Ugly, the Bad, and the Good 120
   The Ugly: Debts to Eliminate ASAP 120
   The Bad: Debts to Get Rid of Sooner Than Later 121
   The Good: Debts to Get Rid of Last 122

Where to Put That Extra Cash 123
  The Highest-Interest-Rate Debts................................*123*
  The Debts with the Smallest Balances........................*124*
  The Largest Balances...*125*
  The Debts That Affect Your Credit Score Most..........*125*
  Accounts That You Plan on Closing...........................*125*
  Those with Nondeductible Interest............................*126*
  The Most Stressful Debts..*127*
Changing Your Strategy Midway....................................127

Part 3: Debt-Specific Strategies   129

13 Credit Card Strategies   131
The Trick to Paying Off Credit Cards.............................132
Stop Using Your Credit Card for Day-to-Day
  Expenditures...132
Keep the Credit Cards out of Your Wallet 133
So That Means I Should Cancel All My Credit Cards?..........134
Silver Bullets for Reducing Your Credit Card Balances..........134
  Negotiate a Lower Rate..*135*
  Transfer Your Balance to Another Card.....................*136*
  Use Your Home Equity to Pay It Off..........................*137*
  Consider Balance Reduction and Debt Settlement........*138*
  Consolidate Your Credit Cards..................................*140*
  Use Your Credit Insurance *141*

14 Mortgage Strategies   143
Getting to Know Your Mortgage 144
  "What If" #1: Interest Rates Adjust...........................*145*
  "What If" #2: Balloon Payment Is Coming Due...........*145*
  "What If" #3: Your Principal Isn't Shrinking.............*146*
Refinancing: A Bad Mortgage's Best Friend 146
  Refinancing an Adjustable Rate to a Fixed Rate..........*147*
  Refinancing a Shorter Term to a Longer Term...........*147*
  Refinancing an Interest Only or NegAm to a Fixed.........*148*
  Refinancing a HELOC into a Fixed Mortgage.............*148*
  Knowing When to Refinance......................................*148*
  Origination, Points, and Closing Costs ... Oh My!........*149*
  Choosing a Lender You Can Trust..............................*150*
When You Can't Refinance...150
Foreclosure: The Final Frontier......................................152

Strategies for Not So Rainy Days...153
The Biweekly Payment..*154*
PMI: Insurance You Don't Need *154*

15 Student Loan Strategies **157**

The Student Loan Stew..158
Stafford Loans *158*
Perkins Loans *159*
PLUS Loans...*159*
Private (for Profit) Lenders...*160*
The Standard Repayment Options...161
Reducing Your Student Loan Payments.................................162
Student Loan Consolidation...*163*
Deferment *164*
Forbearance *164*
Loan Forgiveness Programs..*165*
What to Do If You're in Default 166
Loan Rehabilitation *167*
Consolidation to Fix Your Default..*167*

16 Strategies for Other Types of Debt **169**

Payday Loans..170
Breaking the Payday Loan Cycle *170*
Getting Help with Food Costs...*172*
Car Loan Strategies..172
Pay More Than the Minimum..*173*
Refinance Your Auto Loan...*173*
Pay Off Your Car with a HELOC *174*
Other Expenses..175
Curing Your Medical Bills..*176*
Settling Legal Debts *178*
Dealing with Alimony and Child Support *178*
Standing Up to the IRS 180
The IRS Penalty System *180*
Installment Agreements and Offers in Compromise....................*181*

17 Strategies That Can Backfire **183**

Three Important Questions...184
Taking a Loan from Your Retirement Plan.............................185
Debt Consolidation 186

Debt Settlement 187

Borrowing from Friends or Family 187

Other Strategies to Avoid..189

   Credit Card Checks..189

   Tax Refund Loans...189

   Loans from Pawnshops 189

   Getting Paid Under the Table 190

18 Bankruptcy   191

Overview of Bankruptcy...192

   Chapter 7..193

   Chapter 13..193

   Chapter 11..194

   Chapter 12..194

   Chapter 15..195

The Benefits and Limits of Bankruptcy 195

   What Bankruptcy Will Do..195

   What Bankruptcy Won't Do 197

Recent Changes in Bankruptcy Laws 198

   The "Means" Test..198

   Debt Counseling 199

   Automatic Stays...199

   Not Filing Your Tax Returns.......................................200

How to File for Bankruptcy.....................................200

The Hidden Costs of Bankruptcy 201

   Your Credit Score Will Plummet................................201

   You're Going to Get Asked 201

   Jobs and Apartments May Become Harder to Get......202

   Your Ego and Reputation May Take a Beating 202

Part 4: Protecting Yourself   205

19 Getting Your Creditors Off Your Back   207

Understanding Your Creditors 208

Your Rights Under the Consumer Credit Protection Act........209

   The Fair Debt Collection Practices Act (FDCPA) 210

   The Fair Credit Billing Act (FCBA)............................211

   Restriction on Garnishment Act 212

   Truth in Lending Act (TILA).......................................212

Predatory Lending Laws...213

Usury Laws...214
Face-to-Face Encounters 215
Important Steps in an Auto Repossession.....................215
Important Steps in an Eviction....................................216
Important Steps to Keep Your Utilities On....................217
Reporting Violations of Your Rights 218

20 Salvaging Your Credit Score **219**

Credit Score Basics..220
Your Fair Isaac Corporation (FICO) Score 220
Other Major Credit Scores..221
The Credit Score Formula 222
Payment History..223
Credit Utilization..224
Length of Credit History...224
Credit Inquiries 225
Types of Credit Used 226
So What Really Screws Up Credit Reports? 227
How Long Does Stuff Stay on Your Report? 228
Steps to Raise Your Score 229

21 Guarding Against Identity Theft **231**

Are You at Risk? 232
The High Cost of Identity Theft 233
How Identity Theft Happens 234
Protecting Your Vital Information..............................235
Phishing 237
Spoofing 239
Monitoring Your Identity...239
Checking Your Credit Report......................................240
Credit Monitoring Services 240
Review Every Statement...240
The Next Steps If You've Been a Victim....................241

22 Avoiding Scams and Rip-Offs **243**

Back to the Basics..244
The Biggest Wastes of Money.....................................244
Debt Elimination..245
Debt Negotiation 246
Free Credit Reports..246

Credit Protection...246
Credit Repair..247
Seminars and Workshops 247
Get-Rich Schemes That Don't Work 248
Multilevel Marketing 248
Easy Money in Real Estate......................................248
Day-Trading and Currency Transactions 249
Scams That Are Also Illegal.................................249
Nigerian 419 Scams 250
Chain Letters...250
If You've Been Scammed or Duped.........................251

Part 5: Life After Debt   253

23 You and Debt: Is It Really Over?   255
A Shift in Attitude 256
You Can't Live Without Borrowing..............................256
Budgeting Is Impossible Without a Credit Card 257
Using Credit for Life's Big Purchases 257
It Pays to Have Debt 257
You Need to Borrow to Build Credit 258
You Won't Be Able to Handle Emergencies Without Debt 258
Getting Your Last Hurrah 258
Rules of Thumb for Future Use of Credit...................260
Rules of Thumb for Mortgages 261
Rules of Thumb for Student Loans 261
Rules of Thumb for Car Loans 262
Taking Your Time 262
Debt and Love: Yours, Mine, and Ours 264

24 Tools and Tips for Staying Out of Debt   267
Sticking with What Works...................................268
Your Most Immediate Financial Goal............................268
Planning Ahead to Have Fun 269
Breaking the Auto Loan Cycle 269
Stretching the Useful Life of Your Car 270
Continuing to Make Payments to Yourself 271
Repeat This Healthy Cycle.....................................272
Being Properly Insured 272
Health Insurance 272
Auto Insurance 273

Disability Insurance 273
Long-Term Care.. 274
Homeowner's Insurance and Renter's Insurance 274
Liability Insurance 275
Life Insurance.. 275
Putting an End to Solicitations................................... 276

25 Passing Along Good Money Skills   279

Keep Your Debt from Being Traumatic … 280
Your Debt Is Not Their Fault 280
Avoid Guilt Trips... 281
Don't Use Debt to Say No...................................... 282
Money Attitudes Are Contagious 283
Delayed Gratification... 284
Contentment.. 284
Prudence... 285
Helping Your Kids Manage Debt Wisely........................... 285
Teaching Them to Save 286
Preparing Them for All That Debt Offers.......................... 287
The Myth That They Should Build Credit 287
Co-Signing for Your Child...................................... 288
Get Them Thinking About Retirement 288

Appendixes

A Glossary   291

B Sample Letters   299

C Resources   305

D Student Loan Forgiveness Programs   313

Index   317

Introduction

Managing your finances is like driving a car down a winding mountain road. Take your eyes off the road for just a second and you can end up upside down in a ditch. In personal finance, that ditch is a thing we call debt.

Debt is far more than just a balance or two that you owe to someone. It's a parasite that seems to cling to you, sucking away your energy and joy, continuing to grow and grow even as you do your best to get rid of it.

If that sounds familiar, then I'm glad you found this book. My hope is that it will serve you in many different ways, ranging from emotional support for your situation to tactical advice about the next steps.

The good news is, you're not the only one. Enough of us have gone through this that there are answers about how to end your cycle of late bills, phone calls from creditors, and mounting credit card balances. Even better, this book comes fresh on the heels of the most chaotic economic period of the last three decades. It's written with a new breed of consumers in mind. There's hope and wisdom for the overstretched mortgage owner. There are practical tips for households getting nickel-and-dimed by higher gas prices and other types of inflation. Especially important, there's some tough love for people who need to hear it when it comes to their spending habits.

But before we go any further, let me give you the first and most important lesson in debt reduction. It's hope. Hope that things can be different than they are now. Hope that it'll never be like this again. Hope that you'll regain control and regain your life.

I promise you that if you take and apply the principles in this book, change will occur. Not overnight, as I like to say, but inevitably. One to two years from now, things can and will be so different that you'll look back and laugh about where you are right now.

How's all that going to happen? I've written this book to help you accomplish five main tasks:

- ◆ Understand debt and how it crept into your life.

- ◆ Give you step-by-step instructions for changing the way money flows in and out of your household.

- ◆ Arm you with strategies to deal with each type of unique debt.

- ◆ Educate you on how to protect your credit score, your identity, your sanity with pushy creditors, and what little cash you might have.

- ◆ Prepare you to live in a way that ensures you'll never return to a lifestyle plagued by debt.

How to Use This Book

Like someone working a gigantic jigsaw puzzle, you'll go about these tasks very systematically. Everything you read will be used as the building blocks for the skills outlined in later chapters. While all the chapters are written to be standalone resources if you need them, your best education and highest likelihood for permanent change will come if you read this book straight through.

Part 1, "How Debt Works," helps you establish a vocabulary and working knowledge of the different types of credit and loans. You learn how to break debt down into categories like long- and short-term debt, as well as "good, bad, and ugly" debt. Moving forward without this information would be like trying to work that jigsaw puzzle while blindfolded. You also take a layman's look at the math of debt and a psychologist's look at the emotions that surround dealing with your debts.

Part 2, "Your Debt Reduction Plan," is the meat and potatoes of this book. It's where you find the most important techniques you need to conquer debt. We take a good look at how money flows in and out of your household, why budgets by themselves almost always fail, and how to create a spending plan that virtually assures you make progress on paying your balances off. You also end up with a shopping cart full of tips about how to deal with unexpected financial events and how to tame the paperwork monster.

Part 3, "Debt-Specific Strategies," contains tidbits and wisdom for dealing with each kind of debt that will turbocharge your debt reduction plan. You learn the tricks of the trade that'll help you make significant progress trimming your credit card, mortgage, and student loan balances. You also get armed with a working knowledge of how to attack medical, legal, alimony, child support, and IRS bills. And to make sure you don't get detoured in your quest for financial freedom, we also review some of the popular and much talked about strategies that backfire on a regular basis.

Part 4, "Protecting Yourself," teaches you how to get creditors off your back, keep identity thieves off your trail, and get your credit score to where it should be. You get an insider's view of the mysterious FICO score and a courtroom view of your rights as a consumer and borrower.

Part 5, "Life After Debt," takes everything you've learned and crystallizes it into a new lifestyle. It helps you navigate the future uses of debt that are inevitable, teaches you how to plan for some of life's biggest events so that you don't have to borrow to fund them, and shows you how to pass on healthy money skills to your kids and family.

You'll also find four helpful appendixes that help you address specific debt challenges: a glossary; easy-to-use sample letters to send to your creditors; resources of books, websites, and organizations; and a directory of student loan forgiveness programs.

Extras

As you go into battle against your debt, I want to make sure that you have the best weapons at your side. To help ensure that, you'll find some easy-to-recognize sidebars throughout the book. They contain tips, tricks, key definitions, cautions, and some encouragement to set certain goals.

Dollars and Sense

These are some of the best pieces of advice and follow-up steps I've compiled over my career as a financial planner. Each one will help you trim just a little bit more debt out of your life.

In the Red

One of the most frustrating things is working hard to make progress only to feel like you're sliding backward. These "red flags" will help you identify things that need to change and actions you need to avoid.

Set a Goal

Some of the chapters include an action step that I want you to take right then and there before you read any further. Keep a pen and pad of paper handy, because you'll be writing a lot of these goals down for easy reference!

Debt in America

The assurance that you aren't alone in the journey is crucial to not getting too over-whelmed. Throughout the book, you'll find statistics about credit and debt usage in America.

def•i•ni•tion

Using the proper terminology will help you fully understand your situation as well as let your creditors know that you mean business.

Acknowledgments

First and foremost, I'd like to thank my amazing team at Alpha Books, including a very special thanks to my editors Randy Ladenheim-Gil and Lynn Northrup. I could not have written this book without your patience and expertise.

To my agent, Bob Diforio at D4EO Literary Agency. I will be thankful for the rest of my career for you taking the time and a chance on a newcomer.

To my editors and friends at About.com and Helium.com; you've all contributed so much to me as a writer and a journalist.

To my high school literature teacher, Mollee Merrill; thanks for putting so much amazing literature in front of my face and teaching me the joy of telling stories!

To Josh Beauchaine, a gifted friend and family therapist. I'm deeply indebted to you for everything you've taught me about how to listen to people, hear the hidden messages, and journey with them toward solutions.

To my entire extended family, but especially my dad, Ken Clark Sr. Everything I know about personal finances and being a financial planner is built on the foundation you've laid. Thanks for being an amazing mentor and friend.

To my precious kids, Drew, Price, and Ryan. You got a lot less of me than I wanted to give during the busiest months of writing this book. I look forward to making up for it!

But most of all, to my amazing wife, Michele. In the years when we had the least, you made me the richest man in the world. The debt I owe to you can't be repaid in a lifetime.

Trademarks

All terms mentioned in this book that are known to be or are suspected of being trademarks or service marks have been appropriately capitalized. Alpha Books and Penguin Group (USA) Inc. cannot attest to the accuracy of this information. Use of a term in this book should not be regarded as affecting the validity of any trademark or service mark.

How Debt Works

In his classic book *The Art of War*, famous Japanese philosopher Sun Tzu advises you to "know your enemy." Never is this more true than when you step into the ring to do battle with debt—one of the most formidable enemies of your time.

If you don't understand where your debt came from, how it works, and the things inside of you that hold you back, you'll be like someone throwing stones at a tank. But if you understand how these things work, you can find the weak spot in your debt's armor.

In this part, you'll become familiar with the basic components of the different types of debt. Then, you'll look at how the math of debt slowly sneaks up on you. Finally, you'll do a little battle with your greatest enemy … yourself.

Where Debt Comes From

In This Chapter

◆ Realizing you're not the only one

◆ America's problem with debt

◆ Credit: easy to use, and easier to abuse

◆ Why debt isn't always bad

◆ A change in mind-set

Let me start by telling you what this book is *not*. It is not just a book about how to pay off your loans, lower your credit card balances, or get your creditors to leave you alone. While I do talk about how to deal with all those different types of "debts" that you might owe, this book more importantly addresses the underlying mind-set of "debt." It is meant to help you eliminate both the symptoms of a problem, and the problem itself.

As you'll see, debt isn't just a "thing" you find yourself in, or owing. If it were, it'd be easy enough for you to create a plan to get out of it. Rather, debt for many becomes an action, a cycle, and a mind-set. Some might even call it a lifestyle. "Debt" is the ongoing state of borrowing money to finance a way of life. "Debt" is a way of managing your money so that you can enjoy more than what your income will buy you at a given moment.

And of course, "debt" becomes a weight around many people's necks that results in them drowning financially.

In fact, debt has become a way of life for many people living in the United States. You might even argue that it's one of the things that truly make us American. According to various statistics, everyone from college graduates to senior citizens, from the underpaid to the overpaid, is drowning under the tidal wave of debt. Even trained financial planners like, ahem, the author of this book, have found themselves in debt at some point.

So just like a good plumber who fixes a leak by finding the source, you must first try to understand how you got yourself into this mess. If you don't, chances are you'll make a little progress only to experience a discouraging slide backward. That's what this chapter is all about: taking a look at the source of your debt problems.

Learn from My Story

One of my core beliefs as a financial planner is that you need to separate "guilt" from "shame" when it comes to your personal finances. In other words, we're all ultimately "guilty" for our debt situation simply because it's ours. We're in charge of it and we were participants in each financial decision that added to the chaos.

You shouldn't feel any "shame" over it, however. You don't need to feel stupid, even if people gave you good advice that you refused to listen to. You are not a financial planner or accountant, but just somebody doing the best you can with the knowledge you have.

In fact, even as a financial planner, my wife and I maxed out our credit cards twice in the last 10 years. If anyone should have known better, it would be me. Especially after the first time!

The reality is, debt crept up on me, a well-meaning and savvy financial planner. Not because I was careless or reckless. Not because I decided to blow off some major steam in Vegas or just couldn't live without a plasma screen TV. It was because I was trying to be careful and smart with my money. Oh, the irony!

Straight out of college, my wife and I both had decent jobs. We were newly married and lived a fairly simple life. In fact, it felt so simple that we didn't quite watch the road as well as we should have.

We were trying to save money, so we thought it'd be a great idea to get a credit card that let us earn airline miles for our purchases. That'd surely help us save some money on a vacation down the road, because we wouldn't have to buy airline tickets. All we would have to do was put the necessities on our credit card, and collect miles on what we were already spending each month. Sounds like a great plan, right?

Within a couple of years, a few extra dinners out, an occasional treat at the department store, and a blown transmission added up to a $10,000 credit card balance. We spent a lot of time that year pointing fingers and placing blame, which didn't do a whole lot to actually pay off the card.

With a $10,000 balance, we reached what I like to call the "screw it" point. We'd say things to ourselves like, "We're already $10,000 in debt, we might as well go out and have a nice dinner!" Our $10,000 balance mushroomed quickly from there.

Does all of this sound familiar? I share my story not because I think you're a good listener (although I'm sure you are), but to tell you that it's okay that you are where you are! I get it. I understand. I've been there. You're not a bad person. Even though this is a *Complete Idiot's Guide*, you're not stupid. Debt just somehow crept up on you. But just like me, you've come to the realization that it's time to do something about it.

A Tale of Two Frogs

There's an old analogy about frogs and boiling water that I think applies to your individual struggle with debt. (Please, for the sake of the frogs, take my word for it and don't try this at home.) The idea is that if you drop a frog in boiling water, it will immediately jump out. It senses it is in deep trouble and does what it needs to make a change for the better. However, if you put a frog in a pot of cool water and slowly raise the temperature, it'll sit there until it becomes an appetizer.

Debt in America is no different. Thirty to forty years ago, *cash* was king. People buried it in the backyard in coffee cans and woke up with backaches because they stuffed their mattresses with it. Credit card debt, payday loans, and adjustable rate mortgages weren't part of most people's vocabulary.

Back then, if someone acquired too much debt, especially high-interest debt, they knew it was bad. They would be the talk of the neighborhood and would probably get a scolding from their family. There was an immediate incentive to change their financial behavior. They were like that frog dropped into a pot of boiling water.

def•i•ni•tion

Cash is something I talk a lot about in this book. When we say "cash" in the financial world, we don't literally mean "wads of green." Rather, we mean money in the bank. Just because you can get cash from your credit card or home equity line of credit doesn't mean you are using "cash."

Now, however, credit is everywhere. Not only have you likely been encouraged to use it by everyone from advertisers to financial experts, but you might actually feel scolded if you don't! Young people are foolishly encouraged to build credit. Supposedly savvy investors borrow money to make more money. It's everywhere.

If you grew up and learned the basics of personal finance in this environment, you were like that frog dropped in a nice comfortable pot of cool water. As the water "got hot" and your debts mounted, no one really acted that concerned. All the other frogs in the pot just sat there smiling right back at you. Eventually, your debts got too hot to handle, and here you are.

Stats to Make You Feel Better (and Worse)!

America's recent love affair with borrowing money is truly staggering when you stop and look at the numbers. It's only in the last 20 to 40 years that debt has run amok among the general population.

Considering that the vast majority of wealth in the United States is held by individuals age 60 to 80 (which is ironically 20 to 40 years older than the average reader of this book), trends in debt are worth considering. Remember, solving a problem starts with understanding it.

Let's start with overall individual debt (including real estate loans) in the United States. In 1948, the Federal Reserve calculated that total consumer debt in the United States was approximately $6.5 billion. Sixty years later, in 2008, it is just over $2.5 trillion. That's an increase of almost 350 times, in just 40 years. That means the average amount of debt owed for every man, woman, and child in the United States in 1948 was a measly $97 per person, adjusted for inflation. Forty years later in 2008, the average total debt balance per person has mushroomed to $9,249.

Looking at it from another perspective, the amount of a U.S. citizen's paycheck that goes toward debt is climbing as well. According to the Federal Reserve, the average American in 1980 spent 13.77% of his or her monthly paycheck on monthly debt payments. By 2007, this number had jumped to 18.02%. That's an increase of 30% in just under three decades. That's significant considering most of us can barely make our paycheck stretch to cover all our bills in the first place!

Dollars and Sense _____

What would you give to interview one of the greatest financial minds of our time? Wouldn't you want to find out his or her secrets to success, wealth, and staying out of debt? Look no farther than your grandparents, church, or local senior center. The age bracket that controls the largest portion of wealth in our society is the World War II generation. Buying someone from this generation a cup of coffee and interviewing them about their money habits may be the best financial education you can find!

Businesses and You: Partners in Crime

When we really stop and look at why people are trapped under mountains of debt, the phrase *perfect storm* comes to mind. Ultimately, most debt is created because there is someone who really wants to sell something, and someone who really wants to buy it. We might call the first person a capitalist and the second a consumer. There may not be two more American terms than those!

The success of the capitalist, someone who hopes to make money by providing a product or service, is always going to be limited by the consumer's ability to buy what he or she offers. The consumer, who wages a daily war to both make ends meet and make life enjoyable, must carefully decide how to spend his or her money to achieve those goals.

That's where credit—or the perfect storm, depending on your perspective—comes to the rescue. Even though it might cost them 1% to 5% of the purchase price, capitalists can make it easier for consumers to get their hands on what they want. Because consumers can borrow more money than they actually have at the moment, capitalists can also sell more then they would normally be able to.

Hence, the vast majority of people who find themselves curled up in the fetal position across the room from unopened credit card and loan statements are there for a reason. They use borrowed money to buy what they thought they needed, from people who were happy to sell it to them.

Recognizing this cycle is perhaps the most important first step in beating your debt. If you can't recognize that you got there because you need and want to spend, and also that there are those who need and want you to spend, then you'll likely never make a permanent change.

Not All Debt Is Bad

After everything I've said so far, you may think I'm on a personal crusade to burn all types of debt at the proverbial stake. I'm really not! In fact, debt by itself isn't the core problem. Debt can provide a crucial bridge to allow you to go from where you are to where you want to be.

There's a saying with those who oppose gun control: "Guns don't kill people; people kill people." I think the same could be said for the use of debt and credit cards. Debt and credit cards don't ruin people's finances; people ruin people's finances!

Getting off the debt merry-go-round doesn't mean you need to buy your next house for cash or that you shouldn't have a credit card for emergencies. Rather, it means that you need to learn how different types of debt work, and when are the right and wrong times to use each type.

Good Debt vs. Bad Debt

Just like with cholesterol, there's both "good" and "bad" types of debt. The overall goal of eliminating debt centers heavily around learning to avoid the bad types of debt altogether, while using the good kinds when necessary.

Ultimately, good debt is defined by three factors:

1. The item being purchased is a necessary part of your life.

2. You can afford the monthly payment.

3. It will be paid off in a reasonable amount of time.

Did you notice that I didn't mention anything about interest rates? While interest rates are important (more on this in Chapter 4), it's easy to get seduced by teaser rates. If you're not careful, you'll find yourself struggling with a long-term monthly payment on something that you can't really afford.

Conversely, bad debt is defined by three related factors:

1. You do not really need the item being purchased.

2. It is a stretch to afford the monthly payment.

3. The repayment period is open-ended or undefined.

When you use debt to purchase things that match the "bad debt" description, you're creating the perfect storm of financial chaos. The item you're purchasing may not be that exciting to pay off as time passes, the monthly payment may become a struggle if your economic situation changes, and you can easily avoid making sufficient payments when faced with other more exciting options.

Identifying Your Needs and Wants

I don't know about you, but I've always enjoyed those primetime television medical dramas. If it weren't for the fact that I still don't know what *stat* means, I'd almost consider myself a doctor.

One of the things that I've learned through my years in front of the tube is when a critical patient comes in all banged up, you first have to "stop the bleeding." If you're reading this book, it's because your finances just got rolled in on a gurney after being run over by runaway debt. Your first job in treating the problem is to stop the bleeding. In this case, that means that you have to slow the tide of money leaving your bank account. By doing that, you'll be able to divert this money into paying off your debt and credit cards as quickly as possible.

The gaping hole in most people's finances is that they usually *want* far more than they actually *need*. Don't get me wrong; you're not a bad person because you enjoy the finer things. But you may be stressed out if you've gone into debt to acquire them.

By beginning to limit your purchases to the things you truly need and temporarily cutting back on the things you simply want, you'll be on your way to getting out of debt.

Being able to borrow money is a helpful, wonderful resource when you use it to acquire the things that you truly need. For example, in many parts of the country, a car is a legitimate need to both work and live. If you're like the average person, who does not have $10,000 to $20,000 lying around, an auto loan enables you to get what you need to survive and thrive.

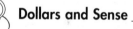 **Dollars and Sense**

The worst time to decide if something is a need or a want is when you're at the store, holding the item in your hands. Prioritizing your purchases before you actually make them may save you a lot of buyer's remorse. Consider making a list of all your potential purchases over $50 for the next year. After a day or two, come back to the list and label each item by whether it is a need or a want.

But even with things like a car or the roof over your head, it's a fine line between using borrowed money to get what you need, and misusing credit cards and loans to acquire what you want or deserve. A medium priced, four-door sedan gets you to work just the same as that sexy import. One is a need, the other is a want.

Appreciating vs. Depreciating Assets

Perhaps one of the biggest rules of thumb as you move toward your goal of eliminating debt is to make sure you only use debt for *appreciating* assets. In other words, using debt to acquire something that will actually be worth more than its cost is usually a safe proposition.

Using debt to acquire a home, an education, or needed medical care will all likely pay themselves back many fold over time. Homes go up in value, education raises your earning potential, and better health increases your productivity and life span. All these things contribute to your financial well-being and can help end the cycle of debt.

On the other hand, using debt to acquire too many things that decrease in value (cars, vacations, clothes, toys, etc.) leaves you struggling to pay for things that will be worth less than what you owe.

There's an old saying: "Your car decreases 50% in value the moment you drive it off the dealer's lot." While I'm not sure the figure is really 50%, the reality is cars do go down in value pretty darn quick. That sports car that you stretched your finances to buy is quickly worth less than what you owe on it. Purchases such as these move your finances backward more than forward.

And it's not just cars. Things like vacations, nice meals, and new clothes all begin losing their financial value the moment you purchase them. They may create great memories, but their value decreases rapidly. If you borrow money to buy these things, it won't be long before you are paying off something that may have become forgotten or worthless!

Avoiding the Unavoidable

A friend of mine who is a psychologist was telling me about how much more difficult eating disorders can be to treat than addictions to illegal drugs. Even though illegal drugs can be chemically addictive, you do not need to use them. Food, on the other hand, is a requirement for living. Someone with an eating disorder has to continually use the very thing that he or she is battling to control.

Debt and money are similar. It would be one thing if you could just plop down on a desert island, where all of your needs are meet out of the island's abundance. You would not find yourself owing a couple of local monkeys 20,000 bananas for some grass skirts you never wear!

But the reality is, we have to spend money on a daily basis. To make matters worse, very few of us actually get paid on a daily basis. If anything, we get a paycheck every couple of weeks and must figure out how to budget it as we go. Credit cards and other types of debt can seem to simplify that process. All you need to do is temporarily "borrow" the money and then pay it off when your paycheck comes, right? Right …

Housing, medical, and college costs are no different. They are all things that many of us believe are key to our survival and happiness. However, most of us do not have the resources to pay for them outright. Yet again, the ability to borrow comes to the rescue.

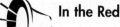

In the Red

Did you use a credit card to buy this book? How many other times today and this week have you used a credit card?

You Bought This Book for a Reason …

My guess is that you bought this book because the anxiety is starting to creep in. The balances are beginning to mount and the phone is starting to ring. Maybe your adjustable rate mortgage payment just reset or maybe you just got denied for an auto loan.

Whatever the cause, you need to commit right now to staying the course. Reading this book will be the easy part. Sticking to the proven principles within its pages will be the challenge. I can't promise you things will magically get easier, but I can promise that you can get out of the debt cycle once and for all.

It won't happen overnight. But, within 12 to 24 months, you can eliminate a significant portion of the anxiety-causing debts you're carrying. In 36 to 48 months, you can significantly repair your credit score. And hopefully, once you've regained control, you'll learn skills that will help ensure this is the last time you have to do this. But it all takes admitting there is a problem.

Set a Goal

Before we go any farther, I want you to set a goal for yourself. You can always change it later as you learn more about the process of getting out of debt. The goal I want you to set is the amount of time it will take for you to be debt-free of everything besides your mortgage and student loans. Six months? One year? Two years?

Grab a few sheets of paper, staple them together, and write "Debt Journal" on the top. (Or buy a special journal for this purpose if you want to get fancy.) You're going to use this a lot. Now, at the top of the page, write your goal: "My goal is to be debt-free in _____."

... So Read It with Purpose!

In the classic movie *Little Shop of Horrors*, a humble florist discovers a cute talking plant and names it Audrey. By accident, the florist discovers that Audrey requires blood to live. As the florist feeds the plant and it grows, it begins to make him famous. This instant fame helps to give him the life he's always dreamed of. But there's a problem: Audrey requires more and more blood to live as it grows. The florist knows it, but can't walk away from the lifestyle his now famous plant is helping to provide. Eventually, the plant consumes the florist and the woman he loves.

Debt is kind of like that. When you discover that you can use debt to improve your lifestyle, it can seem so unintimidating. They give you free toasters and 10% off when you sign up for credit cards and home equity loans. But sooner or later, your debts grow to where it is a daily struggle to manage them.

Twelve-step programs, which are famous for helping people regain control of their lives, often state, "Admitting there is a problem is the first step to solving it." Hopefully, realizing that you are not the only one with a debt problem will make it easier for you to "admit it and move on."

If you want things to change before they grow out of control, you have to start with admitting that you might have overused or accidentally misused debt and credit from the start. You have to acknowledge that, from their humble beginnings, your debts have grown out of control. You have to recognize that, if you want things to change, you need to "nip them in the bud" sooner rather than later.

The Least You Need to Know

- The average amount of outstanding debt and credit per person in the United States has increased 350-fold in the last 60 years.

- Controlling debt is difficult because you still need to spend.

- Debt and credit aren't bad by themselves, but not being disciplined in your use of them can lead to major trouble.

- Beating debt takes more than fancy techniques. It takes a commitment to change your behavior.

- Admitting that you have a problem is the first step toward overcoming debt.

2

Long-Term Debt

In This Chapter

- ◆ Understanding the risks of long-term debt
- ◆ Dream homes and nightmare mortgages
- ◆ Fixed-rate mortgages, adjustable-rate mortgages, and more
- ◆ Studying up on student loans

There are certain purchases and costs in life that most people would not be able to afford, if it were not for the use of debt and loans. For example, no amount of saving would likely get you the funds you need to purchase a home or pay for a college education with cash. Using loans and debt to acquire either of these things can often be considered a "good debt" because it is for something that creates or increases your net worth.

Because of the high cost of these things (often hundreds of thousands of dollars), the repayment of these loans is spread over a long period of time (10 to 30 years). This makes the monthly payment manageable even though the debt is large. Additionally, the payment typically remains the same throughout the loan, making it easy to plan your budget accordingly.

Risks of Long-Term Debt

While the use of long-term debt clearly allows you to purchase the things that help you increase your net worth and employability, they can also present a number of risks. Whether you are considering taking out your first long-term loan, or you are re-evaluating your past choices, there are a number of important risks and mistakes to consider:

◆ **Never paying it off.** It has become increasingly easy to "refinance" your existing debts into new ones. While this might lower your payment, it usually also rolls the clock back to zero. If you constantly refinance, you'll never get a loan paid off and always be paying interest to someone else.

◆ **Forgetting that it's still a debt.** Since there's a lot of talk about long-term debts (mortgages, student loans, etc.) being good debts, it would be easy to forget that they're still loans that cost you interest. Even with the best rates, you're still sending money to someone else as opposed to investing or enjoying it.

◆ **Not deducting the interest.** Unlike credit cards and auto loans where your interest isn't generally deductible, you can actually lower your tax bill by writing off your student loan and mortgage interest. If you take out a long-term loan but fail to properly deduct the interest, if allowed, you could be costing yourself thousands of dollars annually. Check out IRS Publication 936 for the mortgage interest rules, and Publication 970 for student loan interest guidelines.

Set a Goal

In the last chapter, you set a goal to be completely free from your short-term debts within a certain amount of time. Because it would be impossible to pay off your long-term debts in that same time period (unless you win the lottery), you should also set a goal to pay off your long-term debts. Instead of talking months or years, I'd suggest you pick an age at which you'd like to have each long-term debt eliminated.

Grab your Debt Journal and write down your goals for paying off your long-term debts. "I want to have my student loans (or mortgage) paid off by age _____."

Mortgage and Real Estate Debts

According to The Mortgage Bankers Association, in the early 2000s, propelled by a low rates and questionable mortgage products, homeownership soared to a record

68% of U.S. households. Unfortunately, due to a "perfect storm" of factors, including consumers' poor use of debt, homeownership is sliding from its highest point.

There's no doubt that owning a home is part of the American dream. In fact, in the last runaway real estate market, it almost felt like the dream was slipping through your fingers if you weren't able to get into something sooner than later. Now you know that dream can quickly turn into a nightmare.

Mortgages are generally one of those debts that can earn a coveted "good debt" rating, but only under certain conditions. Namely, the payment has to be something that you can afford, that you don't expect to change, and on a property that is "right" for you for years to come.

Many of you may own a property with a mortgage that is just the opposite of that. The payment has become something you can't afford, will likely continue to fluctuate, and the property is more or less home than you truly need.

A key component of getting out of debt is understanding how mortgages work and ensuring that you are in, or getting into, a mortgage that creates net worth instead of destroying it.

Fixed-Rate Mortgages

Once upon a time, a fixed-rate mortgage was the only real option. It may have taken some folks a few years to get to the point where they could qualify for one, but once they did, they were in a good, predictable situation.

In essence, a fixed-rate mortgage has one interest rate for the entire life of the loan. While this interest rate may not be as low as the adjustable-rate mortgages that have contributed to the housing crisis, it's predictable. Owners are not likely to be caught off guard.

In the Red

Don't confuse a fixed mortgage, which is sometimes called a conventional mortgage, with a conforming mortgage. While the term "conventional" refers to a fixed interest rate, usually for 15 or 30 years, "conforming" refers to the requirements for the loan to be resold. A conforming mortgage may have a fixed or adjustable rate, because the term "conforming" actually refers to its ability to be sold by the bank to a corporation such as Fannie Mae or Freddie Mac.

Most fixed-rate mortgages have either 15- or 30-year terms, but are often "refinanced" or replaced, with other fixed-rate mortgages when interest rates decline. It's likely that homeowners will need to try and convert their adjustable-rate mortgages into a fixed-rate mortgage. That stability is key to diverting money to take care of other kinds of debt.

Adjustable-Rate Mortgages (ARMs)

In the runaway real estate market, adjustable-rate mortgages were everyone's best friend. With interest rates that were significantly lower than fixed-rate mortgages, homebuyers could purchase a larger and more expensive home for the same payment as a fixed-rate mortgage. Mortgage brokers and real estate agents loved them because they could sell you a bigger house and earn a bigger commission.

Of course, there is just one small problem with adjustable-rate mortgages ... they adjust! When the rate finally goes from 3–4% to 8–9%, your mortgage payment might double. That's a huge adjustment for any budget—especially if you didn't see it coming.

Debt in America

Pete and Susie found the home of their dreams, but it was a bit outside their price range. Their mortgage broker encouraged them to consider an adjustable-rate mortgage, which offered a lower payment for the first seven years. They were told they "could always refinance" after seven years. Seven years later, the real estate market has gone down and they can't refinance. Their original monthly payment was $1,671 based on a 4.00% annual rate. When their rate readjusted to 7.50%, their monthly payment jumped to $2,447. That's an increase of almost $800 per month, and is a large enough cost that their budget can't be adjusted enough to cover it.

Adjustable-rate mortgages come in two primary types, all of which can leave a homeowner between a rock and a hard place:

◆ **Balloon mortgages.** The monthly payment on these mortgages looks like a 30-year mortgage payment. However, a balloon mortgage requires the entire mortgage balance to be paid off after a short period of time, usually seven years.

◆ **7/1 or 5/1 mortgages.** These mortgages have a lower rate for the first 7 or 5 years, after which the rate adjusts every year for the remaining 23 to 25 years of the loan!

Though the statistics vary by study, it's estimated that one quarter to one third of all home purchases are made with adjustable-rate mortgages. In the beginning, adjustable-rate mortgages were designed for people who thought interest rates were going to go down within a few years of purchasing a home, or those who thought they would move within 5 to 7 years. Someone in either of these situations would benefit by not being locked into a longer 30-year fixed-rate mortgage.

If you plan on being in your current home for more than 5 to 7 years, or you think interest rates will stay the same or climb, you need to think about getting a better loan.

Interest-Only Loans

Interest-only loans are a complete curiosity to me. They defy our goal of eliminating bad debt altogether while using good debt to purchase appreciating assets.

Quite simply, an interest-only loan is one whose payment only covers the interest that accrues each month. No portion of your payment actually goes toward reducing the amount you owe. In other words, 20 years into an interest-only mortgage, you will owe exactly what you owed on the day you bought the home.

That's okay if home prices go up 15% per year. But, if home prices stay the same or drop, you've essentially given someone a down payment to rent a home. That's not even taking into account the costs of selling it again someday or what you could have done with that down payment if you would have truly rented a home.

If you are in an interest-only mortgage, you'll want to seriously consider either increasing your payments or refinancing your mortgage.

> **In the Red**
>
> Just because someone can offer you a low monthly payment doesn't mean the loan is a wise idea. This is especially true when the length of time required to pay off your loan is longer than the useful life of what you bought. Be especially wary of car loans longer than 6 years and mortgages longer than 30 years.

Payment-Optional or "NegAm" Loans

As you fight tooth and nail to get out of debt, there is no mortgage that stands more opposed to this than the payment-optional or negative amortization loan. These loans, if misused, may actually cause your debt to swell past the point of no return.

On the surface, these loans are presented as a homeowner's best friend, because they actually give you the option of deciding what you pay each month. In fact, they usually give you four different options:

1. Pay a minimum dollar amount, less than the interest actually added to the loan in a month.

2. Pay only the interest that was added to your loan balance in a month.

3. Make a monthly payment that's equivalent to a 15-year fixed mortgage.

4. Make a monthly payment that's equivalent to a 30-year fixed mortgage.

While the 15- and 30-year fixed-rate payments would be good choices that move you toward eventually owning your home, the minimum-payment and interest-only options either keep your debt the same or increase it further.

The term *negative amortization* actually comes from the fact that instead of increasing your ownership in the home through an amortized monthly payment, you're actually decreasing it by not covering the basic interest added each month.

If you are in a Payment Option of Negative Amortization, it's critical that you take a good, hard look at this loan and how you're using it.

Dollars and Sense _____

Many people hear about the low rates offered on reverse mortgages, and walk into a bank hoping to score one of these great rates. Unfortunately, reverse mortgages are exactly as the name implies. Instead of slowly buying your house by sending a monthly payment to the bank, the bank is actually buying your house from you by sending you a small payment each month.

Student Loans

As a college diploma has become a virtual requirement for many careers and the cost of a college education has skyrocketed, student loans have become a necessary evil for many young adults. According to the National Center for Education Statistics, the average graduating college senior has just over $17,000 in debt. One quarter of all graduates have at least $25,000, and one tenth have at least $35,000. Sadly, many spend the first decade after college struggling to make the required payments on student loans.

The situation has become even more overwhelming as more students than ever are pursuing post-graduate degrees that can cost in excess of $150,000. Understanding your student loan options and avoiding high-cost lenders and programs are key to eliminating your debt.

Government Programs

Despite what most students and their parents think, government student loan programs make money available to all families, regardless of their income or net worth. These programs offer some of the best options for keeping your borrowing costs down, due to government restrictions on the rate of interest that can be charged.

If you are in school or thinking of going back to school, you'll want to make sure to use these programs first. You'll also want to avoid debt consolidation options that take you out of these programs, instead saddling you with debt that takes longer to pay off.

Private Loans

In the last few years, we have seen explosive growth in the number of private student loan companies. Typically, the schools themselves work hard to keep these companies off their campuses and away from their students, due to their lousy loan terms and predatory lending practices.

However, these companies have begun to bombard students and their parents with TV commercials and Internet ads claiming easy access to large amounts of funds. Of course, they fail to mention that their rates may be two to three times what is available through government programs.

In the Red

Even if you or your family makes a significant amount of money or has managed to save a bunch for college, you can still qualify for government loans. To apply for these programs, you simply need to complete a Free Application for Federal Student Aid (FAFSA) form online at www.fafsa.ed.gov. Beware of companies that advertise student loans or loan application services. Many of these programs use private lenders that charge significantly more than the Department of Education's free application.

While a reasonable number of student loans would normally be labeled as "good" debt (because it can help you increase your earning power), these private loans would definitely be labeled as "bad." If you are considering going back to school, or have a child who is entering school, it will be crucial to your fight against debt to avoid these lenders and their programs. If you are in one of these programs, it is one of the debts you're going to move to the top of your hit list.

The Least You Need to Know

- Student loans and mortgages are usually considered long-term debt because they consist of reasonable payments spread over 10 to 30 years.

- While long-term debt can be considered "good" debt, it can also be reckless if the rate, payment, or purchase price is outside your financial capacity.

- Fixed-rate mortgages tend to offer the most predictable and practical approach to buying a home.

- Interest-only, payment-optional (NegAm), and reverse mortgage loans can dig you into a financial hole for a variety of reasons, and should generally be avoided for most situations.

- With plenty of public student loan programs available, private loan programs should be used as a last resort.

3

Short-Term Debt

In This Chapter

- ◆ Credit cards: buy now, pay later
- ◆ Car loans: the must-have accessory?
- ◆ 401(k) loans: robbing your retirement
- ◆ The danger of payday loans
- ◆ Medical costs can cause heart attacks
- ◆ Legal bills, alimony, and the IRS ... oh my!

In the last chapter, I discussed the use of long-term debt to acquire "assets" that you would not be able to purchase otherwise. Short-term debt on the other hand is used to help you survive day-to-day. While its use is justifiable from time to time (buying a car so you can get to work), more often than not, the purchases are avoidable.

For many people, excessive or impulsive use of short-term debt can create a major roadblock to achieving their long-term goals. Hence, we tend to label this kind of debt as "bad debt."

Credit Card Debt

When it comes to debt problems, credit card debt is the granddaddy of them all. According to CardWeb.com, the average American had $9,900 in credit card debt in 2007. In addition, 61% of credit card users do not pay off their balance each month, with 13% carrying a balance of at least $25,000. If it weren't for credit card payments, many people would be able to successfully deal with an increase in their mortgage, the addition of a car payment, or the temptation to buy that new "thing."

It's very likely that your unique battle to get rid of unhealthy debt will center around the elimination of your credit card balances. But, as you'll see, whether or not you eliminate them is affected by how and when you continue to use them. And how and when you continue to use them will be impacted by your budget and spending plan, which I'll talk more about in Chapters 8 and 9.

The Major Credit Card Companies

Thanks to advertising, mergers, and co-branding of certain company logos, it's hard to separate the major credit card companies from the "fly by night" operations. This is a critical distinction because the larger companies generally work harder to keep their customers and investors happy, as well as stay in the good graces of regulators. While the term "American Express" really refers to just one company, the terms "Visa" and "MasterCard" are used by numerous institutions with varying policies and rules.

> **Dollars and Sense**
>
> When trying to decide on which credit card to keep or use, you should invest a little time online. In addition to reviewing some of the numerous credit card rating sites, visit sites like Epinions.com, where users rate their experience with different credit cards.

When you evaluate which credit cards to keep and potentially use, it'll likely be a card from one of the larger companies, without a lot of the fancy features. It'll simply be a low or no annual fee credit card that you use to do things like book airline tickets. These cards should also have a reasonable annual interest rate, but don't get too hung up on that. Your goal is to pay it off in the same month you make a necessary purchase.

Retail Credit Cards

It's a trap few shoppers can resist. As the salesperson rings up your purchase at the local mall clothing store, he or she offers you a generous 10% to 15% discount off your purchase … *if* you sign up for the store's credit card.

Repeat after me: "Mall and retail credit cards are not my friend."

These credit cards, which earn you that generous discount (on your first purchase only), also charge you some of the highest interest rates. It's not so hard for stores to give you a 10% discount when the annual interest rate on their card is 30%! What's worse is the fact that people always tend to spend more the next time they shop and use that card, compared to paying cash or using a debit card.

To add insult to injury, accepting credit card offers at the mall might significantly increase your future car or mortgage payment. The fact is, having too many retail credit cards can hurt your credit score because they theoretically demonstrate impulsivity on your part. In turn, this lower credit score keeps you from getting the best rates on other loans you may apply for down the road.

Installment Purchases

While this type of credit comes without a fancy card, it is used to buy the same kind of stuff and can overwhelm your finances just as easily. The two most common appearances of this kind of debt are the catalogs we all get in the mail that offer low monthly payments for cool gadgets, and the furniture stores that let you "buy now with no payments until June!"

In essence, both of these are credit cards minus the card. They have minimum payments, high rates of interest (20–30%), and are used to buy things that go down in value over time.

Many of these programs have tricky rules that hike your interest rate retroactively if your debt isn't completely paid by a certain deadline. Again, these should be some of the first pieces of short-term debt on the chopping block.

Other Types of Debt

Virtually everyone I've sat down with over the years who has resolved to get themselves out of debt has a smorgasbord of other types of debt. If all that most people had to tackle were a mortgage, some student loans, and a credit card or two, they'd probably be able to figure out a plan on their own.

By the time you're buying this book or sitting down with a financial planner, you've probably found yourself surrounded on all sides by people demanding you pay them what you owe. These may include medical providers, payday loan companies, ex-spouses, and even the IRS.

Let's take a quick look at these different types of debt, and begin lumping them into the "good" and "bad" categories. Doing so will help you prioritize which ones to eliminate first.

Auto Loans

Cars are a "need" for most people. Without a way to get to and from work, you'd have no ability to earn a wage, pay your bills, or even get out of debt. Yet, many people go a little overboard when it comes to cars.

def•i•ni•tion

Many first-time car buyers don't understand the difference between a **lease** and a **purchase**. In essence, a lease consists of you paying the dealer for temporary (usually two to four years) use of a car. When the lease is over, the car has to be returned with any damage or excessive mileage paid for.

In California, I marvel at how many of us, myself included, approach our auto loans. In fact, it's almost a cliché that many people I know borrow money to *lease* or *purchase* a car, complain and stress out about the payments as they go along, and then get a new car and a new loan as soon as the last one is paid off!

This cycle is especially profound with young people, who have less than stellar credit. Before they actually need a new car, they start wanting a new car. In response to this need, they often do whatever it takes to get that car they want, including using high-interest-rate loans that will take a long time to pay off.

401(k) and Retirement Plan Loans

Over the last 20 years, 401(k) plans have become the primary form of retirement plan used by many Americans. In fact, the Investment Company Institute estimates that Americans now hold 4.5 *trillion* dollars in employer-sponsored retirement plans.

One of the features that makes these plans so attractive for many employees is the promise that they can borrow against their account balance should they need it. While the loan provision was put into the plan to help employees survive true emergencies, 401(k) loans are increasingly being taken to finance large purchases or pay off other debt.

Aside from the fact that a 401(k) loan freezes the growth on the portion of your 401(k) that you borrowed against, 401(k) loans can create a huge tax liability that forces many people further into debt. This occurs when an employee quits or is fired from his job prior to repaying his loan balance.

Whatever balance is still unpaid after a maximum of 30 days of leaving is included in the employee's income, making it subject to income tax and a 10% penalty. This can easily equal 50% of the balance borrowed. Naturally, this often forces people to use credit cards or debt to pay off the IRS.

Payday Loans

I'll be blunt on this one. Payday loans are a ridiculously bad idea! If you've used them, or are considering using them, you're going to need to get out of that cycle right away. These loans, which can seem like a great way to make ends meet in a tight month, can often start someone down an irreversible cycle toward bankruptcy.

You cringe at the thought of a credit card that charges 25% to 35% interest, right? Yet, if you pay $50 to borrow $500 for 30 days, that's an annual interest rate of over 120%. In fact, some payday loans are known to charge anywhere from 500% to 1,000% in annual interest!

To make matters worse, these loans that seemingly solve a problem for you in the current month, create a problem for you in the upcoming months. If you've borrowed money against a paycheck you haven't received, that paycheck will actually leave you with less, and needing to borrowing again. With such high rates of interest and a continual cycle of borrowing against next month's paycheck, an initial loan of $500 can grow to over $2,500 in debt in just 12 months!

Medical Bills

Medical care is a double-edged sword for many Americans. We have easy, instantaneous access to both necessary and elective care. Sadly, we often don't realize the true cost until after procedures are completed.

In your journey to eliminate debt, you've got to be incredibly cautious about adding tens of thousands of dollars in debt overnight. I've seen this time and time again, as someone diligently scrapes to pay off their debt, only to get a $5,000 hospital bill from their child's broken arm because they were uninsured.

It's not just the uninsured who can find themselves facing staggering debts because of medical expenses. Many insured individuals get hit with large unexpected bills because they choose certain procedures that were not covered or pre-approved by their insurance company. Long story short, when it comes to your battle against debt and credit, make sure you're properly protected against surprise medical costs, while simultaneously making sure recommended or desired procedures are covered by your insurance company. The good news, which I'll get to later, is that if you do find yourself in debt to a medical provider, you often have more options than you have with other types of debt, but it requires you to be aggressive in dealing with it.

> **Debt in America** _____
>
> I had a close friend whose situation is a fairly common story for many Americans. Bobby was in between jobs when he first began to feel some pains in his abdomen and lower back. Within another couple weeks, Bobby called me doubled over in pain. I rushed him to the hospital, where after a few simple procedures, he was told he had a couple of kidney stones. He was given some painkillers and sent home, thankful that it wasn't something more serious. What *was* serious was the bill he got from the hospital six weeks later: $9,600 for his two-hour visit and an MRI!

When it comes to keeping astronomical medical debt out of your life, here are a few easy tips:

- **Have adequate coverage.** This can often feel like a no-win situation, because medical insurance can be so expensive. Get caught without it, though, and you'll spend the rest of your life digging out from underneath it. Be sure to look into employer-sponsored plans and low-cost offerings from your state such as Medicaid.

- **Get a pre-authorization.** Even with comprehensive medical coverage, many households still get slapped with a huge medical bill for certain procedures. More and more, insurance companies are requiring you to get "pre-authorization" before you undergo an expensive procedure. If you fail to get this pre-authorization, the insurance company can refuse to pay the bill.

- **Use walk-in clinics.** For simple injuries and minor illnesses, try to avoid the hospital emergency room. A simple broken arm can cost you thousands if you have no insurance. Consider using community walk-in clinics, which often offer much cheaper services if you don't have insurance.

Legal Bills

Just like many medical expenses, legal costs can pop up out of nowhere. Whether you get sued, need to help out a child who gets into trouble, go through a divorce, or even file for bankruptcy, you can quickly rack up $5,000 to $10,000 or more in legal debt. Even worse, owing money to someone who understands his or her legal rights and options can put you between a rock and a hard place.

If you find yourself, or expect to be, in a situation that requires legal help, here are some options to consider:

- ◆ **Call your Employee Assistance Plan (EAP).** Many larger employers now offer their employees access to an Employee Assistance Plan. Most of these plans offer short and confidential consultations on legal and financial matters over the phone. Your EAP can often help you assess what your next steps should be.

- ◆ **Consider prepaid legal programs.** In recent years, there has been a significant increase in the number of companies offering prepaid legal services. For a few hundred dollars per year, you receive a certain number of hours of legal consultation from a lawyer. If additional hours are needed above your maximum, you receive a discounted rate.

- ◆ **Check with your insurance carrier.** Many insurance policies will actually pay for legal representation as it relates to something they cover. However, there's no way for them to know what you've spent, much less reimburse you for it, if you don't understand your coverage and report your losses.

Child Support and Alimony

While no one makes it a goal of their life to owe child support or alimony, you can often find yourself owing significant amounts of money due to someone else's decisions. Because there is often a mountain of emotions tied to these debts, they are some of the easiest to negotiate and find a compromise that works for both parties.

The legal system and states have become increasingly aggressive in pursuing people who fail to pay what they owe. Because of this increased aggressiveness, failure to pay child support or alimony can lead to garnishment of your wages and a debt that follows you even if you declare bankruptcy of move out of the country!

Like legal and medical debts, proactive negotiations can often reduce or even eliminate amounts you owe to other parties. Hence, if you find yourself in this situation, you need to put it at the top of your prioritized list.

The IRS and Other Government Agencies

It's said that the Canadian Mounties "always get their man." In reality, the IRS makes the Mounties look like a bunch of amateurs! No other organization in America has the ability to collect on unpaid debts like the IRS and government agencies. Not only that, they're pretty unforgiving in terms of the penalties and interest they charge to people who don't pay what they owe, when they owe it.

With a tax code that many accountants and financial planners struggle to master, there are hundreds of thousands of individuals who are caught off guard and unprepared by large tax bills. If you find yourself in this situation, it's crucial to begin communicating with the IRS about eliminating this debt as soon as possible.

Set a Goal

Identify your most stressful "short-term" debts. Which ones are causing you the most anxiety, stress, or fear? As part of your journey to get out of debt, I show you how to strike a balance between paying off the debts that makes the most financial sense, with the ones that are causing you the most stress.

So ... flip to your Debt Journal and write the three short-term debts you'd like to see gone ASAP.

The Least You Need to Know

- Short-term debt (due in less than 10 years) usually charges higher interest rates and blocks our long-term goals.

- America is drowning in credit card debt. The people who will thrive financially generally will be the ones who don't use their plastic.

- Car loans are often necessary, but can easily become an overused habit that sucks up your monthly income.

- 401(k) loans can create a huge tax liability if you leave your job before they're repaid.

- Payday or cash advance loans can dig you into a deep hole that is extremely hard to climb out of.

- Medical and legal bills, outstanding child support and alimony, and unpaid IRS balances can often be avoided or reduced with a proactive approach.

4

The Math of Debt

In This Chapter

- ◆ Simple versus compound interest
- ◆ Minimum payments lead to growing debt and credit
- ◆ A "day late"—more than a dollar short
- ◆ Play by the rules or they'll change

By this point in the book, you've probably gotten the impression that I'm ready to take "debt and credit" out behind the shed like Old Yeller when he caught rabies. In reality, though, it is not debt that I hate. What I have a problem with is the interest and fees charged on debt and credit card balances.

If you could borrow money without truly having to pay anyone for the privilege of doing so, would you? Hopefully you answered yes; in fact, you'd probably willingly choose to be in debt up to your eyeballs.

With your interest-free loan, you'd go down to the bank and stick it into a savings account, and why wouldn't you? It doesn't cost you anything to borrow it, and you can turn around and earn money on it. That'd be the greatest deal going.

But that's not how debt and credit cards work. The vast majority of the time that you borrow money or spend using your credit cards, you're charged interest for the privilege. And, almost always, the amount you're charged is significantly more than what you could earn if you stuck the money in the bank. It's this interest, and how it piles up, that makes debt such an uphill battle to get paid off.

How Interest Rates Work

There are two basic types of interest that every person who uses debt or credit cards needs to understand: simple interest and compound interest. Over time, there is a significant difference between these two methods of calculating your interest on a debt. Part of your strategy to eliminate debt will probably involve getting rid of debts that use compound interest first.

Dollars and Sense _____

Often, the rate you're quoted on a loan or a savings account is not what you actually pay or earn. Depending on how often the actual interest due to you or the lender is calculated, your rate may be noticeably higher than the "nominal" or stated rate. APR stands for annual percentage rate, and refers to the actual cost of borrowing the money based on the frequency of the interest calculation. For example, a 6% loan may have an APR of 6.15%, depending on the calculation period. APY is identical to APR, except that it calculates the actual rate that our savings earns, instead of the interest we pay on a loan.

Simple Interest Loans

Simple interest is, well, simple. To calculate simple interest, you would multiply your interest rate by the balance that you owe. Any payment you make, in excess of the interest calculated for that period, is applied toward your balance or "principal."

Let's look at an example. Bob takes out a simple interest loan of $1,000, at 12% per year. If Bob makes one payment, at the end of the year, $120 in interest ($1,000 multiplied by 12%) will be subtracted from his payment *before* it is applied to what he actually owes. If he sends in $500, his balance will drop to $620 ($1,000 balance minus $380 applied to principal).

If Bob waits another full year to make a payment, he will owe $74.40 in interest. That's his $620 balance multiplied by 12%. Whatever payment he makes will have $74.40 subtracted from it for interest, before it is applied to his balance.

That's it! It's that simple!

Most auto loans, many mortgages, and most personal loans from credit unions use simple interest. As you'll see in a moment, these are far more preferable than loans that use compound interest.

Compound Interest

Albert Einstein, perhaps the most brilliant mind of the twentieth century, had an opinion about compound interest. He's quoted as saying, "Compound interest is the most powerful force in our universe!"

Now, I know our old friend Albert was being a little sarcastic, but he's got a semivalid point. Compound interest is a force to be reckoned with. For those who are owed compound interest, it can make them wealthy. For those who owe it to someone else, it can be an anchor around your financial neck.

Dollars and Sense

To give you an idea of the power of money "compounding" on itself, I want to make you a hypothetical offer. Suppose I offer you $1 million cash, or offer you a penny today, with the promise to double the balance every day for the next 30 days. Which would you take? Grab your scratch paper or calculator and start doubling (Day 1 = 1¢, Day 2 = 2¢, Day 3 = 4¢, etc.) Do it 30 times to simulate a month's worth of doubling and see if you made the right choice.

Guess who loves to charge compound interest? You got it ... credit card companies, payday loan providers, and other types of questionable lenders. It's part of the reason that paying off credit cards is a far greater struggle than paying off a car loan—even when they're at the same interest rate.

The magic of compound interest is that you are charged interest on your interest until the loan is paid off. In other words, a little bit of interest is added to your debt every month, week, day, or even every second. Then, in turn, you are charged interest on that new slightly higher balance, during the next period.

Like a car that's lost its brakes on a steep and winding road, it doesn't take long to go over the edge! Let's look at an example of a 12% credit card, with a $1,000 balance, that compounds its interest every month.

For every month that goes by, 1% of the balance (12% divided by 12 months) is going to get added to the balance. The following month, that 1% is calculated on the new balance. For example, after one month, the balance would grow to $1,010. That's $1,000 times 1%.

After another month, with no payments, the balance would grow to $1,020.10. The balance grew not by $10 like the month before, but $10.10. The difference comes from the fact that interest was calculated on the new balance, not the original. It doesn't take long before this interest-on-interest growth of the balance mushrooms beyond control.

It's not hard to see that with higher-interest-rate loans, this can spiral out of control. This is especially true when you are making the minimum payments, getting late fees added to your payments, or even skipping payments altogether. To add insult to injury, many companies begin raising their already-high interest rates when you don't keep your account in good standing.

To make matters worse, most interest is compounded daily, not monthly. This only speeds up the effects of compound interest, and leaves you making much slower progress than you need.

The Minimum Payment Trap

When we talk about minimum payments, we're not just talking about credit cards, which is what "minimum payments" are usually associated with. Many other types of loans, such as "payment optional" mortgages, give consumers a lot of room to minimize their monthly payments, as long as they don't go below a certain dollar amount.

The problem with this is that compound interest continues to march forward on your balance, especially when you pay just the minimum. In fact, your balance can actually grow if your minimum payment was less than the interest that was actually added to our account for that month.

Unfortunately, making minimum payments is human nature. To get out of debt, you're going to have to go against the very fabric of who you are. By nature you instinctually avoid pain, and paying down a debt when there are other fun things that you can use your money for is painful! When given the choice between using all your disposable income to pay off a debt, and using some or most of it to enjoy life, you're going to choose the latter.

In fact, over the years, I've come to observe that when most people open their credit card statements, their total balance is not the first number they look at. People actually tend to check their minimum payment due before the balance!

Minimum Payment—Maximum Time

Let's look at another example. Sally is carrying a $10,000 balance on her credit card. Sally's monthly minimum payment is 2% of the balance, or $200, and the interest rate on the card is 18% annually.

If Sally makes just the minimum payment each month, it will take her 57.5 years to pay off her balance! Not only that, the $10,000 she put on the credit card will have cost her $33,930 by the time she gets it paid off.

But let's say Sally always makes her minimum payment, plus an extra $100, or $300 a month. In this case, it will take Sally just under 7 years, instead of 57.5 years, to eliminate this credit card debt. In addition, her $10,000 that she spent on the credit card will only end up costing her $16,000. That's a savings of over $17,000, which could have been used to eliminate other debts sooner.

Keep in mind as well that this example used a credit card that is charging 18%. With credit cards that charge higher rates (30%+) and things like payday loans, you can spend the rest of your life trying to get caught up. In either case, you've got to take drastic action to cut your debt now.

Fees, Fees, and More Fees

One of the key things to remember is that companies that loan out money are not charities. They're not in this because they feel called by a higher power to loan money for interest. Nor are they in this because they really have a heart for the cash-strapped consumer. They're in it to make a profit. With that in mind, you have to see fees for what they are ... another way for a company to make money off its customers.

Do you think your mortgage lender, auto finance company, or credit card issuer is mad because your payment got there a week

In the Red

Many types of credit or debt accounts that offer low interest rates make up for it through charging exorbitant over-the-limit, late-payment, and cash-advance fees. Likewise, many lenders who specialize in first-time or bad credit borrowers have been known to charge exorbitant fees knowing that desperate consumers have few options.

late? Just the opposite. They love it. It's a great excuse to significantly increase their profits at your expense by raising their interest rates and charging you late fees.

By charging you a $25 fee because your $250 car payment is a day late, they've effectively raised your car payment by 10%. What do you gain in the process? Absolutely nothing. That $25 doesn't lower your balance, and it doesn't make your car any fancier. It does nothing, and that's a major problem if you are working to eliminate debt as fast as you can. The money used to pay that late fee could have been used to pay down one of your other debts.

If you make a habit of paying late, it could easily be costing you hundreds, if not thousands of dollars per year. In fact, making payments late may be adding *years* to the length of time it takes to become debt-free!

Here are the most common reasons some people are overwhelmed with fees:

- They think a bill is paid on time if they mail it or it's postmarked by the due date. It's not. It's got to be there, in the company's hands, by the due date.

- They use electronic bill pay and don't realize that it may take just as many days for the check to get there as if they mailed it.

- They forget that holidays and weekends aren't "business days" for most companies. Payments received on these days don't get processed and credited to your account until the next business day.

- They wait until the day before something is due, and use express pay services offered by their lender. While it avoids the larger late fee, these services usually cost $10 to $20 per transaction.

The Fine Print Isn't So Fine

Few things in life fit the stereotype of "fine print" like loans and credit cards. If the devil is in the details, loan and credit card fine print is his home away from home.

Play by the rules, and everything is fine. Break one of the rules, and all financial hell can break loose. Your interest rate can change and be charged retroactively. Your fees can skyrocket. Your company may even have the right to demand you pay off your debt right on the spot.

Most of us don't break the rules because we're rebels. Rather, we get overwhelmed with life and are too busy or too tight on money to get our payments in on time.

While that's completely understandable, your company feels no pity. It's one more chance for them to make a profit off of you. More profit for them, of course, means it takes you longer to get out of debt.

Be sure to watch out for these famous tricks of the trade:

◆ **Retroactive interest.** That "no-interest purchase" or 0% interest balance transfer was great. Miss a payment, though, and they may go back and add in all the interest you should have paid at an exorbitant rate.

◆ **Changing credit score, changing rates.** Many times, companies that offer great rates on a loan bury this little surprise in the fine print. If your credit score goes down, your payments will go up!

◆ **Annual or inactivity fee.** Sure the loan seems great, until you realize that they charge an annual fee just to have the loan or credit card. Some of the higher-privilege credit cards charge $400 to $500 per year just to keep your account, while some of the lower-cost cards charge you if you don't use them enough!

◆ **Collection fees.** Many lenders and credit cards companies pass the entire expense of collecting your unpaid balance on to you. If they have to hire a collection company or a lawyer, that is coming out of your pocket.

The Least You Need to Know

◆ Simple interest loans are preferable to compound interest loans.

◆ You've got to exceed the minimum payment due if you don't want to spend the next 10 to 20 years making payments.

◆ Fees can chip away at the effectiveness of your goals to eliminate debt from your life.

◆ Reading the fine print of any loan is crucial to avoid hidden fees and conditions that could slow your repayment.

Denial, Acceptance, and Action

In This Chapter

- ◆ The top 10 signs of debt denial
- ◆ How much do you owe?
- ◆ Tracking your progress and staying motivated
- ◆ Getting started on the road to being debt-free
- ◆ Getting professional help

I don't know about you, but I hate going to the dentist. The smells of the office. The sounds of the drills. The really happy looks I see on people as I'm sitting in the waiting room. I'd rather just avoid it. In fact, I've learned that the best way to avoid having cavities is to just not go to the dentist. Makes sense, right? I mean, if I don't go to the dentist, then there's no one to officially tell me I need to change my lifestyle, much less that I need to take drastic action involving needles and drills.

Well, that plan worked for me for about 10 years, until my teeth hurt so bad I had to go in. The bad news: a cavity on virtually every tooth. The good news: they've got drills and high-priced procedures to take care of that … Your debt situation is no different—you can pretend like there's no problem, but in reality, the problem only gets worse with time.

Debt and Denial

For some people, "denial" isn't just a river in Egypt. They have made it a way of life—avoiding opening their mortgage statements and ignoring late payment fees and climbing interest rates. All the while, they continue to go out to dinner with friends, slapping down the card like usual.

Even right now, as you read this book, there's probably a part of you that is thinking you're doing what you need to do to eliminate your debt. I mean, c'mon, you're reading a book about debt!

Well, unfortunately, the techniques in this book aren't going to come naturally to you just because you read it. There's no such thing as "financial osmosis," where you read a little and your habits are magically transformed. To make your debts disappear, you've got to face this thing (and your fears, habits, and unwillingness to change) head on. Ready?

Don't think you're in denial about your debt situation? Go through the simple checklist below and check each box that applies to you and your household.

❏ You don't open credit card statements immediately upon arrival.

❏ You can't name, within a few hundred dollars, what your credit card balances are.

❏ You can't accurately guess, within one to two months, when your car will be paid off.

❏ You made late payments in the same month you've spent more than $50 on clothes, a meal, or a night out.

❏ You're mad at your lender or credit card company because of all the fees they keep charging you.

❏ You are afraid to share with your spouse, partner, or friend that you recently applied for a credit card or did a balance transfer.

❏ When making a purchase, you silently wonder whether or not your purchase will be approved.

❏ You feel like one more small purchase isn't going to make a difference in how much you owe.

❑ You think you have "bad luck" when it comes to money and bills.

❑ You think your debt was unavoidable.

So are you in debt denial? Do you already know the answer even before I tell you how to score the quiz?

If you checked one or two questions, you're in the early stages of debt denial. If you checked three to four questions, you've got a major problem brewing. If you checked five or more, it's official: you own beachfront property on a river called Denial!

In the Red

Sometimes, financial struggles aren't the main problem but evidence of a bigger problem. For someone with a gambling problem, compulsive spending issues, or any type of deep emotional wound, money problems may be evidence that a different kind of help is needed. Many times, when a person's feelings of loss, inadequacy, anger, or emptiness are dealt with, his or her money problems begin to take care of themselves. If you think you or someone you share finances with should talk to someone, visit the website for the American Association of Marriage and Family Therapists (www.aamft.org).

How Bad Is It?

When it comes to eliminating your debt, we've arrived at that point. It's time for you to pull back the sheet and see how ugly this thing really is. It's time to grab pen, paper, and calculator and get the numbers on paper.

For now I just want you to break down your debts between long- and short-term debt. If you'll recall from Chapters 2 and 3, long-term debt includes your mortgage and student loans, while short-term debt includes credit cards, car loans, medical bills, and everything else.

Add everything up and record the numbers here:

Total short-term debt: $_____

Total long-term debt: $_____

What Is Your Monthly Debt Service?

As big and bad as these numbers may be, it's probably not the balance that is causing you the biggest problems. Rather, it's probably your monthly payments or *debt service*. Virtually everything in your financial world, from bills to paychecks, operates on a monthly basis. Injecting $200, $500, or $1,000 of debt service can make surviving month to month utterly exhausting.

def•i•ni•tion

Debt service refers to the total of the required monthly payments to keep your accounts in good standing.

Just as you did with your total balances, add up all your required payments before you try and pay any extra, breaking them down into those categories again. Short-term monthly payments (car, credit card minimum payments, medical, etc.) and long-term payments (mortgage, student loans, child support/alimony).

Record those numbers here:

Total short-term debt monthly payments $_____

Total long-term debt monthly payments $_____

I ask you to consider the short-term debts, because they tend to be the easiest to eliminate, while simultaneously having a large impact on your budget. Even though your mortgage or student loan balance may be 10 to 100 times your credit card balance, the lower interest rates and longer repayment schedule make it relatively painless.

Paying down $10,000 on a $250,000 mortgage is not going to change your monthly cash flow that much. Paying off $10,000 out of your $25,000 credit card balance, which is charging you 30% interest per year, will make a huge difference.

Could You Get a Loan If You Needed It?

Another important measure and motivating factor as you do battle with debt is whether or not you could get *pre-qualified* or *pre-approved* for a loan if you really wanted one. What if your car needs a major repair and you'd rather just buy a new one instead of repairing the old? What if you found the house of your dreams?

def•i•ni•tion

Many people often confuse getting **pre-qualified** and **pre-approved** for a loan. They're quite different, and a misunderstanding of the terms often leads to some major disappointment. Pre-qualified simply means that based on the answers to a couple of simple questions, you seem like someone a lender would choose to do business with. Pre-approved means you've actually submitted all the required paperwork, have been deemed worthy of a loan, and the bank is ready to hand you a check.

Aside from credit cards, which companies seem to hand out like candy on Halloween, many loans are approved based on a couple of key ratios that consider your monthly debt service. Now granted, you still have to have a good credit score, but many lenders would not approve someone with the best credit score if they fell outside these ratios:

- ◆ A *front-end ratio* is a comparison of your loan payment for the purchase you're making against your total household pre-tax monthly income. For example, a $500 payment compared against a $2,000 per month income would give you a front-end ratio of 25% ($500 divided by $2,000). For most car and home loans, the front-end ratio needs to be in the ballpark of 30%, though this changes based on the lender and the size of the loan.

- ◆ A *back-end ratio* is a comparison of the payment on the loan you're applying for plus all your other types of monthly debt service, compared against your income. (This is the one that gets most people denied for a loan.) For example, the back-end ratio on a new monthly car payment of $500 and an existing monthly mortgage payment of $1,000, when compared against $2,000 in monthly income, would be 75% ($1,500 divided by $2,000). For most auto and home loans, the maximum back-end ratio is 50%, though 35–40% is common.

So what is your back-end ratio? Let's figure them out:

Total monthly debt payments (short + long term) $_____

Total monthly income before taxes $_____

Back-end ratio (monthly debt payments divided by your income) $_____

Tracking Your Progress

It's important to stop and assess if your debt problem is getting worse by the day, or if you've managed to stop the bleeding. If your monthly debt service is steadily climbing each month, that's the dead opposite of trying to get rid of debt. If more water is leaking into the rowboat than you're bailing out, it's only a matter of time before you sink. In other words, you've got to take decisive action.

To make sure you're not taking two steps forward and three steps back, make a chart where you start tracking your short-term balance, long-term balance, monthly debt service, and credit score. It'll look something like the following chart.

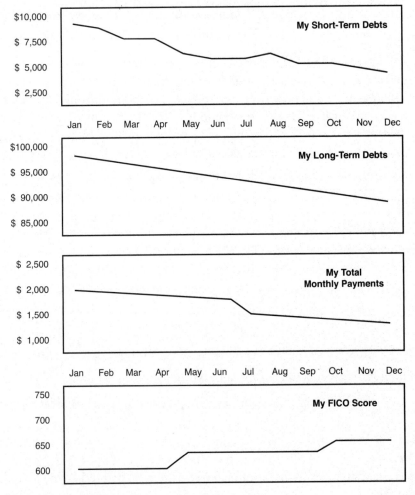

A chart to track your progress.

It doesn't matter how you create this chart. If you know how to use a computer spreadsheet, you can do it there. If not, go steal some paper and crayons from the closest kid you can find. Whatever you do, make sure it's got a graph that plots your progress or decline. I promise this will go a long way to keeping you motivated and on track.

What's Your Credit Score?

Remember, this chapter is all about getting started. It's your pep talk to get you over the hump. So while we're breaking it all down, let's look at your credit score (we'll discuss it more in Chapter 20). It's a great measure of how bad your debt situation is.

If your debt situation is worse than you care to admit, your credit score will help to bring you back to reality. It'll also help you measure your progress in the eyes of lending professionals.

I'd suggest that you check your credit score once a quarter as you're trying to clean up debt. It's kind of like standing on the scale when you are trying to lose weight. It's where the rubber meets the road. Either your overall situation is improving, or it isn't.

Getting your credit report isn't the same thing as getting your credit score. Ideally, you would check both two to four times per year. You can receive your free credit report, which shows your account history and should be checked for errors once per year by visiting www.AnnualCreditReport.com. Your credit score, which is actually computed for lenders by private companies like the Fair Isaac Company (creators of the FICO score), is not required to be given to you for free. However, you can visit websites such as www.MyFico.com and pay a small fee to view this score that determines your rates on loans.

Here are the basic ranges and ratings for the FICO credit scores:

- **700–850.** You've got "Very Good" to "Excellent" credit depending on where you fall in that range. Getting a loan is usually no problem for people with scores in this range, and borrowers with these scores usually get the best rates and terms.

- **680–699.** You've got "Good" credit. With a score in this range, you can usually get a standard loan as long as your other factors, like income and down payments, are solid.

- **620–679.** You've got "Okay" credit. You can usually get a loan for smaller purchases without a co-signer or a major down payment, but you're going to pay for it. Borrowers in this range and below start getting charged higher interest rates and fees.

◆ **Below 620.** It's official, you've got "Bad" credit. You may or may not get approved for a loan based on how far below 620 your credit score is. If you do manage to get approved, the further your score falls, the higher the interest rate you'll typically pay.

Credit Scores and Monthly Payments

As you battle to get out of debt and to use debt wisely, it's of the utmost importance to realize how your credit scores affect your situation. In fact, there is nothing that may affect the money that flows in and out of your household more than your credit score.

I'll discuss the importance of salvaging your credit score in Chapter 20, but suffice it to say, you've got to start guarding that thing like it's the president!

> **Debt in America**
>
> According to Experian, one of the largest credit reporting companies in the United States, the average credit score of the American consumer is 674.

Your credit score is a rating of how "safe" you appear to be to a potential lender (i.e., how likely you are to pay off the money that you borrow). The higher your score, the safer you are. The safer you are, the more friendly your interest rate and repayment terms are going to be.

In fact, two people with different credit scores will be required to pay a noticeably different monthly payment on the same loan. The following table contains six different credit scores along with what the corresponding mortgage ends up costing them. For this example, I've used a 30-year fixed-rate mortgage on $250,000.

FICO Score	Interest Rate	Monthly Payment	Total Interest
720–850	5.888%	$1,481	$283,132
700–719	6.011%	$1,500	$290,232
675–699	6.548%	$1,588	$321,705
620–674	7.698%	$1,782	$391,540
560–619	8.531%	$1,928	$444,000
500–559	9.289%	$2,063	$492,952

As you can see, the failure to show tender loving care to your credit score results in some major money disappearing from your life. In fact, the difference in total interest paid between the best credit score and worst is over $200,000. This is money that could be used to pay off your other debt and save for your other goals. Heck, that's enough money to buy a second home!

Is Someone Making It Worse?

I was watching one of those funniest home video shows a while back. There was an adorable video of a dad digging this big hole in the backyard. Right behind him, just out of his line of sight, was a little kid with a shovel, throwing the dirt right back in the hole.

That's what it's like trying to get out of debt sometimes, when you share your finances with another person. In fact, it can be the source of a lot of tension in your relationships.

You may be the most determined person in the world when it comes to getting out of debt. But if someone else refuses to slow down their spending, or even worse, continues to incur new debts, you're going to get nowhere. If change is going to occur, you're going to need to sit down and have a serious talk with them about the changes that you think need to take place.

Debt in America

Despite the stereotypes of women being impulsive spenders, my professional experience suggests that men are just as prone to irrational purchases. The difference is that men tend to go months without being frivolous, but then make one large frivolous purchase. Women tend to make smaller purchases as they go along.

Here are some points to consider when having this less-than-fun discussion with someone you care about:

- **Don't place blame.** The moment you make someone else the whipping post for your frustrations is the moment he or she will probably stop listening. Even if you know you're right, you may need to swallow a little pride to get your plan moving.

- **Take a lot of blame.** Heck, take all of it if you can. The more you make this about you, the less defensive and resistant to change someone else will be.

- **Use "I" statements.** As you talk about your money stress, be sure to speak in the first person. Chances are, the other person cares about you a lot, too. When he or she sees the true extent of your stress and anxiety over your finances, the part of him or her that cares for you will want to step up and help!

◆ **Talk about temporary changes.** Permanent changes will send most partners who are struggling with denial running for the hills. Talking about a temporary change lasting 6, 12, or 18 months is a lot more palatable. Usually, by the time you get six months into it, your partner gets fired up about the change as well.

◆ **Ask for input.** Nobody likes to be bossed around. Handing someone your completed debt reduction plan without getting his or her input may get you some dirty looks or a few nights on the couch. Attempt to invite your loved one into the process and get his or her input.

The In's and Out's of Change

All right, enough talk. Let's get down to the brass tacks of changing your debt situation. Specifically, let's talk about how long it's going to take, when you should start, and how to get help if you need it.

Change Your Lifestyle and Your Spending Habits

One of my favorite quotes on hard work and change comes from Thomas Edison, who was asked about his successes in life. Edison said, "Opportunity is missed by most people, because it dresses in overalls and looks like hard work."

I think this is a great place to start when you think about getting rid of debt once and for all. There's about a million different ways you can tweak your life to move yourself toward being debt-free. You can make the process as comfortable or as strenuous as you want.

But be assured of this: there is a direct relationship between how much you are willing to change your lifestyle and spending habits, and how soon this debt will disappear. If you do it little by little, only a little bit will get done. If you are willing to make drastic changes, even *delaying gratification* in certain areas of your life, you can usually get all this behind you in two years or less.

How much will you need to change your life to get rid of debt? It all depends on how quickly you want to put all this behind you.

def•i•ni•tion

Delayed gratification is one of the most important concepts in the psychology of personal finance. It's the idea that your overall enjoyment of something will be greater if you're able to wait a certain period of time until you purchase or pay for it. This is especially true with debts and compound interest, where the reverse can often be true. By borrowing money to enjoy something now, you actually may create more stress and anxiety in the future. If you knew what the true emotional cost was of your purchases, you might be more careful before you spent.

Reward Yourself Along the Way

A good debt reduction plan will have some fun built into it. Just like a workable diet that lets you order the nachos with extra cheese once in a while, a good debt reduction plan is going to let you blow off some steam to keep you sane. Don't start packing your bag for Tahiti just yet, though.

An important part of sticking to your debt plan is going to be finding alternative ways of enjoying life without having to spend the big bucks. Start by treating yourself every time you eliminate a piece of debt. When you get the car paid off, go buy a new outfit. When that credit card balance hits zero, go out to a nice dinner. When you finally get your house paid off, take a vacation. Reward yourself for your hard work—just make sure the reward is relative to the accomplishment! You don't get a new Lexus for paying off the $400 balance on your Macy's credit card.

Start Today

Did you know that there is one day of the week that is statistically proven to be the worst for starting a successful diet? Any guesses? The worst day to start a diet is … tomorrow!

The longer you wait to put your plan into action, the less likely it is to have a permanent effect. If you truly want to resolve yourself to getting rid of debt, you need to take the first step today. I don't care if you're reading this book on a lounge chair in the Bahamas on your vacation, you can begin making immediate changes. Just say no to that souvenir.

Set Realistic Goals

Perhaps the only thing worse than dragging your feet on getting started is setting completely unrealistic goals. We've all known those people. They're the ones you see a few days after New Year's Day, and they inform you that in their quest to get in shape, they've signed up for a triathlon. Now, you know this person. You know that they haven't run a lap since high school. You know they don't know how to ride a bike. Worst of all, you know they're afraid of water. It doesn't take a lot of guesswork to figure out that this person will probably give up on their goal after a few weeks.

The same holds true with your debt reduction plan. You've got to learn to crawl before you can walk, and learn to take control of your spending piece by piece, before you can start paying down large amounts.

As you embark on your quest to get rid of debt, here are some tips on setting realistic goals:

- If you've got more than a couple thousands of dollars in debt, you shouldn't expect to eliminate it in less than a year. A more realistic goal is 12 to 24 months for your short-term debts, and 10 to 20 years for your long-term debts.

> **In the Red**
>
> If your debt reduction plan can only happen if one or two other things fall into place (like a raise, tax refund, or inheritance), there's a good chance it will fail. While miraculous increases in income are always welcome, most successful debt reduction plans have their foundation in cutting expenses by a small but increasing amount each month.

- I'd love to see you cut your expenses in half if you can, but most people won't be able to do that. A more reasonable goal is to cut your expenses by 10% to 15% until you get out of debt.

- Suddenly increasing your debt repayments is kind of like stepping on the gas real hard when your car is standing still on a gravel road. The wheels are going to spin for a bit before you finally get some traction. As you begin to make increased payments, it may not feel like you're getting anywhere for a few months. Keep your foot on the gas, and you'll get some traction before long.

The Need for Accountability

A few years ago, one of my friends talked me into a 5k "mud run" at the Marine base near us. This was a day that the base let nonmilitary folks come and run the boot-camp obstacle course for prizes.

My friend, who plays competitive soccer, left me in the dust after the first mile. After another mile, which included a long, winding, uphill dirt road, I decided to walk a little. I hadn't been walking 20 seconds when I heard screaming behind me.

"Why are you walking!? Who told you that you could walk!?" It was a big, burly Marine drill sergeant, and he was clearly talking to me. I'm not sure whether it was fear, shock, or respect, but my feet started moving.

"I want you to keep running, son. And, if you even think about walking again, you come find me first. I'll talk you out of it." I ran the entire rest of the race, though I nearly puked my brains out afterward.

You need accountability when it comes to this plan. You need someone to talk you out of giving up. You need someone to pat you on the back as you succeed. You need someone who can see that you are moving toward the finish line, even though you feel like you're barely crawling.

My biggest recommendation in finding an accountability partner is to find someone who also wants to get out of debt. That way, you two can run this race together. Here are some other practical pointers on choosing an accountability partner:

- Unless you have a spouse who is really excited to get out of debt as well, you should find someone who is emotionally separated from your debt. Even other close family members may make poor choices, because they may not be able to be completely honest.

- True accountability takes hearing and saying the hard things sometimes. Your relationship should be secure enough that your accountability partner can give you a hard time without you taking it personally.

- A good accountability partner will be able to grab coffee with you once a month, at a pre-arranged time. They'll be able to review your Progress Chart from earlier in the chapter with you, and ask the critical questions about why and how things are changing.

Dollars and Sense

If you cannot find an accountability partner on your own, or you think your use of debt may truly border on compulsive, the Debtor's Anonymous (DA) program may be for you. Modeled after Alcoholics Anonymous and other 12-step programs, this program helps people stop using debt, one day at a time. You can find more info about a DA group near you on their website at www.DebtorsAnonymous.com.

Should I Get Professional Help?

It's easy to see why you'd want to hire a professional to help you get out of debt. Just sorting out the paperwork can feel like you need an advanced degree. But unfortunately, most of what a financial planner or a debt counselor is going to tell you is either common sense or something you'll learn by the end of this book.

On top of that, a professional, no matter how good they are, can't do the most important part for you. They can't make you spend less. They can tell you to spend less, but you've still got to put the plan into action. If you are willing to make dramatic, but temporary, changes in your budget, getting out of debt is as easy as falling off a log.

Unfortunately, though, there are a lot of people out there who prey on people in desperate situations. We'll go into it more in Chapter 22, but people with a ton of debt make great targets for scam artists.

When it comes down to hiring professional help, I generally think you should try reducing your debt on your own before hiring anyone. Give yourself 6 to 12 months. But if you know there's no way you'll do it on your own, or you haven't made much headway after 12 months, consider getting help from a pro. Here are some things you should look for in a debt professional:

- **Focus on budgeting.** I know I repeat this ad nauseam, but getting out of debt is all about controlling the flow of money in and out of your household. A professional who can help you gain control of this is going to be the best kind to hire.

- **Pay a flat or hourly fee.** The best professionals to work with are the ones who charge you for their time, not their results. Professionals who get rewarded to cut your debt by as much as possible, as soon as possible, may offer you advice that is not in your long-term best interest.

- **Consider a CFP or a CPA.** Both Certified Financial Planners (CFPs) and Certified Public Accountants (CPAs) have gone through extensive training and licensing procedures. They may not be the cheapest professionals to hire, but you are guaranteed a certain minimum quality.

- **Try your Employee Assistance Plan.** Many employers now offer Employee Assistance Plans that give their employees free or low-cost access to a variety of financial and legal professionals who will get you started on your way.

◆ **Consider Consumer Credit Counseling Services (CCCS).** CCCS is a non-profit organization that offers free budget counseling over the telephone as well as at numerous locations throughout the United States. Additional services beyond the free budget counseling are available for a reasonable fee. You can locate an agency near you by visiting www.NFCC.org.

The Least You Need to Know

◆ You need to ask yourself the tough questions to determine if you are in debt denial.

◆ To get an accurate picture of your financial situation, you need to add it all up: short- and long-term balances, monthly payments, and credit score.

◆ A progress chart that tracks these numbers from month to month will help keep you on track.

◆ The sooner you start making changes in your lifestyle and spending habits, the sooner you'll start putting debt behind you.

◆ If you haven't been able to reduce your debt after 12 months of trying, consider hiring a professional to help you.

Chapter 6

Sticking to Your Plan

In This Chapter

- ◆ All debt comes with an opportunity cost
- ◆ Your most important financial goal: saving for retirement
- ◆ Planning for college costs
- ◆ Why paying interest is a waste of money
- ◆ Debt-related stress and your health

When my wife and I went to the hospital to deliver our first son, our doctor recommended that we hang up his first little outfit in the delivery room. The theory was that, if in the middle of the labor pains, my wife could see the outfit our son would soon wear, it would make the labor much more bearable.

This is actually based on a widely embraced personal growth and athletic theory called "visualization." In essence, by envisioning the results, it both keeps you focused enough to achieve them, as well as eases the struggle and pain to get there. Getting out of debt is no different.

Now, I know you bought this book because you wanted to get out of debt. You're sick of the monthly payments, afraid of your finances collapsing, and are breaking out in cold sweats every time the phone rings. But, to truly achieve your goal of getting and staying out of debt, you'll need to keep the "why" at the forefront of your mind as you struggle to learn the "how."

Opportunity Costs: Understanding What You Are Missing

Opportunity cost is a concept from economics that states whenever you make a choice to do something, you are also making a choice not to do many other things. Oftentimes, those other choices had benefits attached to them that you will now miss out on because you chose another seemingly good option.

Great examples of opportunity costs in action can be found on any number of TV games shows like *Who Wants to Be a Millionaire* or *Deal or No Deal*. In these shows, a contestant has to make a tough choice between taking a sure thing like $25,000, or taking a chance of winning $1 million or going home broke. If you choose the $25,000, it costs you an opportunity to possibly leave with a million bucks. If you choose to roll the dice and you lose, you missed an opportunity at a guaranteed $25,000.

def•i•ni•tion

Opportunity cost refers to the opportunity missed when one choice is made over another.

Everything in your personal finances has an opportunity cost. If you pay down your debt, you lose the opportunity to do all kinds of fun things with your extra cash, from spending it to investing it. However, if you pay down your debt, you'll likely be debt- and stress-free much sooner.

So what are some of the largest opportunity costs when you don't pay down your debt? The biggest missed alternatives are the ability to save toward other goals, pay less interest in the future, and be a healthier person.

Dollars and Sense

One of the best ways to approach the opportunity cost of debt is to consider your interest rates as "potential rates of return." In other words, if you had to choose between putting $100 per month toward a savings account paying 2% and a credit card charging you 15%, you should pay down the credit card. Even though you won't earn the 2% annually on your $100, you avoided paying 15% on the same amount. For the savings account to make more sense, it'd have to have a higher interest rate than your credit card. In short, this means paying off a 15% credit card is roughly equivalent to earning 15% on your money!

Opportunity Cost #1: Your Future Goals

As a financial planner who spent the first part of my career helping people save and invest money, this opportunity cost is the single scariest. It is not just a missed opportunity that you'll someday kick yourself for, snap your fingers, and say "Aw Shucks!" Rather, it's an opportunity cost that will determine the day-to-day existence of possibly one third of your entire life. I'm talking about retirement.

Now, a good percentage of you reading this book will say something along the lines of "retirement is so far away that I'm not worried about it" or "I'll worry about retirement when I get out of debt." But, the key thing I want to pound into your head is that retirement planning is monumentally less painful the earlier you do it. In fact, if you wait until 15 to 20 years before retirement to start planning, you may not be able to pull it off.

Why is it such a big deal? Well, the biggest problem is that people are living longer and longer, and our employers and Social Security system are giving us less and less. In fact, it is very possible that you might retire at age 65 and live to be close to 100 years old. That means that 35 years, or one third of your life, will be spent without income from a job. If you are hoping Social Security is going to cover even the majority of that, think again.

I don't mean to scare you, but rather hope to give you some major motivation for moving forward. Just like my wife kept her eyes on that little sailor outfit during delivery, you need to keep your eyes on retirement as you try and decide what to do with each and every penny of your income and expenses.

Retirement: The Mother of All Financial Goals

Before we get much farther in this book, I want to tattoo this concept on your brain. Not that I want you to spend every dime you have for the rest of your life saving for retirement, but you've got to do what you've got to do. Period.

I'm not going to show you step-by-step how to calculate the exact amount you should save each year, but I do want to give you a rule of thumb and show you how painful procrastination is.

My rule of thumb, based on a decade as a retirement planner, is that you'll need to have 20 times your "unmet income need" for your first year of retirement in the bank on the day you retire. In other words, if you think you'll need $50,000 per year for the rest of your life, and Social Security is going to give you $20,000, you'll need

$600,000 in the bank ($50,000 minus $20,000, multiplied by 20). This amount would provide you with a large enough nest egg to live off just the interest of your investments. Not using up the investments themselves is crucial because none of us know how long we're going to live.

Dollars and Sense

Determining how much you need to save for retirement each month or year is an advanced calculation that involves the "time value of money." Luckily, there are some great calculators online that can do the work for you in a matter of seconds. Check out your company's retirement plan website, www.RetirePlan.About.com, or Finance.Yahoo.com for some easy-to-use online calculators. I also list a few in Appendix C.

So, for example, if you are 25 years old and want to accumulate $600,000 by age 65, you'd have to save about $175 per month (assuming 8% annual growth). Over your entire life of saving, this would translate into about $84,000 out of your pocket that grew to $600,000. Not too shabby.

But what if you wait until age 35 to start saving toward your $600,000? Then you'll need to save about $410 per month, or more than double, to accumulate the same $600,000 at retirement. And even though you saved for retirement for 10 years less than the 25-year-old, you'll end up dishing out about $147,000!

Debt in America

If you are aged 45 to 65, you are now part of what historians are calling the "sandwich generation." Members of the sandwich generation are faced with unprecedented financial pressures as they plan their own retirements in the midst of trying to help their own children pay for college and simultaneously care for their own aging parents.

At age 45, your monthly savings number jumps to $1,000 per month that you'll need to save for retirement, or about $242,000 out of pocket.

See the point? If you're not saving toward retirement early, you will have to pay for it exponentially later. If you are spending money instead of saving, whether it is going toward vacations or interest on your debts and loans, there's an opportunity cost. Getting your debts paid off as soon as possible means that you'll be able to put money toward these goals while they are still within reason.

Four Immediate Retirement Strategies

It's a question that comes up almost every time I sit down to help someone dig their way out of debt: should I wait until I'm out of debt to start saving toward retirement?

Unfortunately, the answer doesn't consist of a simple yes or no. Rather, the answer is probably a combination of "maybe" and "some."

For the most part, we want to free up everything we can to get rid of our short-term debts before we dive headfirst into retirement planning. But there are four things you should be doing today, even if you are putting the majority of your free income toward paying down debt:

1. **Take the 401(k) match.** If your employer is willing to match your retirement plan contributions, I'd recommend contributing up to the point where they stop matching. Even if they only match you fifty cents for every dollar you contribute, that's like getting a 50% interest rate on your savings in the first year.

2. **Take the IRS match.** Did you know Uncle Sam will also match you for saving money into a retirement plan or an IRA? The Retirement Savings Contribution Credit effectively gives you a bonus on your tax return in the form of a tax credit. This credit ranges anywhere from 10 to 50% of the amount contributed for unmarried wage earners who make under $26,000 ($52,000 for married filing jointly). Check out IRS Publication 590 for more details.

3. **Buy your company's stock.** If your employer gives you an opportunity to buy shares of your company stock at a discount, this may be worth doing. Often, companies offer their employees a substantial discount on the current purchase price of their stock—sometimes as much as 15%. Additionally, the IRS may offer additional tax benefits in retirement to employees who invest a portion of their 401(k) or employer-sponsored plan assets in company stock. Of course, if you think your company's stock is headed south, you'll probably want to steer clear. Talk with your investment and tax advisor for more details.

4. **Stay put at that good job.** Do you have one of those increasingly rare jobs that promises to pay you a monthly pension when you retire? If you do, I'm jealous. Before you jump ship and go searching for greener pastures, find out how much longer you need to stay to lock in your future benefits. Another couple years at the same desk may be a worthwhile trade-off for that monthly check at retirement.

College Costs

I'm not going to bore you with every possible financial goal, but if you plan on putting yourself or someone else through college in the future, it's imperative that you begin to save for that now. Again, to save adequately, you'll need to eliminate your monthly debt obligations as soon as possible.

Failure to plan for college expenses has two major effects in my experience. First, many people who have not planned and saved adequately usually stop saving for their other goals while scraping to pay for tuition. Even a small delay in getting started on saving can have a huge impact on what you'll have to save later to play catch-up.

Second, the failure to plan for college usually results in the accumulation of more debt in the form of student loans. While these are often a necessary evil, they can be one more financial weight around your already exhausted neck. (See Chapter 15 for more on student loans.)

> **In the Red** _____
>
> Every year, college costs are increasing faster than just about any other expense, with the possible exception of gas. In fact, while normal inflation in the U.S. economy averages somewhere between 2% to 3% annually, college costs are increasing at an average of 6% per year. This means that they're doubling every 12 years. Considering that four years at a public school can easily cost over $50,000, the cost of a public education a decade from now may be well over $100,000. Will you be ready?

By getting your debts taken care of as soon as possible, you can begin taking care of this goal, so that it, too, doesn't overwhelm you later. After all, your goal is not to just eliminate debt or save for the future, but to do what you need to do, so you can get on with enjoying today.

Just like with retirement, there are things you should be doing today, even in the midst of getting out debt, to help prepare for future college costs:

◆ **Move to a different state.** Just kidding. But there are some states that offer their residents a matching contribution for putting money into a Section 529 plan. For example, the Arkansas Aspiring Scholars program will match a $250 contribution to their state savings plan with up to $500 (depending on income). Check with your state treasurer's office to see if such a plan exists.

- ◆ **Contribute toward college for holiday and birthday gifts.** Consider opening college accounts for your kids at your local brokerage house and asking the grandparents to divert some of their holiday spending there. Trust me, your kids will appreciate it way more than a pair of socks.

- ◆ **Use UPromise and BabyMint.** Both of these services are free to sign up for, and set aside money into a college account for your child every time you shop. It doesn't actually increase the cost of your purchases, but instead is a way for stores to reward you for your loyalty. You can also have your friends and family register their cards to contribute to your child as well. Check out www. UPromise.com and www.BabyMint.com.

Opportunity Cost #2: Paying Less Interest

Okay, I get it. Money is fun to spend, right? Would you be surprised if I told you that I agree and love to spend money? I do.

Ultimately, my beef with debt is that it forces you to send your money to someone else for something you bought in the past. I'd much rather get to spend it on things I truly want now or will need in the future (like a retirement or a college education for my kids).

You have to shift your mind-set from "I don't want to miss out on fun today" to "I want to have even more fun tomorrow." It's one of those "is the glass half empty or half full" type of moments.

By scrambling to pay off your debts now, that means interest does not accumulate as fast. That in turn means your debt gets paid off even quicker. This of course means the money you waste on debt each month will now be freed up for you to spend on whatever you like!

Let's look at someone with $25,000 in combined short-term debts (a payday loan, a few credit cards, and some medical bills), with an average interest rate of 20%. Take a look at their total interest costs based on some different fixed monthly payments.

Monthly Payment	Months Until Paid Off	Total Interest Paid
$500	109	$29,202.43
$750	50	$11,795.88
$1,000	33	$7,610.73
$1,250	25	$5,665.32
$1,500	20	$4,534.18

What a difference $250 makes as you raise your payment from $500 per month to $750. It cuts your repayment period by more than half and saves $18,000 in interest!

For what you saved in interest by paying off your debt as quickly as possible, you could go out and pay cash for a new car. If that doesn't make the case for an opportunity cost of using your money for other things besides paying down debt, I don't know what does!

> **Debt in America** _____
>
> At the time of this book's writing, the Consumer Confidence Index has hit a 16-year low. Ironically, but not surprisingly, personal debt is at an all-time high. There's no doubt that these two factors are linked, and a major conclusion can be drawn: America is stressed out by its debt!

Opportunity Cost #3: Your Health and Sanity

What would you think if I told you study after psychological study ranked financial pressure as the one of the leading causes of stress, anxiety, unhappiness, and relational discord? And what if I also told you a joint study done by the Universities of Virginia and Arizona linked physical health problems to financial stress?

My guess is that most of these problems didn't come from having too much money, or even just enough money. Instead, it probably came from owing a whole lot of money to other people.

As you clean up your debt situation, I'll bet that you'll begin to see noticeable differences in everything from your emotions to your physical health. While it can't replace a healthier diet, regular exercise, or a trip to the doctor, it can sure help the underlying problems!

> ### Set a Goal
>
> To help you visualize the rewards of all your hard work, I want you to sit back, close your eyes for 60 seconds, and imagine a debt-free life. In fact, I want you to imagine the number-one thing that will change. Do it now, I'll wait right here for you!
>
> Now, grab your Debt Journal and sum up that change in three or four words. Write it really big and circle it. This is your opportunity cost of failing to reduce your debt. By not getting your debts paid down, this is what you're missing out on. Strive to keep this at the front of your mind!

The Least You Need to Know

- Every choice you make with your money also represents another choice you missed out on, or an "opportunity cost."

- Pay down debt as soon as possible so you can tackle your other financial goals.

- Monthly debt payments rob from your retirement.

- Failing to plan for college costs can lead to significant debt.

- Increasing your debt payments by a few hundred dollars can save tens of thousands over 7 to 10 years.

- Debt causes stress, and stress affects your health. Get your debt under control and your physical health will improve.

Part 2

Your Debt Reduction Plan

The road to financial hell is paved with good intentions. So if you want to make any significant change, you'll need to arm yourself with a lot more than intentions—you'll need an action plan. A solid debt reduction plan leaves nothing to chance, not even your own ability to put it into place. In this part, you're going to do everything from putting your past expenditures under the microscope to developing a strategy for money if it falls into your lap.

By the time you move on to the next part, you'll be armed with a payment strategy and will have a solid idea of how you're going to get rid of the balances that are driving you nuts.

Chapter 7

Controlling Your Cash Flow

In This Chapter

- ◆ Increase discretionary income, reduce debt
- ◆ Fixed expenses and variable expenses
- ◆ Tips for increasing your income
- ◆ Tips for decreasing your fixed expenses
- ◆ Tips for decreasing your variable expenses

The most important thing I've learned in all my years of school, training, and professional experience can be summed up in a phrase uttered by my final college professor. He said, regarding everything from large corporate budgets to our personal finances, "Cash flow is king."

In other words, those who have more money "flowing" in than out will ultimately control their destiny. Those who run a negative cash flow each month will become subject to others (in the form of debt).

Never is this so true as for those of you reading this book. You've found yourself in a situation where you are enslaved to balances you owe someone else. To break free, you must minimize those balances. Short of winning the lottery, the only surefire way to lower those balances is to increase your net cash flow each month.

Discretionary Income Is the Key

With an increase in positive cash flow, you can direct more toward your debt. The more debt you pay down, the less interest accumulates during the following week, month, or year. The less interest accumulates, the greater the amount of your next payment that gets applied to the balance, and so on.

By increasing your positive cash flow, you can ultimately increase your debt payments. Instead of being caught in a downward and negative spiral, you find yourself in a positive, upward spiral. There is a name for this "positive cash flow" that you need to increase in order to eliminate your debt. It's called discretionary income.

While the term sounds complex, it's simple when you stop and think about it. It's the income that's left after all your required bills have been paid; you choose how to spend it. To accelerate the process of getting out of debt, you ultimately have to increase the amount of discretionary income left at the end of the month.

In the Red

Nonsufficient fund (NSF) fees on your bank account can actually cause you to start the month with a negative balance in your bank account. This can put you into a cycle where part of each paycheck immediately goes to pay your negative bank balance and the mounting fees. Consider using an FDIC-insured bank that doesn't charge overdraft fees or that offers an overdraft protection. Doing so can protect hundreds, possibly thousands, of dollars in cash flow each year.

The Formula for Discretionary Income

Calculating discretionary income is simple. There's no need to get out your protractor or call your friend with a Ph.D. in Economics. It's a simple three-part formula that requires basic arithmetic. Once you burn this formula into your brain, you'll begin to see every dollar that flows in and out of your household in a different light.

Discretionary income is calculated by taking your household total income and subtracting two kinds of expenses from it: fixed and variable expenses, which I'll discuss in a moment.

On paper, it looks like this:

Total monthly income

– Fixed expenses

– Variable expenses

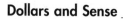

= Discretionary income

That's it!

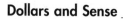
Dollars and Sense

If you consistently get a tax refund every year, it means that you are having too much withheld from the paychecks that come into your household. While it's always fun to have the government hand you a big check, it essentially means that you've loaned them some of your discretionary income, interest-free, for a year or more! If this is your situation, you need to talk to your accountant, financial planner, or employer about adjusting your withholding on your W-4. To calculate the correct number of exemptions to report on your W-4, visit the IRS website at www.IRS.gov and use their online withholding calculator.

Fixed vs. Variable Expenses

While you could just lump all expenses into one category, I think it is crucial to separate them. The reason for this separation has to do with how you spend money, and more specifically, how you chip away at your discretionary income.

Fixed expenses are not just those expenses that are the exact same amount every month, but they are the ones that don't change if you are reckless, lose control, or rationalize. Essentially, you pay them every month and the amount due isn't determined by your emotions or psychology. Some examples of fixed expenses are rent or mortgage, car payments, utility bills, and tuition.

Variable expenses, on the other hand, are expenses that can vary widely from month to month, depending on your money attitudes and willpower. When you're having a hard time breaking even each month, much less creating discretionary income to pay off debt, variable expenses are usually the culprit. Variable expenses can include things like clothes, dining out, groceries, gifts, and leisure activities.

Ways to Increase Discretionary Income

If there is a punch line to this book, a must-do for your action plan or a secret to getting out of debt, increasing your discretionary income is it. You've got to make this your central mission. You need to realize that every dollar flowing in and out of your household affects your discretionary income.

With that in mind, there are only three real ways you can increase your discretionary income. While there might be a million different tips and tricks, they all still fall under one of these three categories:

- **Increase your household income.** If you increase the amount of money coming in, there's a good chance you'll increase the amount of money left over. But it's also one of the hardest things to do. It requires getting a raise or second job, or developing some type of passive income like owning rental property.

- **Decrease your fixed expenses.** Our fixed expenses are often some of our biggest, which means we can make a huge impact on our discretionary income by lowering them. But finding a lower-rent apartment, getting rid of a car payment, or eliminating your child's preschool tuition is a big decision that requires major life changes. Chances are, you'll adjust your fixed expenses over the long-term, not overnight.

- **Decrease your variable expenses.** Decreasing your variable expenses is the only real change you can make today. You can choose to say no to the iced mocha, skip the big birthday gift for Mom, or pass on that "thing" you think you really deserve. But let's face it, that's all the fun stuff. Knowing how hard it'll be to cut these expenses, it's important to remember that this change is temporary, and also to reward yourself as you make progress.

> **Debt in America**
>
> Frugal living refers to a growing movement of people who make it their mission to cut their costs so they can reach their financial goals as soon as possible. In an ironic shift from the consumerism of the 1980s and 1990s, people now brag about how much they save instead of how much they spend. You can find a never-ending supply of frugal living tips just by searching the Internet and online blogs.

Twelve Ideas for Increasing Income

While the opportunities to increase your income are really only limited by your creativity and motivation, here are the top ideas I've seen work for people over the years:

1. **Volunteer to pick up extra shifts.** Instead of sitting around the house wondering how to get out of debt, pick up an extra shift at work. Working one extra 8-hour shift every two weeks, at $10 per hour, would be $2,080 a year.

2. **Ask for a raise.** If you've been the model employee, now is definitely the right time to ask for a raise. Try phrasing it to your boss in the form of a question like, "What are the important things for me to do to get a raise as soon as possible?"

3. **Get a second job.** There's all kinds of stuff you can do on the weekends or at night for some extra dough. Consider getting a job at a place you already shop since many employers offer discounts to their employees. If you have days off during the week, consider getting a job as a substitute teacher.

4. **Pick up seasonal work.** Many businesses need extra help at different times of the year and pay a great hourly wage because it's hard to find quality help. Check with local tax preparers in the early part of the year, resorts during the summer, and the mall at Christmas.

5. **Have a garage sale.** It's time to get rid of some of that stuff you charged on the credit card years ago. A good garage sale can easily put $500 to $1,000 in your pockets. For large and more unique items, try EBay or CraigsList.

6. **Rent out a room.** If you own a house or are renting an apartment by yourself, you might be able to seriously knock down your debt by renting out a room to someone else. An extra $300 to $500 per month goes a long way!

7. **Start blogging.** You can start an online diary of your own, with ads built right into them, or you can sign on to blog for someone else. Blogging for someone else can pay anywhere from $3 to $20 per post, especially if you have a unique perspective or skill.

8. **Freelance.** If you have certain job skills or talent, ranging from bookkeeping to website design, you can make significant money working from home. Go to Google and search for "freelance websites" where you can bid on projects people need completed.

9. **Tutor.** Were you that kid who always got 102% on the math tests? Do you love American History or Spanish verbs? There are a lot of kids who don't, with parents who are happy to pay $20 per hour for good tutoring. You can tutor on the weekends at your local coffee shop.

In the Red _____

Watch out for scams! If it sounds too good to be true, it probably is. Be wary of work-at-home and money-making scams. Be especially cautious of any home business or income opportunity that requires you to pay an upfront fee or make an investment. The best home businesses most often seem to be ones where someone uses an existing skill to meet a demand in their neighborhood or community.

10. **Turn your hobby into a home business.** When we were really poor, my wife learned how to make beaded jewelry at her preschool mom's group. We started using her creations in place of store-bought gifts, and it wasn't long before people were asking how to buy them. She works when she wants and makes an extra $2,000 to $3,000 per year.

11. **Open a home day care.** If you are already a stay-at-home parent, taking care of a few extra kids besides your own can bring in significant money. After a few required classes and a safety inspection, you can start providing day care for other children at $8 to $15 per hour, per child!

12. **Recycle.** For years, I was that parent scooping up all the cans and bottles after my kid's baseball games and at my office. The $10 to $20 per week I'd earn on Saturday mornings helped me overcome the weird looks I'd get from my co-workers.

Twelve Ideas for Decreasing Fixed Expenses

Decreasing your fixed expenses can result in a huge jump in your discretionary income. Oftentimes, though, getting rid of or lowering a fixed expense can take a major lifestyle adjustment. But when you are battling to eliminate debt, the thousands of dollars you may save might well be worth it. Here are some ideas:

1. **Ditch the ride.** Over my years as a financial planner, I've seen few things that suck up as much discretionary income as a car payment. Add in the other costs such as gas, insurance, and maintenance, and you can easily spend $5,000 to $10,000 per year for the privilege of sitting in traffic. One to two years of riding the bus or subway, or even carpooling with your accountability partner (Chapter 5), may get you completely out of debt!

2. **Put a smaller roof over your head.** There are a lot of reasons why you may have needed a bigger house or apartment in the past. But since the kids moved out, the dog ran away, and you've sold a bunch of your stuff at a garage sale, you

could make do with less space. A few hundred dollars less per month in rent will go a long way toward getting you out of debt.

3. **Cancel your PMI.** Mortgage insurance is required by most lenders when they loan you more than 80% of a home's value. However, when your mortgage balance drops below 80% you are no longer required to pay PMI. Oftentimes, companies will continue to charge it until you ask them to stop. Canceling your PMI as soon as you're eligible can save hundreds each month.

4. **Cancel unused subscriptions/memberships.** Whether it's the gym or the newspaper, there are a lot of things that slowly nickel-and-dime us to death every month. A couple of canceled memberships or subscriptions could easily save $50 per month, or $600 per year!

5. **Shop your insurance.** If you haven't updated your life, health, auto, or home insurance in the last few years, now may be a great time. Besides making sure you don't have too much insurance, you may also find significant savings as you shop.

6. **Go green.** A few years ago, our son, who was in kindergarten, started giving us a hard time about all the energy we waste. To humor him, we started working really hard to shut off the lights when we walked out of a room, bought more energy-efficient appliances, and got rid of that second, inefficient fridge in the garage. Our monthly utility savings were $50 to $100 per month.

7. **Get rid of cable.** Cable TV, while a fun luxury, can easily cost $50 or more per month just for the basic service. When you add in digital cable, HDTV, and those digital video recorders, it can easily cost you $100 or more per month. That's $1,200 per year. That's a lot of debt you could pay off!

8. **Get rid of a phone.** In this day and age, it feels like a little bit of overkill to have a house phone and a cell phone. Consider getting rid of your house phone and using the $20 to $40 per month to pay off your debts.

9. **Quit smoking.** Don't get me wrong, I enjoy the occasional fine cigar. But heavy smokers are costing themselves a ton of money. A pack a day will cost you over $1,000 per year, plus the increased insurance and out-of-pocket medical costs. It may help lower your stress, but so will being debt-free!

10. **Use regular gas instead of premium.** For most light drivers, the difference in quality will be negligible. Most car experts would also agree that it doesn't make any difference in how long your engine lasts. Saving 20¢ per gallon, with one weekly fill-up, could easily save you $150 to $200 per year.

11. **Send your kids to public school.** Private school tuition can run anywhere from a couple hundred dollars per month, into the thousands. Consider putting all your kids in public school at a certain age, and using the thousands of dollars in savings to pay off debt and save for college.

12. **Buy from the source.** I have many friends, both in the city and suburban neighborhoods, who buy fresh produce straight from the farm. In fact, for $30 per month, one friend gets two huge baskets of fresh produce delivered straight to her door. It's fresh, healthy, and about 50% less than buying from the local supermarket. Other companies do this for meat, poultry, and fish, offering similar savings. A good place to start is your local farmers' market.

Twelve Ideas for Decreasing Variable Expenses

Variable expenses are simultaneously the easiest to cut and the hardest to control. If you fail to pay attention to your variable expenses, your debt-reduction plan will feel like it's going nowhere. If you get creative, you'll reach your goals faster than planned. Here are some ideas:

1. **Use grocery coupons.** No one decision may decrease your variable expenses like using grocery coupons. Consistent use may cut your monthly grocery expenses anywhere from 35% to 60%. In fact, my wife consistently purchases about $1,000 worth of groceries for about $400 each month. Be sure to check out websites like TheGroceryGame.com and CouponMom.com to maximize your savings.

2. **Always use a 2-for-1 coupon.** Whether you are going out to dinner or going to a theme park, don't go anywhere without using a discount voucher or coupon. Order an Entertainment Discount Book (approximately $40) for your area at www.Entertainment.com.

3. **Always go "off-peak."** While you should be trying to cut back on your expenses, you and your loved ones may still need that occasional escape. When that time comes, always try to go "there" when no one else can or wants to. Most bed and breakfast inns are 50% off if you go Monday through Thursday.

4. **Set gift limits.** A lot of people with credit card problems can trace it back to holidays, birthdays, and anniversaries. Consider setting an agreed-upon dollar limit with the people you're exchanging gifts with. Consider giving gift cards or writing a letter to tell someone how much they truly matter to you.

5. **Trim clothing costs.** One person can easily spend over $1,000 per year on clothing. To help lower your costs, consider shopping at the end of the season when clothes are on sale. Also look around your local second-hand store—there are great bargains to be found, especially on kids' clothing.

6. **Download the song, not the album.** One of the great blessings of the technological age is websites like iTunes. Instead of buying a $15 album just to get that one song, you can download the one you want for 99¢.

7. **Make your own cup of coffee.** Even if you made your own coffee half of the time, it might save $10 to $15 per week, or over $750 per year.

8. **Take your lunch.** Whether it is the "taco truck" or the factory cafeteria, eating out can easily cost $5 to $10 per day. Bringing a lunch just twice every week could save $500 to $1,000 per year.

9. **Go camping for your next vacation.** Two nights at a three-star hotel with a view of the parking lot … $198. Two nights beachfront in a tent listening to the waves and the birds … $28. Getting your credit card paid off sooner than later … priceless.

10. **Avoid dry cleaning.** Getting five items dry-cleaned per week can easily cost you $10 or more per week, or over $500 per year. By wearing your washer-friendly items, as well as not buying new dry-clean-only garments, you can save a bundle!

11. **Wash your own car.** The full-service carwash can be a money trap. Between the carwash, the tip, and some snacks while you wait, you can easily spend $20 every couple of weeks. By washing it yourself, you'll save $400 to $500 per year and get a free workout.

12. **Donate goods instead of cash.** If you feel called to give to charity, consider emptying out your house or closet instead of your wallet! You can still take a tax deduction, and use the cash to pay down your debts.

> ### Set a Goal
>
> Without even completing a budget, you probably have some idea where your expenses are getting you into trouble. While you don't need to set a dollar amount yet, take a moment now to pull out your Debt Journal and make a top five list of the expenses you know you need to cut.

The Least You Need to Know

◆ Increasing your discretionary income is key to eliminating your debt.

◆ You can only increase your discretionary income by making more money or spending less.

◆ Increasing your income may allow you to cut fewer expenses.

◆ Cutting fixed expenses is a major decision, but yields big results.

◆ Variable expenses are the easiest to control, the least missed, and can be started today!

Chapter 8

How to Make a Budget

In This Chapter

- ◆ What will a good budget do for you?
- ◆ Ideal, actual, and compromise budgets
- ◆ Tracking your historical expenses
- ◆ Key steps to creating a workable budget
- ◆ Budgeting pitfalls

One of my favorite moments as a financial planner is bringing up the "B" word. All you have to do is say "budget" and many people start looking for the door. If you were tempted to skip this chapter, or are prone to think that this will mostly apply to other people, you've got plenty of company.

Just like those little army tanks in the *Godzilla* movies, denial is quickly crushed by the creation of a thorough budget. Perhaps that's why most of us start squirming when we begin talking about one. We know there is nowhere else to hide. We know that the financial "rubber" is about to meet the road.

The Purpose of a Budget

To help you better understand where I think budgets fit into your life, I want you to imagine your journey to get out of debt as a road trip. You're the driver, and it's up to you to get us where we need to go.

Most people, when I use this analogy, want to think of the budget as the front windshield. They think that it shows us where we're going. I would argue that it's just the opposite; it's a rearview mirror. A good budget shows us where we've *been*, as much or more than where we need to go.

Most successful budgets are not built on speculation about what you will spend. Rather, they're built on a thorough knowledge of what your past spending habits are. From there, you often kick yourself and swear to make changes.

In your journey to get out of debt, I want you to imagine budgets as a hindsight tool. They're not the front windshield, and they're not their steering wheel.

Set a Goal

People talk and talk about needing to do a budget, but most never get around to it. Because accurately doing your budget is going to require you tracking down your bank and credit card statements, let's go ahead and set a date to get this done.

Grab your calendar and your Debt Journal. Pick four times in the coming year, including one in the next week, when you will do or redo your budget. Title it "Budget Review Dates" and write these dates under the other goals you've set for yourself.

What a Budget Is—and Isn't

First and foremost, let me assure you that a budget is not a whip that I will encourage you to beat yourself with on a monthly basis. Some people might use it for that, but I'm not convinced it does them any real financial good.

Secondly, a budget is not meant to be something that restricts your fun or cuts out of life the things you enjoy most. While you may need to make some of those choices, and a budget may help you to see where, it does not exist solely for eliminating joy in life.

A budget, when used properly, is the basis of what you're going to learn about in the next chapter. It's the foundation for a spending plan, which is a system that takes all the guesswork out of how much to spend on certain things.

A budget, when used properly, helps us decide in advance how much discretionary income we want to have left over at the end of the month. Pair this decision with the structure of an effective spending plan, and I can almost guarantee that you will get yourself out of debt on schedule with your goals.

The Basic Ingredients of Any Budget

I've seen quite a wide variety of budgets over the years, ranging from three or four things written on the back of a cocktail napkin, to high-tech spreadsheets that would make NASA look stupid.

More often than not, they're either too simple or too complicated to be effectively used. If they are too simple, you lose the ability to understand exactly where your money goes and why. If they are too complex, you overwhelm yourself with data to the point of becoming paralyzed by all your options.

I'd suggest a middle road that starts with our formula for discretionary income (see Chapter 7). In other words, there are three categories that all budget items fall into: income, fixed expenses, and variable expenses.

Within each one of those categories, you will break down your expenditures by company, payee, or store. In other words, you'll put everything you buy at ABC Supermarket on one line, instead of breaking it down into further categories such as dairy, meats, cleaning supplies, etc.

The Three Types of Budgets

While I'm sure that there are a million different approaches to creating a budget, there are three related techniques that I'd encourage you to use. Each has its purpose, and they are all used in conjunction with one another. In fact, they all build off of each other.

The three main types of budgets are the ideal, actual, and compromise budgets. The Three-Budget-System Worksheet at the end of this chapter shows you how to set up the three budgets.

The Ideal Budget

The first budget you should make is the ideal budget. I call it the ideal budget because it is the one that you make without actually looking at the numbers. Its primary purpose is for comparison with the actual budget, to see where your estimates of what you should spend are dramatically different from what you actually spend.

For many people, the reality of our old spending habits hits home as we answer "I don't know" to a lot of the categories. Add this to the fact that our total expenses under our ideal budget are often more than we earn each month, and we've got a great source of motivation for changing things.

Dollars and Sense

The best budgets include a miscellaneous category for the random expenses that can't be predicted or don't fit neatly into another category—things like Little League sign-ups, an unexpected trip to the vet, or a cracked windshield on your car. For an individual, this might be $50 to $100 per month. For a family, it might be $100 to $250 per month.

Here are some tips for completing your ideal budget:

◆ **Be honest.** It doesn't do you any good at this point to start guessing low on your expenses or high on your income.

◆ **Go with your gut.** As you complete each line of your ideal budget, go with the first number that pops into your head. Usually the first number that pops into your head is also the same number that guides your purchasing decisions each month.

◆ **Don't feel bad.** The whole point of this exercise is to get you out of debt. The ideal budget is a tool to help you move forward, not beat yourself up with.

The Actual Budget

Of the three budgets, this one usually provides the biggest shock to our system. As opposed to the ideal budget, where we are estimating what we spend each month, the actual budget adds up the real receipts.

Pay close attention to this budget as you do it. It likely contains many of the reasons you find yourself in debt, and are now are struggling to get out.

To construct your actual budget, you're going to need to gather everything that shows money flowing in and out of your household. This includes your pay stubs, your bank and credit card statements, and your check register.

Once you have these things, grab a separate sheet of paper and a highlighter. Now, go through and begin dividing up the expenses for the month into the categories on the Three-Budget-System Worksheet at the end of this chapter. As you add up your totals, transfer the result to your actual budget worksheet. Be sure to highlight the transactions you've already included on your statements or check register. This will keep you from accidentally doubling up.

Remember, you don't need a separate line on the budget for each place you spend money. Rather, you're going to combine like expenses into the same categories. For example, instead of having a separate line for McDonald's, Burger King, and Taco Bell, you'll just have one category called "Eating Out."

In the Red _____

With the growth of the superstore concept (places where you can find everything you need under one roof), it's getting harder to separate how much of each purchase falls into a specific expense category. For many people, a trip to a store like Wal-Mart or Costco can suck up money with impulsive buys (like purchasing a DVD or a piece of clothing on a trip to get groceries). Make sure you either save your receipts from these stores so you can break down your purchases, or have the cashier separate your items into two or three purchases.

Here are a few additional tips on constructing your actual budget:

◆ **Average three to six months' expenses.** If you only use one month's expenses, there's a good chance your numbers will be too high or low. This comes from the fact that certain months require you to spend more on certain items like cleaning and grooming supplies, occasional spikes in utility bills, and seasonal price differences. By adding up three months' expenses for a category and then dividing by three, you'll get a more accurate number.

◆ **Consider using software.** I'm a big fan of programs like Quicken or Microsoft Money. These programs can greatly speed up the process by automatically downloading all your transactions from your bank. In addition, they print very handy reports that help you see exactly where your money went and when.

◆ **Keep an eye on your cash.** One of the black holes of many people's budgets is the ATM machine. They get out a $20 bill to pay for an $8 lunch, and the other $12 eventually evaporates. Make sure you save your receipts so you can accurately track your cash expenditures.

The Compromise Budget

This compromise budget is what makes my Three Budget System so effective. It is where you take what you think you spend, compare it against what you actually do spend, and begin making compromises. These compromises will become the foundation of the choices you make to hopefully increase your discretionary income, and in turn allow you to pay down debt.

Because you are putting the numbers from all three budgets on one piece of paper, with each category compared side-by-side, it becomes easy to begin going through and making adjustments. But before you make any actual compromises between what you want to spend and what you really can spend, you need to remember your goal to eliminate debt by a certain date or age.

As you are making compromises, the most important one to make is the size of your "excess debt" payment. This is your personal goal for how much additional you will be trying to pay toward your debts each month. While you'll get a better handle on what you want this amount to be in the next few chapters, I want you to get you used to the idea now. I'd hate for you to create a compromise budget that you love, only to be told you've got to cut it more if you really want to eliminate debt from your life!

Dollars and Sense

Before you even begin thinking about the dramatic steps you're going to take to eliminate your debts, consider the simple act of "rounding up." When you round up, you commit to always rounding your debt payments up to the next even increment. For example, if your car payment is $239 per month, you'd try to make a habit of writing the check for $250. This little bit of extra discipline usually shaves a month or two off the amount of time it takes to repay a loan. For debt payments under $250 per month, round up to the nearest $25 dollar increment. For debt payments between $250 and $1,000, round up to the nearest $50 dollar increment. Lastly, for debt payments over $1,000 per month, round up to the nearest $100 increment.

Time to Do Your Budget!

At the end of this list is my Three-Budget-System Worksheet. It's got all the main categories of expenses down the left-hand column, plus a few blank lines in case there is anything I missed.

Across the top, you'll see column headings for your ideal, actual, and compromise budgets. Here's how to use the worksheet:

1. **Make some copies of this budget.** Don't get me wrong, it's your book, you can write in it. But you'll probably want to redo and rework this budget a few times as you get started, as well as in the future. With that in mind, use a pencil to fill in figures so you can go back and erase them if needed.

2. **Gather all your paperwork.** You'll need all your credit card and bank statements, as well as your check register and receipts, to accurately complete your actual budget.

3. **Complete your ideal budget.** Just work your way down the column called "Ideal" budget, writing in what you think you spend each month in these different categories. After you've filled in all the categories, subtract your total expenses from total income. Were you in the negative? If so, you're already spending too much!

4. **Complete your actual budget.** Go back and total your receipts and statements, and write the amounts for each category in the second column, just to the right of the "Ideal" column. Again, after you've filled in each line, go back and subtract your total expenses from your total income. If you are in the negative, you've probably found the source of your ongoing debt problems.

   Before you move on, grab your highlighter and mark the categories where your actual expenditures were significantly greater than your ideal expenses. These are places you can begin cutting back immediately.

5. **Start making compromises.** Take a look at the "bottom line" on your actual budget. How much do you need to cut out to not dig yourself in a hole each month? How much would you need to cut out to have an extra $100, $250, or $500 to put toward your debt?

   Write in your new compromise amounts in the last column, and add up the bottom line. Are you still in the negative? Didn't find any extra money to save? Get out the eraser and cut a bit further.

6. **Review and update regularly.** While we've got more uses for these budgets which we'll talk about in the next chapter, you should make a habit of going back and revisiting these three budgets at least every six months. Additionally, you should revisit and rework these budgets every time you get a raise or are considering taking on a new loan payment or debt.

Three-Budget-System Worksheet

	Ideal	Actual	Compromise
Monthly Income			
All jobs			
Businesses			
Alimony/child support			

continues

Three-Budget-System Worksheet (continued)

	Ideal	Actual	Compromise
Rental property			
Gifts			
Miscellaneous:			
_____			
_____			

Fixed Expenses

Mortgage/rent

Student loan(s)

Car payment(s)

Credit card min.

Excess debt payment

Alimony/child support

Tuition

Gasoline

Car insurance

Health insurance

Home/property insurance

Life insurance

Homeowner's association

Gas (heating)

Electricity

Water/sewer

Trash

Home phone

Cell phone

Cable

Internet

Newspaper subscriptions

Prescriptions

Gym membership(s)

Retirement plan(s)

	Ideal	Actual	Compromise
Other loans			
Irregular fixed expenses (divided by 12)			
Property taxes			
Miscellaneous:			

_____

_____

Variable Expenses

Groceries

Dining out

Entertainment

Clothing

Gifts

Beauty/barber

Business expenses

Charity

Miscellaneous:

_____

_____

_____   **Total Income**

_____   (–) Total fixed expenses

_____   (–) Total variable expenses

_____   = Discretionary income

Avoiding Budgeting Pitfalls

Making a budget, like any other process, can break down at numerous points. In order to keep yourself on track, consider the following tips:

◆ **Give a copy to your accountability partner.** One of the main places an accountability partner can really help you is in the formation of your budget. Sometimes it takes a fresh set of eyes from someone who knows you really well to tell you something is unrealistic. Whether it is spending too much or too little, your accountability partner can help you gauge your level of denial.

◆ **Review it regularly.** The best budget will be the one that you look at on a regular basis. Whether you review it once per month, per quarter, or semi-annually, you've got to burn the numbers into your brain. Some of the most successful debt warriors I've met put a copy on their fridge or make it the "wallpaper" on their computer screen.

◆ **Budget for irregular expenses.** Whether it's Christmas gifts, new brakes for the car, or surprise medical bills, there are plenty of things we must pay for that occur on an irregular basis. Failing to budget, or set aside, a little bit each month for these expenses invalidates even the best budgets.

The Least You Need to Know

◆ The best budgets are built on your past spending habits.

◆ All expenses on a budget fit into one of our discretionary income categories: income, fixed expenses, and variable expenses.

◆ The ideal, actual, and compromise budgets should be used in conjunction with one another.

◆ Keep your budget on track by giving a copy to your accountability partner, reviewing it regularly, and factoring in irregular expenses.

Chapter 9

Spending Plans: The Key to Beating Debt

In This Chapter

- Why budgets alone fail
- Why spending plans work
- Using your budget to create a spending plan
- The two-account system
- The three-account system for shared finances
- Adjusting your spending plan

Budgets are a lot like New Year's resolutions. They're something that you make in response to a situation you're unhappy with. You feel empowered and proactive as you make them. Yet budgets so often fail within a short period of time.

The reality is, for most people, budgets alone do not work.

Why Do Budgets Fail?

Budgets can fail for many reasons, but it is usually not because you lacked commitment or motivation. Motivation and commitment was what it took to make the budget in the first place. Rather, most times that you fail, it comes from a breakdown somewhere between the budget and the actual spending. If you can find a way to address these breakdowns, there's a good chance you'll actually stick to your budget.

There's Too Much to Remember ...

In the last chapter, you made a budget using the Three-Budget-System Worksheet with at least 30 to 40 lines of expenses. Each on of those lines might have been made up of 5, 10, or 20 different places where you spend or send money. That's a lot of information to keep track of!

Even if you have made the most aggressive compromise budget you could imagine for yourself, there is still a lot to remember. Perhaps, if you lived a life of leisure, you might be able to mentally track what you are supposed to spend and where.

> **Debt in America**
>
> A recent survey of Americans found that 64% of us claim to use some kind of budget. Yet a much larger percentage than the 36% of people who admit to not using a budget is struggling with debt. If a budget is only a mental commitment to spend less than we make, it is not likely going to make a huge difference unless we are naturally a frugal person.

But most of us don't lead lives of leisure. We've got about 8 million other things to remember, are generally in a rush, and lead lives where one day blurs into the next. To expect yourself, within that chaos, to remember how much you can spend on gourmet coffee this month, compared to what you've already spent, would be impressive. To remember all 30 to 40 lines of your budget, and track your spending in your head, is downright impossible.

A big part of the reasons budgets fail is that you can't remember where you are mid-month. As you stand in line at the cafeteria, you can't recall how much of that $1,591.23 balance in your bank account is already spoken for. Not knowing, you usually spend blindly, hoping that it'll all work out. Or even worse, you use credit cards so you can delay having to work it out.

Dollars and Sense _____

Automatic bill pay can be your spending plan's best friend or worst enemy, depending on how it's used and monitored. The great part about using automatic payments for your bills is it makes sure the money gets out of your account before you can spend it, while also helping you avoid late fees. Be sure to monitor your bank accounts closely, though. Automatic withdrawal programs, like those for a gym, are famous for wasting hundreds of dollars before you get around to canceling them. Additionally, automatic withdrawals can pile on the NSF (nonsufficient funds) fees if your bank account is running on empty for the month.

No Barriers to Impulsive Spending

There's an old saying that for some people, "money burns a hole in their pocket." In other words, if you've got money in your pocket, all of a sudden you find all kinds of ways to spend it. Sadly, if you didn't have money in your pocket, you would have never treated yourself to some extra sushi, just because.

Even though you've created a budget, with all these neat little divisions of what you should spend, there is nothing to keep you from going nuts or spending impulsively. Ironically, most of us don't waste our money $500 at a time, but $5 at a time.

The best budgets also often fail, even for those of you who are the most determined, because there is no barrier between your money and your spending habits. While I'm about to show you a system that helps create a "barrier," here are some of the reasons people make impulsive spending decisions:

◆ **They're in a rush.** Salespeople love hearing your stories about the washing machine that just blew up or the tire that just went flat. These stories indicate you need something and you need it now, otherwise life will be disrupted. Not taking (or having) the time to shop around, much less "sleep on" your purchase decisions, often leads to impulsive overspending.

◆ **They don't want to miss out.** Being afraid you'll miss the good deal, the hot trend, or the chance to ever buy this item at this price leads to impulsive spending decisions as well. Begin keeping track of how many going-out-of-business or 72-hour sales you see. It doesn't take long to realize that good deals are a dime a dozen, and it's just a matter of time before another one comes along.

- ◆ **They carry cash.** I've said it before, and I'll say it again: cash evaporates. If you're like most people, you probably don't guard your cash very closely. In fact, many people act like the cash in their pocket is "extra" money, because it's not part of their account balance. Keep cash out of your pocket and you'll likely cut down on your impulsive spending.

- ◆ **They use credit cards for impulsive purchases.** If you keep a credit card in your wallet, it's almost guaranteed that you'll struggle with some level of impulsive decision making. Credit cards allow you to "buy it now" and figure out if you can afford it later. I like to refer to this as "shoot first, ask questions later" shopping. Lock the credit cards in a drawer at home, and I can guarantee your impulsive spending will drop.

- ◆ **They shop online.** While there is a lot of merit to the potential time savings of shopping online, it can be quickly offset by some sly marketing techniques. Whether it is quantity discounts (e.g., spend $50, get 10% off) or free shipping offers, there are plenty of ways retailers encourage you to spend more than you need. Even worse, shopping online is almost *too* convenient—you can "flop and shop" when you're bored or can't sleep!

Spending Plans to the Rescue!

If you can move from having just a budget to having a spending plan, your success at getting rid of debt is almost guaranteed. A spending plan will ultimately help you enforce what I've said from the start is the true secret of getting out of debt: spend less and pay more toward your debts.

At its simplest, a spending plan is some type of system that forces money to go where you've already predetermined it should go. In other words, it ensures that the amounts you filled in on your compromise budget (see Chapter 8) get to where they need to, and don't get exceeded. Unlike a budget, which mostly operates in a rearview mirror role, the spending plan acts like the front windshield.

A good spending plan does this by rescuing you from the two primary sources of budgetary failure: having too many things to remember and being an impulsive spender. It overcomes your short-term memory challenges by setting aside certain amounts in advance for each category. When those set-aside amounts are used up, you know you're done. There's nothing to remember but zero. When you hit it, you're done.

It also overcomes your impulsive spending by setting apart amounts you need to protect—namely, your discretionary income. If you decide what your discretionary income should be before you ever spend, there's a lot better chance it'll be there when the smoke clears at the end of the month.

Dollars and Sense

For anyone raising kids (or caring for older parents), I can almost guarantee you've said some version of it at least once: *Money doesn't grow on trees.* Yet when you are shopping with your kids (who you only want the best for) or your parents (who you owe so much to), it's easy to overlook your own boundaries out of love, guilt, or obligation. Consider using a mini spending plan with them to help keep your spending plan from derailing. Don't tell your kids, "Hey, let's go pick you out some clothes." Rather, tell them, "Hey, I've got $100 to spend, let's go see what we can find!"

Using Your Compromise Budget to Create a Spending Plan

Because your compromise budget is (in theory, at least) a budget that will work for you and move you toward your goals, we've got to make sure it gets put into action. The spending plan you are now going to construct is going to be based on the amounts you've used in your compromise budget.

While you could try to figure out a way to separate single expenditures, so that all your gourmet coffee is tracked under one part of the spending plan and all your groceries under another, I'd like to suggest an easier format. It actually goes back to the formula you learned for discretionary income, where you had three real simple budget pieces.

What I'd suggest is finding a way to have all your fixed expenses come out of one pile of money, and all your variable expenses out of another. Remember, this is based on the premise that for the most part you don't act impulsively when it comes to paying your car payment or electric bill (both fixed expenses). More often, your discretionary income is chipped away by the total effect of your variable expenses.

Set a Goal
Setting up a spending plan usually takes a little more legwork than sitting at the kitchen table with a pad of paper and a calculator. If you use my system in this book, or even create your own, it'll at least take a couple hours of your time. With your calendar in hand, open your Debt Journal and go to your growing checklist of goals. Write something like: Spending Plan Workday _____ (fill in the date). Make sure your Spending Plan Workday is a few days after your Budget Workday. That way, you can sleep on your numbers before you put them into action.

The Envelope System

The most classic way of creating a spending plan that separates your fixed expenses from your variable is the envelope system. You may have seen (and maybe even laughed at) your parents or grandparents using this system back in the day. But remember, they're typically the ones who aren't in debt, so there's some merit to it.

Under the classic envelope system, you'd have an envelope for each expense category stashed away in a safe place in your house. When you received your paycheck, you'd cash it and put your compromise budget amount for each category into each envelope.

When the grocery envelope was empty, you knew you were done buying groceries for the month. If there was some extra money in the entertainment envelope on the last weekend of the month, you went out on the town. It's simple, but it works.

My only problem was that my kids figured out where I kept the envelopes! That's led to me creating a modern version of this using a couple of different bank accounts.

The Two-Account System

For a variety of reasons, such as ability to earn interest on your deposits and avoid theft, the envelope system is a tad outdated. With the ease of online banking, bill pay and automatic transfer, you can accomplish the equivalent of the envelope system will less hassle.

Let's start with looking at the steps a single person might take to use two bank accounts to help enforce their spending plan.

Step 1: Open Two Bank Accounts

Find a bank that offers free online banking, interest on its deposits, and FDIC insurance. I'd recommend looking at some of the online banks like ING Direct or HSBC. Ideally, you'd look for a bank that has no monthly fees, no overdraft charges, allows free transfers between accounts, and even pays you interest on your balance. As always, make sure the bank is insured by the FDIC. Check out bank comparison and rating sites like Bankaholic.com and BankRate.com to find a suitable bank in your area.

Once you've found a bank, open two accounts and set one up to receive your paycheck by direct deposit. This account is now going to be called your fixed account, while the other will be called your variable account.

Step 2: Use the Fixed Account for All Your Fixed Expenses

The fixed account, the one into which your paycheck gets directly deposited, is the same one you'll use to pay all your fixed expenses. This will include the minimum payments on all your debts. This way, you'll always ensure that the most important bills get paid first.

Step 3: Transfer Your Variable Expenses to the Second Account

This step is the real magic of the spending plan, and will take much of the guesswork out of your monthly spending. You're going to add up what your variable expenses should be under your compromise budget, and transfer this amount to your variable account. This amount will include everything from your $5 lattes to groceries to clothes. In essence, you are giving yourself an allowance in a separate account.

Step 4: Keep Your Eye on the Bottom Line

Now, when it comes to your variable expenses account, your only job is to not go below zero. On the 15th, 21st, or 29th of the month, when you are trying to decide how much to spend on groceries or poker night, you just need to check how close you are to zero.

If there is room to go, and you can't think of any other major expenses before you reload the account, you can spend freely. Again, the amount of mental gymnastics required to keep out of trouble is minimal, because the money for your fixed expenses stayed in the other account.

Step 5: Decide What to Do with Your Discretionary Income

Yeah! This is the best part. Because you decided in advance what your variable expenditures are and put them in a separate allowance account, you likely will have some discretionary income left over in the fixed account at the end of the month. Now you can decide how you should use this money: make an extra mortgage payment, pay more toward a credit card than the minimum, keep it in the fixed account as a buffer for next month, or even give yourself a small reward for doing such a great job.

The beauty of this plan is that you've created a barrier in spending between you and the all-important discretionary income. You've forced yourself in advance to live off a certain amount of money.

The Three-Account System for People Sharing Finances

It's virtually inevitable that, at some point in your life, you will share bank accounts and financial responsibility with another person. With the likelihood of shared finances being extremely high, so are the chances of confusion and personal conflict. In fact, many marriage counselors would tell you that a high percentage of marriages experience financial conflict, most of the time related to debt.

The three-account system works just as well as the two-account system, but is designed to help two people control spending and protect discretionary income. In fact, it'll go a long way to eliminate fights, power struggles, and accidental overspending.

In the Red

Many couples choose to have two bank accounts and let each person be responsible for some of the bills. While this seems to make sense on the surface, this can lead to fights or resentment if one spouse begins to earn more or certain bills rise. Using separate accounts can also lead to an increase in impulsive spending. This happens when one spouse feels cheated or entitled and begins spending money only as benefits him, instead of considering the household's overall needs and goals.

To implement the three-account system, divide the variable expenses according to the person who is typically in charge of them, and place them in a separate account for each person.

For example, my wife is in charge of the groceries, the kids' clothes, and the gifts for our friends. The total of these variable expenses adds up to $750 per month. This amount, in turn, is deposited into an account my wife is in charge of. Likewise, I'm in charge of the family's entertainment budget and dining out. The total of these variable expenses is $250 per month, and is deposited into an account that I'm in charge of.

The balance of our money remains in our fixed account. While we do not pay every bill together, nothing additional gets spent out of this account that is not agreed upon in advance. We make joint decisions about the discretionary income and whether it is used to pay down debt or on other expenses.

Just like the two-account system, each person in the relationship can spend his or her account down to zero each month. When each person hits zero, if more money is needed, it has to be agreed upon by both parties. Additionally, if one person is able to minimize the variable costs he or she is in charge of without it affecting the household, that person is free to spend the balance of the money as he or she sees fit. This is often the case with my own wife and grocery coupons, and provides her with some great incentive to be frugal in our choices.

Adjusting Your Spending Plan

Now that your spending plan is in place, it should be a fairly automatic process from month to month. However, the unique factors that make up your life might change from time to time. Whether it is the cost of gas or rent going up or your entertainment costs going down, you'll want to incorporate these changes into your budget as soon as possible.

Failure to decrease your variable expenses after a drop in income can result in you not having enough funds in your fixed account for your regular bills. Failure to increase your variable expenses after an increase in income or paying off your debts can result in you living a stricter lifestyle than needed.

Just as I'd suggest you revisit your spending budget every six months, I'd also suggest that you revisit your spending plan at the same time.

The Least You Need to Know

◆ Budgets often fail because of the amount of information you're required to remember as you spend.

◆ The absence of some kind of spending plan will make it hard to keep from spending your discretionary income.

◆ A spending plan puts your compromise budget into action.

◆ The best spending plans will separate your variable expenses from everything else.

◆ The two-account system works well to keep a single person's spending in check and protect discretionary income.

◆ The three-account system provides all the benefits of the two-account system to a couple, and helps minimize confusion and disagreements.

10

Expect the Unexpected

In This Chapter

- ◆ How unexpected expenses can wreck the best-laid plans
- ◆ Preparing for the unexpected
- ◆ Strategies for when you're caught off guard
- ◆ The smart way to deal with unexpected windfalls

One of the games I loved as a kid was Chutes and Ladders. In the game, your goal was to wind your way up a path on the game board. If you landed on a ladder, you were allowed to skip ahead a few levels. If you landed on chute, which looked like a big slide, you had to go back down a few levels. A few spaces before you reached the finish line, there was a giant chute that took you almost all the way back to the starting line.

Large unexpected expenses and windfalls can be the financial equivalent of Chutes and Ladders. An unexpected windfall, such as a gift, tax refund, or property sale, can greatly speed up your march toward financial freedom. Likewise, an unexpected medical expense, car accident, or home repair can undo months or even years of financial progress.

How you prepare for and respond to the unexpected will have a huge effect on how soon you find freedom from debt.

The Problem with the Unexpected

One of my early mentors often reminded me that "a failure to plan is planning to fail." In other words, if you're not looking down the road, planning for the "what if's" of life, it is just a matter of time before life's details overwhelm you. And when you find yourself overwhelmed, you often resort to your old ways of handling money.

When a large unexpected expense pops up, you are more apt to take care of it by slapping down your credit card, accessing your home equity, or skipping other crucial payments. You then add more debt to your existing debt, wasting all those previous months of cutting costs and paying off more.

In the same manner, if a large windfall suddenly comes your way, you tend to take an entitlement mentality. You're more apt to treat yourself to something that won't last more than a couple of years than you are to pay off debt you'll be battling for the next decade.

The Top Five Expenses That Catch Us Off Guard

While some surprise expenses (like the cost of gas) slowly nickel and dime our discretionary income to death, they often allow us enough time to make some adjustments. Large one-time expenses, however, leave us no chance to adjust and can throw our finances into chaos seemingly overnight. Here's a list of the top five expenses that I've seen surprise my clients:

◆ **Medical.** An uninsured trip to the emergency room can easily cost you $5,000 to $10,000 or more. Even with basic coverage, the deductibles and co-pays on certain procedures can cost $500 to $1,000.

◆ **Automotive.** When a tire goes flat or the transmission goes out, it doesn't feel like you have much choice but to fix it. With labor costs running $25 to $50 per hour, even a minor repair can cost $500 or more.

◆ **Property taxes.** Many first-time homeowners are shocked when they receive their first semiannual property tax bill. With national rates hovering about 1% per year, this can easily stall your plans to get out of debt.

◆ **Weddings.** Whether it is your own, your child's, or your friend's, a wedding can cost you a pretty penny. Even being a bridesmaid or groomsman can cost you hundreds in new clothing, gifts, and travel expenses.

◆ **Holidays.** It's hard to imagine that days that are on the calendar all year long could catch you by surprise. But as you add new friends, co-workers, and kids to your lives, what you spend on cards, stamps, gifts, food, and other holiday traditions can skyrocket.

The Five Biggest Windfalls We Tend to Waste

One of the keys in preparing for surprises is to look around at your world and anticipate what might be coming your way. It's no different in dealing with unexpected windfalls than it is with expenses. By making decisions on what to do ahead of time, you'll help ensure that you don't squander a great opportunity. Consider these potential windfalls:

◆ **Tax refund.** Sadly, you might view your tax refund as free money. In fact, it is money that Uncle Sam held for you all year (without paying you interest) only to return it later. Of course, the months of April through June are great for retailers because many people go shopping with those refunds.

◆ **Inheritance.** While you will probably never inherit millions, more than likely you'll inherit a small sum once or twice in your life. The tendency is to splurge, often rationalizing your actions by saying something like, "Uncle Bob would have wanted me to enjoy this money."

◆ **Bonuses.** It's easy to get used to receiving bonuses or overtime pay from your employer, assuming this income is always going to be there. To make matters worse, you often might splurge at Christmas under the assumption that the check is in the mail.

◆ **Settlement.** If you are hurt on the job or laid off unfairly, you will probably end up receiving some type of financial settlement. To a large degree, these settlements are meant to cover expenses. However, the money often burns a hole in your pocket and you end up using debt again.

◆ **Severance.** If you are a long-term employee, you'll likely receive a sizeable severance package if your company downsizes. Many times, you'll receive one week's pay for every year at your company. Instead of using this windfall to eliminate debt or to live on while you find another job, it's tempting to "reward yourself" for years of hard work.

Was It Really Unexpected?

I'm famous in my family for the drama that seems to surround every car I've ever owned. While I'd like to chalk it up to ridiculously bad luck, my wife is faithful in reminding me that her cars never had problems before she met me. But then again, her family actually believed in things like oil changes, regular maintenance, and slowing down for speed bumps.

When an engine would blow up or a transmission would fail, I would huff and puff and complain about the inconvenience of this unexpected expense. My wife, from a safe distance, would remind me that this is to be expected if you don't take care of your cars.

The moral of the story is twofold: first, unexpected expenses are usually either predictable or avoidable. If they're predictable, then we should have been setting money aside for them. If they were avoidable, well then, we should have avoided them. Second, if you take care of your investments, they'll generally return the favor. It's usually cheaper to keep something in the best of shape than to return it to that state after it's fallen into disrepair.

A big part of keeping your debt reduction goals on track is the need to prepare for the predictable and avoid the avoidable.

Set a Goal

What are the five big expenses in your own finances that you know are waiting to get you? What would you say, as the foremost expert on yourself, are the biggest financial catastrophes waiting to befall you? While you can't foresee every surprise, it would be irresponsible to not begin planning for the ones you've got a gut feeling about. Open your Debt Journal and write down, "I need to plan for the following five unexpected expenses …" and then list them.

Strategies for Dealing with Unexpected Expenses

Even if you do the best job preparing your finances for the unexpected, it's only a matter of time before something catches you off guard. How you deal with these unexpected events will determine whether your debt reduction plan keeps chugging forward or grinds to a halt.

The worst way to deal with an unexpected expense is to create new debt. Not only will this move you back to square one mathematically, but it will go a long way toward breaking your spirit.

Pay It All Now

The single best way to handle an unexpected expense is to pay it all right now, out of your current cash flow if possible. Even if it means having to tighten down every other expense for the next couple of months, getting rid of the expense now will allow you to move on sooner rather than later.

The idea of paying it all in one chunk can definitely seem overwhelming if you compare it to one month's budget. For example, it may seem impossible to pay a $500 car repair bill out of a budget that barely breaks even each month. But if you imagine that amount coming partly from this month's budget and partly from the next, it will begin to feel more survivable.

To absorb that $500 car repair, perhaps you cut your groceries by $150 this month and next by trying to use up everything you already have in the pantry and fridge. That's probably around $300 right there!

Then you could cut $25 out of your dining-out bill each month ($50 more), skip any new clothing items for the next two months (maybe another $100 total), and borrow recently released movies from your local library instead of going to the theater (another $50 over two months). Voilà! There's your $500. I know that's not as fun as spending that money, but it's a lot more fun than adding it to your credit card and paying it off over a few years!

Dollars and Sense

Many times, your local church or faith community will have something like a "Deacon's" or "Elder's" Fund. These funds are specifically there to help members of that community who find themselves in a financial bind. Especially if you have extenuating circumstances, like a spouse in the military, a disability, or you are a single parent on a fixed income, it's worth making a call to your church office to some folks who are more than happy to help.

Request a Payment Plan

You'd be surprised how many businesses offer payment plans. Actually, I take that back. You're reading this book because you've discovered that everyone does offer payment plans!

However, many smaller companies and service providers, unlike larger companies, provide payment plans with very lenient options. While you should always ask if they have a formal arrangement with a medical financing company, many smaller practices will just let you spread your payments over a few months to help you out.

I've discovered this with many smaller dentists and medical offices. Do you remember how I told you I hate going to the dentist? I promise, I wasn't trying to be cute by saying that. I really hate going.

When my mouth finally began to throb after a 10-year absence from the dentist's chair, I finally visited the dentist our daughter works for. The cost of stopping the pain ... about $2,500.

When I told him that I couldn't get all the work done at the time due to the cost, he simply asked me, "Do you think you'd be able to pay for it over the next few months?" When I told him I could, he offered to just do it all now as long as I paid as much as I could until the bill was paid in full.

> **In the Red**
>
> If you are planning on spreading out your payments, don't do it without first getting a business's permission. After a certain amount of time, if you haven't explicitly asked them for some extra time, they may turn you over to a collection agency.

If You Have to Borrow ...

If you have to use debt to finance an unexpected expense, you should seek to minimize the setback to your debt reduction plan. This means that you want the debt to cost you as little as possible and to be placed on an existing account. With caution at the forefront, here are some guidelines for using debt to absorb an unexpected expense:

- By no means should you open a new credit card or debt account to pay for this expense. If you do, chances are you will eventually max out that credit card as well!

- If you have access to a home equity line of credit (HELOC), this would be the only time to use it. With a flexible repayment schedule, interest rates that are significantly lower than credit cards, and potentially deductible interest, a HELOC can save you a lot of money.

- If it's unlikely that you'll be able to pay off the balance in two to three months, you'll want to make sure you charge it on your lowest-interest-rate credit card. The more interest that is added to your original purchase, the longer it will take to eliminate.

◆ Consider putting the expense on the account with the largest balance. As I'll discuss in Chapter 13, getting rid of as many incoming statements as soon as possible provides sanity and motivation. Putting unexpected expenses on an almost paid-off card prolongs its life and your stress.

Many people never realize that different transactions on a credit card carry different interest rates. Grab one of your statements and check it out. There's a good chance there'll be one interest rate for purchases, another for balance transfers, and yet another for cash advances. One card may have three or more different rates ranging from under 10% to over 30%.

Learn from the Experience

As I mentioned earlier in this chapter, most unexpected expenses are really not unexpected. In reality, they could have been avoided through proper planning, or their effects minimized through deliberate saving. But there's no sense in beating yourself up for what you should have known.

But now you know! So you need to take a good hard look at this expense and whether or not it was avoidable or could have been lessened through preparation. Whatever you decide, you need to incorporate it into your budget and spending plan going forward.

Just like the best football teams, in their preparation for the next big game, watch their previous games over and over, it'd be in your favor to step back and think through previous unexpected expenses.

Grab a piece of paper, number it one to five and then list the last five big unexpected expenses you incurred. Now, go through and answer the following questions about each expense:

◆ **Could it have been predicted?** If it could have, you need to stop right now and predict when it'll happen again. If you couldn't have predicted it, you need to evaluate whether or not an emergency fund (more on this in Chapter 24) would have saved you a lot of heartache.

◆ **Could it have been avoided?** If it could have, then it can be again. What do you need to do to keep this expense from reappearing or being as large as it was?

◆ **Did your response put you further in debt?** If it did, what will keep you from responding that way in the future? Based on what you've read in the last section about dealing with the unexpected, how could you, in your situation, have dealt with it differently?

Strategies for Dealing with Unexpected Windfalls

Whether you come across a large windfall by inheriting money, hitting it big at the slot machine, or winning a lawsuit, I can almost guarantee that you'll have your turn. How's that for good news?

> **Debt in America**
>
> Are you still spending a few dollars a week on lottery tickets, hoping to hit it big and solve all your financial problems? Think again. The odds of winning the lottery are approximately 1 in 50,000,000! Even if you did win, studies estimate that one out of three lottery winners are broke within five years of winning!

The bad news is that for most of us, it isn't $2 million, but usually in the thousands or tens of thousands of dollars. The even worse news is that the majority of people mismanage large sums of money suddenly handed to them, often ending up worse off than they were before.

If you find yourself on the lucky end of a financial windfall, you need to take a deep breath and do some serious thinking. You've got a great chance to eliminate your debt and take a giant leap toward financial freedom. But it takes having a strategy and bringing some method to the madness and excitement.

Think About How Much You'd Save

Before I start telling you to spend your windfall, you've got to realize the "opportunity cost" of not paying off debt. If there's a motivating factor that will talk you out of spending any of the money, this will be it.

In fact, I'd go so far as to say that by paying off certain debts, it might cost you nothing! What you save in interest over 5 to 10 years may easily be more than you pay initially!

Let's revisit our minimum payment calculation for Sally from Chapter 4. In that example, someone with a $10,000 credit card balance at 18% who only made the minimum payments would pay almost $24,000 in interest (above and beyond the $10,000 they borrowed on their card) by the time it's paid off in 57.5 years. If I had just won $10,000, I would save $24,000 by paying off $10,000 right now.

In other words, by paying off high-interest debt now, you're not losing the use of your money, you're actually gaining it! Granted, that $24,000 savings in interest would be spread out over a long period of time, but it is still $24,000 that you saved. That means you'd get your original $10,000 back, plus $14,000 more!

Eliminate Debt Once and for All

Could you imagine what it'd be like if all your debts (both short- and long-term) went away overnight? How much money would you save each month? Hundreds? Thousands?

Yet the vast majority of lucky folks I've encountered do just the opposite. They use their windfall to create more debt. To make their windfall "stretch" (especially if it is a smaller one) they'll use a portion of the amount as down payments on new purchases.

For example, I knew a guy who got a $50,000 inheritance. He paid off a couple thousand on credit cards, then used the rest to make a down payment on a new car and a ski cabin. What he didn't seem to understand is that he just spent all his money and picked up $1,000 per month in new debt payments. How does that possibly make long-term sense? Within 12 months, he had to sell the car and was trying to rent the cabin out on weekends to cover the mortgage.

Don't get me wrong. If you get a windfall, I want you to enjoy it, but in a different way than my friend. I want you to get rid of debt once and for all, and then, out of the extra discretionary income you have every month, go have fun!

My friend, for example, could have paid off all his debts, including his existing mortgage on his first home, and created an emergency fund. Then out of the $1,000 dollars that he didn't have to spend on debt every month, he'd be able to enjoy spending his increased discretionary income.

I could find a lot of things to do with an extra $1,000 per month, couldn't you? Rather than go out and blow $50,000 in one shot, I think I could find it in myself to enjoy being debt-free with an extra $1,000 in discretionary income each month!

In the Red

One thing that leaves many recipients of windfalls in deep debt trouble is taxes. Even though a mandatory withholding of tax may have been done on your winnings (usually 20%), that doesn't mean you're done being taxed. Consider it a down payment against what you are going to owe later. This is even true with inheritances that may be subject to estate taxes or income tax (if withdrawing from an inherited IRA). Find a good financial planner or accountant who can help you navigate these issues.

Decide on a Formula in Advance

In Chapter 5, I talked about people's tendency to abandon diets that have no fun built into them; to avoid the same pitfall, I do think you should live it up just a little with your windfall. Not a lot, but just enough to keep you from blowing the whole thing.

To do this without losing control, you need to decide in advance how much it's going to be. You need to come up with a formula; otherwise, you'll probably keep talking yourself into just "a little bit more."

While you are free to come up with your own formulas, I'd like to suggest some starting points based on my experience and the different types of debt you might have. The following percentages refer to how much you can go out and enjoy, not the other way around:

◆ If you have any type of short-term debt, I'd suggest you take 10% of your windfall and live it up. Remember, by getting rid of your short-term debt, you are also going to significantly increase your monthly discretionary income.

◆ If you've got a nice assortment of both short- and long-term debt and the windfall is substantial, I'd say go enjoy 15% of it. That'll make sure that your short-term debt disappears, and your long-term debt is significantly reduced.

◆ If your debt consists more of long-term debt, such as student loans or a mortgage, you can consider using up to 25% of the windfall for some rest and relaxation.

◆ If you're that lucky person who gets your debt paid off just before you get a windfall, I'd consider having fun with roughly one third of it. Now, as with all these numbers, that's a maximum amount. If you have a significant windfall and no debt, you need to talk to a financial planner. When you see the long-term growth potential of that windfall, you may opt for an early retirement over that Mercedes with the personalized license plate.

In the Red

Especially if you have other friends or family members who have been struggling with debt, it's easy to get your heartstrings pulled into helping them out as well. The problem, of course, is that unless they are committed to staying out of debt, all you're doing is giving them a chance to run it right back up. I'd recommend you help them out of the increased discretionary income you receive each month instead of losing an opportunity to erase your debt or plan for your future.

Talk About It and Sleep on It

Last but certainly not least when it comes to windfall strategies and your debts is the need for wise council and a deep breath.

If you are lucky enough to have a significant amount of money fall in your lap, take your time making any decisions. Sleep on your choices for a few weeks or months. A little bit more interest is a lot less costly than a bad or rushed choice.

I'd also consider talking to the following people as soon as possible:

◆ **A fee-only financial planner or accountant.** A good financial planner will help you understand your long-term options and opportunities with this money. A good accountant will help you estimate the taxes you might owe. Because they charge a flat fee (not a commission), you don't have to worry as much about being taken advantage of.

◆ **Your accountability partner.** If you've taken the wise step of choosing an accountability partner for your journey out of debt, as discussed in Chapter 5, he or she would be a great person to bounce your ideas and plans off of.

◆ **A psychologist, counselor, or therapist.** If you haven't realized it by now, I really believe that money and psychology are deeply intertwined. A windfall can start playing games with your head, especially if it comes from an inheritance, lawsuit, or major life change. Processing your emotions may help you keep control over your spending and other related behaviors.

The Least You Need to Know

◆ Large unexpected expenses can put you back at square one of your debt reduction plan.

◆ Many large expenses can actually be predicted or avoided.

◆ A spending plan puts your budget into action.

◆ The best strategy for unexpected expenses is to tighten your belt and try to absorb them into your budget.

◆ Windfalls can actually lead to more debt if you're not careful.

◆ Have a plan in place for dealing with windfalls so you don't get carried away.

11

Getting Your Debt Organized

In This Chapter

- ◆ Being aggressive with paperwork
- ◆ Creating a filing system
- ◆ Using technology to get organized
- ◆ When technology hinders rather than helps

If your debts are weighing down on you, there's a good chance that you hate the mail carrier more than the noisy dogs in your neighborhood. In his hand he holds the ability to totally ruin your day, freak you out, or leave you feeling financially hopeless. He is the bearer of bad news … your credit card and loan statements.

I've seen people who are so overwhelmed with their debt that they simply stop opening their statements. When they finally walk into my office with their still-sealed statements, it's because they've started receiving weekly phone calls from their lenders.

Taming the paperwork monster is the key to you not living in denial, as is developing a payment strategy and staying encouraged as you make progress.

Taming the Paperwork Monster

Tackling your paperwork head-on is a multistep process. It ultimately requires you deliberately interacting with those painful reminders of how deep in debt you are. But doing so is going to enable to truly use the Progress Chart you created in Chapter 5.

Debt in America _____

Over the years, the people I've worked with who get out of debt ahead of schedule are the ones who know exactly what they owe and where. The ones who languish in debt are the ones who walk in with a grocery bag filled with unopened statements. They usually say something semi-ironic like "I don't understand why I can't get out of debt." Knowledge is power. As such, you need to become an expert on your own debt if you ever hope to be victorious over it.

The most important steps in taming the paperwork monster are to …

1. **Open your bills immediately**. Don't hide from them; attack them like a kid attacks presents on Christmas morning. Before you look at the catalogs or flip through your favorite magazine, you must open your bills and read through them.

2. **Review the details**. After you've patted yourself on the back or kicked yourself in the tail, it's time to look at the actual details. Were all the transactions necessary? Were they worth it? How about your interest rates—did they change?

3. **Transfer the balances to your chart**. This is always the scariest part, like stepping on the scale when you've been on a diet. Did you lose debt? Did it actually grow? You need to copy over your balance, connect the dots, and look at the trends.

4. **Write next month's payment now**. Part of the purpose of your spending plan was to keep money from evaporating with careless spending. So you should write the check or schedule the payment now to create a mental commitment in your mind.

5. **File your essential paperwork**. Do you throw your statements in the old round file (a.k.a. the trash can) or stick them all into one overflowing drawer? Neither of these helps you make solid progress because you lose the ability to review statements on a whim. You need to come up with a better system.

6. **Shred the rest.** Even if you don't have any debt and practice good financial habits, identity theft can turn your world upside down. In this day and age, when you throw away anything with your personal info, you've got to minimize the chances that someone else can use it to rip you off.

Let's take a closer look at each of these steps.

Set a Goal

When you look at that list of steps for taming the paper monster, what are your glaring weaknesses? Which do you do well? Before you go any further, I want you to pick a debt organization date. It could be today or it could be a week from now, but it needs to be set in stone. Open your Debt Journal and write it under the rest of your goals. "On _____, I will spend two to three hours getting my paperwork sorted out, organized, and stored safely."

Open Your Bills Immediately

When you get in the habit of not opening or not looking at your credit card and debt statements, you set yourself up for failure. By not looking at these love notes from your lenders, you have no way of gauging whether or not you're making sufficient progress.

Did you catch that I said "sufficient progress"? When you tighten the screws on your spending and make the minimum payments on your debts, you assume you're making sufficient progress. In reality, though, you're only chipping away a small amount of debt and may spend the next 30 years and a whole lot of money getting nowhere fast.

By taking a look at the status of debt frequently, your goals, motivation, and progress stay at the forefront of your mind. You can see how that little extra added to your payment made a difference. You can also see how that night out that you "deserved" basically wiped out any forward progress you could have made this month.

Dollars and Sense

Which bill do you most fear each month? Which one stresses you out the most? Are there any you delay opening or hide from your partner? Make a mental note of this bill. Make this one of the bills you tackle first, even if there are other bills that make more financial sense.

There's even scientific proof for this kind of behavior. The University of Minnesota did a study of 3,000 adults who were attempting to lose weight. One of their most basic conclusions was that people who weigh themselves regularly tend to lose weight faster than those who don't. From my experience, I very much believe the same thing is true with your debt. If you continue to measure your progress, you'll continue to make progress.

Review the Details

Don't just open your debt statement, try not to throw up, and then move on with life. Instead, open your statements with a highlighter in hand. With nonrevolving credit accounts (everything besides the credit card), go through and highlight your balance, due date, minimum payment, interest rate, and any fees you were charged.

For credit card statements, you should also highlight any transactions you now realize in hindsight that you could have lived without.

If you share finances with someone, you should be reviewing all your statements together. Two sets of eyes are more likely to catch the important details. Also, having to answer for your expenditures provides a greater incentive to control your spending in the moment. If you know you'll have to explain why you went to Starbuck's when the other person isn't supposed to, you'll probably think twice.

Transfer the Balances to Your Chart

In Chapter 5 you created a Progress Chart to track your progress toward your goal of eliminating debt. Now, after you open each month's statements and highlight the crucial information, you should transfer your balances to the chart. Be sure to connect the dots with a ruler, so you get a general feeling of whether or not you're making progress.

Make sure this chart stays in plain view throughout the month, ideally in a place where you can view it daily. It'll keep you from being that person who walks into a planner's office with a bag full of statements and a look of panic.

Write Next Month's Payment Now

I picked this one up from my dad. Whenever he'd get a new bill, he'd write the check for it right on the spot, stick it in the envelope and seal it up. He'd then write the date he wants to mail it by right where the stamp will eventually go. Then, he'd keep them sorted by mailing date on his desk.

The magic of doing this is that you commit yourself to your payments ahead of time, right after you looked at the debt you are passionate about eliminating. In doing so, I can almost guarantee you that you'll make larger payments on your debts. If you wait until the end of the month instead, you'll likely write your check based on how much money you have left.

In the Red

One of the silliest reasons to ever be late on a payment is that you ran out of checks. Surprisingly though, I hear it all the time. Someone was doing a good job of getting out of debt and then, a week before all their bills were due, they realized they were out of checks. The result? About $300 to $400 in late fees. Make sure you have plenty of checks and that you order your new ones at least four weeks before you'll need them!

File Your Essential Paperwork

When I sit down with someone trying to get out of debt, especially the ones with grocery bags full of statements, I'm amazed by their inability to quickly show me their most recent statement. They look around confused, frantically sorting through their mounds of unsorted paperwork.

To make matters more confusing, they haven't done a good job of differentiating between the essential paperwork and the junk. They've got stacks of unused payment envelopes, those free offers for junk like $9 weather radios, and offers from companies they don't even borrow from.

To make any progress on your debt, you're going to have to create a solid filing system. This system will separate your statements by company or lender, and help to keep them in chronological order. They're also only going to contain your statements; none of that other junk.

On the front of each envelope, write which company the envelope is for. Each month, after you're done reviewing and paying your statements, stick the statement in the envelope. Ideally, everything in the envelope will be paper-clipped into one giant stack, with the most recent statement on top.

Your important financial documents should be easy for you to grab and hard for others to steal. This is especially true if you have roommates or share an apartment with someone else. Ideally, you would be able to grab all your important financial documents in the event of an emergency, like a fire. But you'd also like them to be safe and

secure from prying eyes. I'd recommend a medium-size "fire box" which you can purchase at any office supply store. These boxes, which offer some protection from fires,
also have a lock and can be easily carried short distances in a hurry.

Shred the Rest

Believe or not, I'm actually going to give you permission in this book to go out and
buy something. Unfortunately, it's not going to bring you much immediate joy or help
you look more attractive as you stroll through the mall.

In fact, it's just the opposite! A good paper shredder will help you avoid a whole lot
of pain by appearing less attractive to those who steal identities. Identity theft is the
fastest-growing crime in America. It can take years and thousands of dollars to get
sorted out, so you need to do everything you can to avoid it.

Can you imagine finally getting all your credit cards paid off only to discover there are
10 more cards someone else has been running up in your name?

A nice, medium-grade shredder will cost you between $50 to $100. Ideally, you'll purchase one that creates little squares of confetti instead of those long strips. You'll also
purchase one that has some kind of guard to keep little fingers out of the shredder.

Don't shred your statements; those should be locked up safe somewhere so you can
review them as needed. But shred anything and everything else that comes to your
house with your name on it, from credit card offers to expired library cards. Heck,
you should even shred the payment envelopes so thieves don't know what companies
you're a customer of. They'll use anything they can get their hands on to begin stealing your identity.

Using Technology to Simplify

When it comes to getting your debts organized, technology and the Internet can go
a long way toward simplifying and taming the paperwork monster. In fact, if used
wisely, it may actually speed up the process of getting out of debt. It can also eliminate
a good amount of your month-to-month anxiety.

Get Your Paycheck Direct Deposited

In this day and age, you'd be the exception to the rule if you weren't already receiving
your paycheck by direct deposit. The advantage, of course, is that your paycheck gets
deposited into your account immediately and doesn't have to "clear" with the bank.

By getting your money into your account as soon as possible, you'll help ensure that you can make your payments on time. This will help you avoid those dreaded late fees that can cause debt to mushroom. You'll also have cash in your account for your living expenses, which will remove the temptation or need to use your credit cards.

If you're not set up for direct deposit, you'll need to contact your employer's human resources or payroll department. They'll need your bank's routing number (the nine digit number found on your checks), your individual bank account number, and probably your signature. Sometimes they'll just ask you for a voided check, since it contains most of this info to begin with.

Pay Your Bills Online and Automatically

Most banks offer free bill pay services nowadays. If your bank doesn't, you should probably think about switching. Online bill payments and automatic payments (which are two different things) offer you a number of advantages.

Online bill pay, which lets you sit down and schedule your payments for the coming month, helps to ensure your money gets there when you want it to. As a bonus, you save the cost of a stamp, which adds up over time.

There are two primary types of transfers bank use to move money from your account to another. Many times, when novice online banking users pay bills online, they accidentally use one of these other methods, which are usually different than a "bill pay" service. ACH or Automatic Clearing House transfers are usually free or have a low fee, and take two to three business days. A federal funds transfer can take place the same or next day, but usually cost anywhere from $15 to $30 per transfer.

All these features will help ensure that you stick to your debt reduction plan, pay your bills in a timely manner, avoid late fees, and protect your credit score. Even with all those benefits, though, there are a couple of drawbacks to be cautious of:

- Every bank is different, so you'll need to look closely at how yours works. The bill pay feature of my account with ING Direct tells me when the check will be mailed. My wife's bill pay with Bank of America tells her when the check will get there. Either way, make sure you plan ahead and allow adequate time for your check to be delivered.

- Depending on how your bank functions, it may or may not make a scheduled payment unavailable for other spending or withdrawals. In other words, if I schedule a $500 payment for two weeks from now, it may or may not remain available to be spent elsewhere until then. It's easy to accidentally spend that money and then have the bill pay go out, resulting in a NSF fee at your bank.

Use Online Account View and E-Lerts

While you might already access your bank account online, there's a good chance you're not taking advantage of this service for your other debts. Nowadays, everyone from your credit card company to your mortgage lender let you view your account online.

Now, while you could use this to obsess daily over your balances, the point is actually to make educated spending decisions. When you are shopping online at work (who does that?) or aren't sure if your car loan payment has been received, looking online can save a lot of heartache. By taking a few moments to login, you can decide if you've already spent too much on the credit card or if you should drive your car payment over to the bank to avoid a late fee.

Even better, many accounts are now offering e-mail alerts (a.k.a. E-lerts) to notify you of everything from missed payments to suspicious activities. If I were you, I'd sign up for every free E-lert I can get my hands on.

> **Dollars and Sense**
>
> Account aggregation is a relatively new feature offered by banks and other third-party companies. In essence, you are able to view all your accounts, from multiple banks and lenders, on one screen. As a rule of thumb, I'd consider using this feature if it was free, and skip it if I had to pay for it. Remember also that if there are any technical problems between your other accounts and your account aggregator, the information you see may not be accurate.

Personal Accounting Software

Software like Quicken or Microsoft Money can go a long way toward helping you understand your spending. The thing that makes them so powerful is that most banks now offer a download feature that automatically posts your transaction to your software.

These programs are easy to use and learn, and can usually be purchased for $25 to $50. In fact, there may be a free version on your computer that was installed when you bought it, so take a look before you spend. Additionally, they often come prepackaged with other software such as tax preparation programs.

Note that while programs like Quicken, Microsoft Money, TurboTax, and TaxCut are all great programs, their "premium" versions are not typically worth the money. Many times you'll see deluxe or premium versions available for $10 to $50 more than the basic version, with a bevy of cool features. Realistically, most of these features are beyond what the average beginning user needs.

When to Avoid Technology

As much as technology can help expedite your debt reduction plan, it can also help you further your denial or make significant mistakes. If technology is causing your overall plan to take a detour or taking a whole bunch of your time to learn, you should skip it.

One of the biggest places I've seen this is when people spend more time and energy learning and mastering the new technology than they do actually cutting their expenses or increasing their income. In psychology this is called an avoidance behavior—doing something that seems important to avoid doing the truly important.

Technology will help you to perform debt reduction tasks better, but will not do the essentials for you. With this in mind, here are some of areas to be cautious in using technology.

Don't Rely on Online Statements

While it might seem both efficient and environmentally responsible to get your statements electronically, it can lead to a pile of problems. Most importantly, you lose the ability to highlight and write all over your statements, like you need to do to accurately chart your progress. Additionally, you run the risk of your statement being overlooked, accidentally deleted, intentionally ignored, or getting trapped by your junk mail filter.

Avoid E-Mailing Your Creditors

If you have a complaint, dispute, or question, you need to contact your lender by phone. For serious matters, you should use registered mail or a shipping service that can verify delivery. There have been numerous times when a client of mine swears that he or she talked to someone at a company about an important issue, only to have the company claim they have no record of the phone call.

Even more importantly, many identity thieves are now using e-mail to dupe their victims. They send an e-mail link with your bank's logo, saying that something is wrong with your account and you need to click on the enclosed link to view the transaction. When you do, it looks just like your bank's sign-in screen, but instead sends your info to the identity thieves.

If you ever get a curious e-mail like this, call your bank!

> ### Debt in America
>
> Using trackable communications and keeping a log of your contacts with a company are extremely important. In the last couple of years, I've cancelled a number of credit cards. It comes as no surprise that my initial requests, even though I talked to a live person, were resisted or ignored. Months after I requested the cancellation, I was still receiving statements on accounts with zero balances! In all of these cases, it took an additional call or even a written request, often mentioning the name of the person who failed to execute my request the first time, to get the card finally cancelled.

Avoid Shopping Online

Many people, in an attempt to save money and cut expenses, start shopping online. While you can often find great deals online, you can be lured into wasting a lot of time and money. If you are the kind of person who can't say no to a good deal, or who has a hard time closing your wallet once you've opened it, it may be wise for you to avoid shopping online.

The Least You Need to Know

- Being deliberate with your debt paperwork will speed its elimination.

- You need to open and review bills the day you get them.

- You need to separate and file essential paperwork, and destroy the rest.

- You should write the check for next month's payment the day you receive your bill.

- Use technology to make payments and check balances before making purchases.

- Avoid technology if it's going to take you a lot of time to master, or if it's going to help you avoid dealing with the reality of your debt situation.

Chapter 12

Creating a Payment Strategy

In This Chapter

- ◆ As much as you can, as soon as you can
- ◆ Using the roll-down method
- ◆ What to eliminate first in your debt "hit list"
- ◆ Strategies for leftover cash
- ◆ Changing your plan

I love "barbershop" sayings. You know, those little nuggets of advice you'd get if you were hanging around with the much older, much wiser crowd. Things like "don't count your chickens before they hatch" or "a bird in the hand is worth two in the bush." For some reason, all these philosophers love poultry-based wisdom ....

Perhaps one of my favorites, because it applies to so many aspects of personal finance, is "If you don't know where you're going, any road will get you there." Nowhere is this more true than with getting out of debt.

You've taken a big step by reading through the last few chapters, making mental commitments, setting goals, and trimming your expenses. But without an actual plan about "how much" goes where, you won't get very far.

That's what this chapter is about—deciding which debts to tackle first with the extra cash you manage to scrape together.

As Much as You Can, as Soon as You Can

You'll recall from earlier chapters that increased discretionary income is the real key to getting out of debt. In other words, you have to begin adjusting your cash flow (income and expenditures) to ensure that there's extra money left over at the end of each month. If you don't, all you'll probably ever do is continue making minimum payments, which translates into decades of repaying debt.

So as you read the strategies in this chapter, realize that they all revolve around the idea that you've managed to scrape together some extra cash flow each month. If you haven't, you need to revisit the budget chapter and continue to rework the numbers until you've found something extra to apply toward your debts.

Dollars and Sense _____

For years, marketers have used the "daily cost" of something to make it seem more affordable to borrowers. They'll say things like "for just 87¢ per day, you can have affordable life insurance coverage." Of course, when you multiply that per day cost times 365 days per year, we're talking about hundreds of dollars. You should use the same mind-set when cutting your expenses in order to pay off more debt. Adding $100 per month to your credit card minimum payments only costs you $3.33 per day, less than the cost of many gourmet coffee drinks!

Use the Roll-Down Method

This is one of the most important parts of your debt reduction plan, and is the place that you'll actually find yourself getting excited about the difference your hard work is making.

In essence, the roll-down method requires that when one debt is paid off, the amount that had been going toward that debt is now added on top of the next debt on your list.

For example, let's say you have three credit cards you're paying down, all with minimum payments of $50. Your total minimum payments are $150 per month, but you've cut your expenses enough to be able to put $250 toward your debts each month. This means that after you make your minimum payments, you've still got an extra $100 per month to put toward the debt you'd most like to get rid of.

Once that debt is paid off, you take the entire $150 you were paying (the $50 minimum payment plus the $100 extra) and start paying that toward the next most hated debt. Of course, this is on top of the minimum payment you are used to making on the second debt.

Suddenly you have $200 per month going toward that debt ($50 minimum payment plus the $150 from the first debt). When that debt is paid off, you divert the entire amount you were paying on the second debt to the third.

As you can see, this accelerates your debt payments, and provides a very exciting turbo boost each time a debt gets paid off.

	Jan. Payment	Feb. Payment	Mar. Payment	Apr. Payment	May Payment
Account #1	$200 ($50 minimum + $150 extra)	$200 ($50 minimum + $150 extra)	Paid Off		
Account #2	$50 minimum	$50 minimum	$250 ($50 minimum + $200 from above)	$250 ($50 minimum + $200 from above)	Paid Off
Account #3	$50 minimum	$50 minimum	$50 minimum	$50 minimum	$300 ($50 minimum + $250 from above)

The roll-down method of paying debts.

As you can see in this table, in February, all the money that was going to the first account gets rolled down to the next, which helps it get paid off faster. In March, all the money that had been going toward the first and second accounts (which are now paid off) gets applied to the third, accelerating its payoff.

No matter how much discretionary income you can free up or how you prioritize your debts for elimination, you should plan on

Dollars and Sense

Snowflaking is another term for this "roll-down" reduction strategy. A quick search for "snowflaking" on the Internet will turn up tons of websites and blogs devoted entirely to helping you find ways to add momentum to your goal of getting out of debt.

using the roll-down method. If you don't, and you choose to spend the money you were paying on a now eliminated debt, the debt elimination process will take forever.

Debt Elimination: The Ugly, the Bad, and the Good

Before you do anything else, you need to first break your debts into three simple categories. Basically, all your extra funds will go toward paying off the different debts in one category before you move on to the next.

Essentially, there are debts you want to eliminate as soon as possible, debts you want to eliminate sooner than later, and debts you can save for last. That extra cash you have left over each month should be applied to those categories, in that order.

The Ugly: Debts to Eliminate ASAP

The debts you want to eliminate first are those that have the greatest potential to compound your debt problem if not taken care of immediately. While this can be any type of debt, depending on our lender's terms, they'll typically be debts with double-digit interest rates, no deductibility, and no relation to long-term assets or the creation of net worth.

Most typically, the debts you'll want to take the axe to first will be …

- **Payday loans.** With interest rates ranging from 100% to 1,000% per year, these are the equivalent of financial quicksand. If you don't get out of them now, you're going to be doomed. Typically, every available dime above your other minimum payments needs to go here until eliminated.

- **Credit cards.** With their high interest rates and hidden fees, as well as their effect on your credit score, these are also going to be some of the first debts to go.

- **The IRS.** While the IRS isn't the most brutal creditor when it comes to interest rates, they are one of the most effective when it comes to collections. There are few things that are as anxiety-provoking as the IRS garnishing your wages and sending you threatening letters. Remember, these are the folks who finally got the famous gangster Al Capone locked up … for tax evasion!

- **Anything in collections.** While they don't have the reach of the IRS, collection agencies can do a lot to make your life hell. If any of your debts have gone to collections, you'll want to get these taken care of immediately.

◆ **Medical debts.** The last people you want to have mad at you are the ones you depend on for your health! If you owe money to a doctor, dentist, or hospital, these will also be a priority. Not only might a bad debt damage your ability to get medical care, but many medical practices are also quick to hand over debts to collection agencies.

◆ **Child support and/or alimony.** Aside from the relational issues that these kinds of debts can cause, they can also create substantial legal problems. Many states will not let you perform simple tasks like renewing your driver's license if you owe money. Some states now even have "deadbeat dad" laws that can actually levy jail time against either parent for failing to pay support.

In the Red

In recent years, the IRS has started accepting credit cards for unpaid tax balances. While this may keep the IRS from breathing down your neck, think carefully before you whip out the plastic. The interest rate charged by the IRS for failing to pay (which is different than failing to file) and underpayments is generally under 10% annually. This is usually significantly less than the interest rate you'd pay if you shifted that balance to a credit card.

The Bad: Debts to Get Rid of Sooner Than Later

The debts you want to get rid of sooner than later are the ones that might have lower rates of interest (under 10–12%), but are used to purchase assets that will eventually become worthless.

Unlike many of the debts you scheduled for immediate execution, these debts will have a specified term (a certain number of years) until they are paid off. If you continue to make the minimum payments, they will take care of themselves a lot sooner than other debts like your credit cards.

These debts, which you'd only put your extra cash toward if the ASAP debts are taken care of first, typically include:

◆ **Installment debt.** This might include furniture, electronics, vacations, or other non-necessary purchases that you have committed to making monthly payments on. Usually, the interest rate on these is less than your ASAP debts, but is still not as attractive as some of your other debts.

◆ **Car loans.** Car loans are a necessary evil for many people. In many parts of the country, a car is an absolute necessity when it comes to working, going to school, and having anything that resembles a life. But, because these are depreciating assets, you'll want to eliminate them sooner than later.

◆ **401(k) and retirement plan loans.** While these loans offer fairly generous terms (low interest rates, reasonable repayment periods, etc.), they also slow your journey toward retirement.

◆ **Home equity line of credit (HELOC).** While these loans usually offer fair interest rates (though not as low as your primary mortgage or many student loans), which are also usually deductible, they still don't have a set repayment period. As such, it is easy to let these linger and slowly suck money away from your other financial goals.

In the Red

A withdrawal from a 401(k) that must be paid back over a certain period is a "loan." However, if your employment is terminated by you or your company for any reason and you do not repay the loan by the end of a specified period, any unpaid balance becomes a "distribution." While 401(k) loans are not taxable, distributions are. The IRS requires you to pay federal and state (if applicable) income tax as well as a 10% penalty on any outstanding balance.

The Good: Debts to Get Rid of Last

Generally, I'm against paying interest to anyone when you could be using that money to enjoy life or reach your other financial goals. But there are certain types of debt that are crucial to helping you reach your long-term goals. These debts have a reasonable rate of interest, a set repayment schedule, and are generally deductible with regard to your interest costs. Because of these favorable factors, they should be the last to go.

That's not to say that there aren't lousy versions of these loans out there. If your interest rate is high compared to similar loans, or can adjust significantly, you'll want to move them up in the order of elimination.

The two types of loans that will typically be the lowest priority as far as receiving your extra cash are …

◆ **Student loans.** With tax-deductible interest rates that are locked in by the government, these loans may be the least painful mathematically. Though the balance may feel large, it will not compound against you nearly as fast as most of your other debts. Additionally, their impact on your credit score is far less than many other types of debt.

- ◆ **Mortgages.** While you might need to look at upgrading from an adjustable rate mortgage to a more stable fixed-rate loan, this is still one of the best kinds of debt to have. Its deductible interest compounds slowly and represents ownership in a tangible asset that should increase in value over time.

> **Set a Goal**
>
> Grab your Debt Journal and break down all your debts into the three categories I've just discussed: Eliminate ASAP, Eliminate Sooner Than Later, and Eliminate Last. Put the book down, go grab your journal, and spend five minutes doing it. I'll wait right here for you.

Where to Put That Extra Cash

Okay, so you've broken down your debts into three categories. Now you have to decide where any extra money should go within these categories and subcategories. If you have 2 (or 10) credit cards, which one do you pay off first? What about the different car loans you have?

The truth is, any method that is used consistently will help you make progress. The trick is to find the method that encourages and motivates you the most.

How fast you actually make progress will be affected most by your willingness to trim your expenses and increase your payments. Aside from that, the amount of time it takes using any one method versus another won't vary by more than a month or two.

As always, it makes a great deal of sense to take care of all past-due amounts first and foremost. You want to avoid collections if at all possible, as well as preserve your credit score.

The Highest-Interest-Rate Debts

The most traditional wisdom on eliminating debt is to eliminate the highest-interest-rate debt first. In fact, this strategy goes beyond wisdom or preference … it actually makes the most mathematical sense.

At the core of this strategy is the reality that the faster interest piles on, the less of a dent each payment makes in your principal. So if you can get rid of the debt that is adding interest the fastest (not the most dollars, but the highest percentage), you will get around to paying down your principal sooner.

Let's look at a simple example of three, $1,000 debt balances with three different interest rates:

Balance	Interest Rate	Annual Interest
$1,000	10%	$100
$1,000	15%	$150
$1,000	30%	$300

Which one of these is causing your total debt to grow the fastest? That's right, the one at 30%. On an absolute mathematical basis, this will be one you'd want to target first with your extra cash.

Dollars and Sense

Do you want to know how your interest rates stack up against the national average? Many of the large personal finance websites track average rates across the country for different types of debt. Check out BankRate.com, Fool.com (the Motley Fool website), and Money.com. If your rates are significantly above the national averages, consider asking for a lower rate or switching cards if it's going to take you more than six months to eliminate the balance.

The Debts with the Smallest Balances

Though eliminating your smallest debts first may seem the opposite of common sense, it's actually my favorite method. Though it won't eliminate debt quite as fast as paying off the highest interest rates first, I've found that it creates a mountain of motivation.

The benefit comes from the fact that the number of your incoming bills will quickly dwindle by putting all your extra cash toward the smallest balances. This creates the equivalent of getting on the scale and realizing you've lost a few pounds through your hard work and discipline. For most of us, that'd be an encouragement that you're not wasting your time and to keep pressing forward.

Chances are, if there are 10 companies you owe money to, some will have large balances and some will be just a few hundred dollars. By devoting your extra cash to those smaller ones, you'll quickly go from 10 statements per month in your mailbox down to 4 or 5. What a stress reliever that would be, to have half of your creditors off your back and to get to cut up those cards once and for all!

The Largest Balances

For some of us, the greatest stressors are the biggest numbers. They feel like Mount Everest compared to all your other financial molehills. By taking care of them, or rather, by making a dent in them, you feel like progress is being made.

The risk to this method is that after 6 to 12 months, you could also feel like you've really not made any progress. This is especially true if the largest debt is also one of your higher-interest-rate debts, meaning that it compounds on itself relatively fast.

If you choose to use your extra cash to tackle the largest balances first, you'll also need to be super-diligent about not adding anything additional to that debt or creating others. Both of these may cause you to throw in the towel as your debts seemingly continue to mount.

Debt in America

People in some states seem a lot more prone to running up credit card balances than others. According to TrackCards, a service of PlasticEconomy. com, Colorado residents who use credit cards carry the highest total combined balances at just over $13,700. North and South Dakota residents using credit cards are virtually tied for the lowest spot, with just over $2,000.

The Debts That Affect Your Credit Score Most

This method essentially focuses extra cash on debts that weigh down your credit score. For example, you might focus your extra cash on your retail credit card as opposed to your auto loan, because the first makes you look like a greater risk to lenders than the second. Other debts in this category would include payday loans, installment loans, and government debts.

You might also focus on getting your maxed-out cards paid down, since that can reflect positively on your credit score. Because many lenders look at the "balance-to-limit" ratio, or how much of your potential limit you've used, it's in your favor to not appear overextended. In fact, when you apply for a new loan, it would be ideal if your balances were less than 50% of any account's limit.

Accounts That You Plan on Closing

In the short term, any type of cancelled debt, even if it was closed at your request, can translate into a black mark on your credit score. However, over the long run, closing accounts will help your credit score as well as take temptation out of your pocket.

With that in mind, it makes some sense to devote your extra cash toward the debts you're going to get rid of anyway. Get them off the books as soon as possible, let your credit score heal, and get on with life. Best of all, once they're cancelled, you'll have one less debt that you can run back up.

Those with Nondeductible Interest

Because some debts are deductible on your tax return, they may be more favorable than others when it comes to deciding which ones to eliminate last. Most often, deductible debt is limited to student loans and mortgage debt. Occasionally, though, other types of debt are deductible if they are related to a business or investment activity, but you need to consult your local tax guru to make sure.

To decide if you should keep a deductible debt as opposed to a nondeductible one, you'll need to know your income tax bracket and how to use a calculator.

Here's how it works:

1. Add your federal and state tax brackets together and convert them into a decimal. For example, a 20% federal income tax rate and a 5% state income tax rate would equal 25% or .25.

2. Subtract this amount from 1. For example, 1 minus .25 equals .75.

3. Multiply this amount by your deductible interest rate to find your "after-tax" interest rate. For example, if your deductible interest is 10%, you'd have an after-tax rate of 7.5% (10% times .75).

4. Compare the "after-tax" interest rates of your deductible accounts with the actual rates of your nondeductible accounts. Consider paying off the ones with the lowest rates last.

Dollars and Sense

Interested in estimating your federal income tax bracket? Go to www.IRS.gov, find the Search box, and type in "Tax Tables." Then, select the most recent year available. It'll usually open a huge document, but don't fret. Just scroll down to the last page, and it'll show you the tax rate schedule for your filing status and income level. Disregard the dollar amount; the percentage listed for your income range is all you need to estimate your after-tax interest.

The Most Stressful Debts

From a strictly psychological point of view, I'd definitely advise people to eliminate the debts that cause the most stress first. While there may be others that make more mathematical sense, staying encouraged is the most important thing.

But before you devote your extra cash to a debt that's stressing you out, ask yourself the following question: *If you take care of the one that bothers you the most, will you care about any of the others?*

Changing Your Strategy Midway

One of the things I've learned as a writer is that I do a better job if I change my scenery every few hours. I also do better if I write about something else every couple of days. If I try to sit still in the same place for a day, or write about the same thing for a week straight, it will lull me to sleep like driving through the desert at 2 A.M. By changing my scenery, method, and focus, it keeps me on task and moving forward.

Getting out of debt may be that way for you. That's okay! I'm giving you permission to feel "blah" about your strategy after a while.

One of the most important things to remember about your debt repayment plan is that it is not set in stone. You are allowed and encouraged to be responsive to changes in your situation and your anxiety, especially if it will keep you making some kind of forward progress.

If, in the middle of funneling your extra discretionary income toward the largest balance, you decide that it's not the best method, then switch! Be proud of yourself for making a dent in the largest debt, then move on to something else. You have my blessing to take a break from one method, as long as you choose another. Just keep doing something!

In addition to years of working as a Certified Financial Planner, I've worked with hundreds of people doing behavioral counseling. One of the things I've noticed in both my own behavior and others, is that I "know" well in advance of when I'm going to cheat on a diet, exercise plan, or budget. In hindsight, my getting off track was never really a surprise. There were always signals and warning signs that I was about to give up on something. As I've become a little older and wiser, I've begun to tell these things to my accountability partners sooner. In turn, they've been able to encourage me and keep me focused. What are your "red flags"? How do you know when you're about to cheat, be bad, or cut loose? Be sure to share your thoughts with someone so they can help watch out for you!

The Least You Need to Know

◆ The most crucial debt elimination strategy remains the same: pay as much as you can, as soon as you can.

◆ Use the roll-down method to accelerate your debt reduction.

◆ Prioritize your debts between eliminate ASAP, eliminate sooner than later, and eliminate last.

◆ Develop a strategy about where to apply your extra discretionary income each month.

◆ It's okay to change strategies as long as you keep doing something!

Part 3

Debt-Specific Strategies

There's a legend about Tiger Woods shooting an entire round of golf with only his putter. He used the putter to tee off. He used the putter to get out of the sand trap. And of course, he used the putter to putt. At the end of 18 holes, he had played a better round of golf than I'll ever play, even if I use every club in the bag.

When it comes to eliminating debt, there's no need to use just one "club." There are different techniques that will help you eliminate different kinds of debt faster. Specifically, in this part you'll learn strategies for reducing your credit cards, mortgages, student loans, and other types of debt. You'll also learn when to consider bankruptcy as an option. Knowing when and how to use these different strategies will ensure you get out of debt sooner than later.

Fore!

13

Credit Card Strategies

In This Chapter

- ◆ It's simple: decrease spending and increase payments
- ◆ Stop using credit cards for daily expenditures
- ◆ Don't carry the cards with you
- ◆ When you need to have a credit card
- ◆ "Silver bullets" to use in paying off your card

Have you ever watched any movies or TV shows about the armed forces? One of my favorites is the old Richard Gere classic, *An Officer and a Gentleman.* One of the staples of the boot camp training in that movie is the obstacle course. At the center of that obstacle course is "the wall," which is this monstrously tall obstacle that most people, until they figure out the trick, can't seem to get over.

If getting rid of your debt is an obstacle course, then credit cards are your "wall." They're right at the center of this thing, and you can't finish the course until you learn how to get over them. If you can't lick your credit card debt, it doesn't matter if you whip your mortgage into shape, outlast your student loans, or pummel your auto loan into submission. Because credit card debt is simultaneously easy and expensive to use, the wall only gets bigger as you put off dealing with it.

Are you ready to deal with your credit card debt? Get pumped up! Get angry! Let's take a full-speed run at it!

The Trick to Paying Off Credit Cards

Okay, there really is no trick. I just said that to keep you reading. In reality, your credit card balances will only disappear by you paying more on them than what gets added to them each month. Even if you pay off what you spend, your balance will still grow because of the interest charges for the month.

Now I know that seems like commonsense knowledge, but for some reason, most of us can't put it into action. So let's break it down into two real simple rules. If you can do these two things, I guarantee that your credit card balances will begin to shrink:

1. Don't make another purchase on your credit card.

2. Pay an amount greater than the interest charged to the account for each month.

Remember, if all you are doing each month is making the minimum payment on the credit cards, your credit cards will take decades to pay off. Further, if your payment isn't at least the amount of interest that was charged to your account, you'll literally never get your credit cards paid off.

When you scan down your credit card transactions, what are the first things you usually see? Chances are, it's the payments and returns you've made. One habit I've seen people get into is buying something on a credit card, later returning it, and then taking a cash refund instead of having it credited back to their card. Then, of course, the cash "evaporates." I know it's tempting when that clerk asks you if you'd like your refund in cash, but this is the one time I'm encouraging you to whip out your credit card!

Stop Using Your Credit Card for Day-to-Day Expenditures

I've talked at length in previous chapters about using a spending plan to free up money (discretionary income) so you can direct it toward your credit card and debt balances. But I haven't talked much about the first rule of thumb you just learned: don't make another purchase on your credit card.

That may feel impossible for you. It may seem unrealistic. After all, how else would you pay for something if it weren't for plastic? Shouldn't you just try to minimize what you spend on the card?

To be blunt, no, you should not. Continuing to use your credit card comes with a whole host of problems. First and foremost, it allows you to continue being impulsive and rationalizing. Having an "I'll figure it out later" type of attitude is probably part of what got you into this mess in the first place.

Second, it continues to perpetuate the cycle of you borrowing money, at a ridiculous rate of interest that you may or may not be able to pay off at the end of the month. Remember, this is where your good intentions got you into trouble from the start, Once you're even slightly behind, your balance begins to grow exponentially.

Keep the Credit Cards out of Your Wallet

So what's the alternative? Cash. Don't get me wrong, I don't think you should be walking around with a roll of hundreds in your pocket or purse. But I mean that you should find a way to limit your spending to the cash you have in your bank account and savings.

For our household, this means that we use debit cards (which take the money immediately out of your bank account) for everything. When that account hits zero, whether it is the 3rd or the 23rd of the month, we're done spending. We may have to skimp for a week, but we'll never be playing catch-up with our credit cards.

In fact, I think you need to stop carrying a credit card altogether when you're just going about your daily life. You have my deepest professional promise that you can survive without it. Generations before you managed to do it, so can you!

In the Red

It only takes one or two times of being hit with an overdraft fee on your debit or ATM card for you to be open to just about any solution. So when the bank offers you overdraft protection for a minimal monthly fee, there's a good chance you'd take it. Unfortunately, many overdraft protection services turn your debit card into a credit card. When you go below zero in your account, the bank loans you a fixed sum, such as $100 or $250. Aside from the fact that it charges you a fee and interest for the privilege, there's an additional drawback: you usually end up spending the excess they deposited!

So That Means I Should Cancel All My Credit Cards?

Well, I didn't quite say that. I said that you should stop carrying credit cards in your wallet or purse. Doing that is going to help you rein in your spending everywhere from the grocery store to the mall. But I do think it is wise to have one credit card, just in case.

A credit card is a necessity if you decide to drive across the country, rent a car, book airfare, visit a foreign country, and for life's true emergencies. Those situations are examples of moments that you cannot afford to be without one. But again, you need to create some barrier to using it when it's not one of those times.

In our household, when we were getting out of debt, we froze our credit card into a block of ice. No, really, we did. For years, there was a Styrofoam cup sitting in our freezer, filled with frozen water and a credit card. The only time we got the blow dryer out was for special occasions like travel.

You don't need to go that far, but you need to find a barrier to use that works for you. Maybe you keep it locked in a drawer, sealed in an envelope, or give it to a trusted family member.

You might want to look into getting a secured credit card. This type of credit card functions very similar to a prepaid gift card, but it is issued by your bank and can be used anywhere major credit cards are accepted. It's ideal for people who need a credit card, but either need to control their spending or have had their credit card frozen due to debt problems. Quite simply, a secured credit card will only let you spend as much as you have deposited in advance with the issuer. That's similar to a debit card, but a secured credit card will typically avoid those dreaded overdraft fees while simultaneously helping to rebuild your credit.

Silver Bullets for Reducing Your Credit Card Balances

As I've said, the only tried and true way to fully eliminate your credit card balance is to pay as much as you can, while spending as little as possible. However, there are some "silver bullets" you can use to give yourself a head start on eliminating your credit card debt. I call these techniques silver bullets because they're to be saved for special occasions when you really need them. You may only get to use some of them once before your credit card company tells you exactly what you can do with your request.

A number of these silver bullets come with significant disadvantages, primarily in how they affect your credit score for the next five to seven years. If you think you are going to need to get a loan of any kind in that time period, you'll want to give serious thought to whether or not these techniques are worth using.

Negotiate a Lower Rate

This is one of the easiest techniques to turbo-charge the process of eliminating your credit card debt. What this technique entails is requesting your credit card company lower the rate of interest that you're paying on your outstanding balance. The savings can be considerable.

Consider a $10,000 credit card balance with an annual percentage rate of 30%. The interest you'll pay over the coming 12 months will be in the ballpark of $3,000. If you can somehow get that rate lowered to 15%, you would avoid paying almost $1,500 in interest. That money you save could then be put toward your balance, which would result in a significant decrease!

So how do you get your credit card company to magically lower its interest rates? How do you convince the company that making less money off you is a good idea for them? It's simple. You just need to convince them that you'll be taking your "business" elsewhere.

Every credit card company is aware that every other credit card company is trying to steal their clients. Whichever company has the biggest pool of money owed to them by consumers is the one who will likely make the biggest profit. Hence, a lot of effort goes into getting and keeping your business.

Dollars and Sense

Most consumers don't realize that all those fees you get slapped with are as open to negotiation as the interest rate. Oftentimes, you can even get fees waived in hindsight. When you have the conversation with your credit card company, be sure to mention these as a reason you're thinking about switching or if you think they were applied unfairly. It only takes a click of a button and a consumer who refuses to give up to erase substantial charges.

You're probably used to the steady stream of e-mails offering you much cheaper interest rates on your balance if you just transfer it to the XYZ Company. Sometimes, all you need to do is let your existing credit card company know that you've seen them.

Here's how the conversation goes:

> You: Hi, I was calling about my account with your company.
>
> Them: Yes, thank you for being a loyal customer and allowing us to pillage your finances for the last 10 years.
>
> You: Yes, well about that. I really like you guys, too, but I got this offer in the mail.
>
> Them: (Silence)
>
> You: They're offering me 10.99% to transfer my balance to them.
>
> Them: (Silence)
>
> You: So anyway, I like you guys a lot, and I'd love to keep my business with you, but I was hoping you could give me a rate that competes with XYZ Company.
>
> Them: Um … Hold on … Let me talk to my manager …

That's about all it takes. The worst they can do is say no and then all sit around and laugh at you after you hang up. But, based on my experience with clients, you will get some type of lowered rate almost 50% of the time.

This one is a freebie as far as negative consequences. It doesn't show up on your credit report and it shouldn't have any negative effects on your existing account if you get denied.

In fact, I think you can probably ask for it about every 12 months if your rate climbs back up. Remember, the reality is, many companies would rather keep you paying 15% than lose you because you were paying 30%.

Transfer Your Balance to Another Card

A balance transfer is another great way to speed the repayment of your credit cards, because it may reduce your interest for 6 to 12 months, even more than negotiating a lower rate. But this is one of those techniques that can backfire on you if you're not really careful.

On the upside, transferring your balance may cut your interest rate temporarily from as high as 30% to as low as 0%, sometimes for up to one year. On a $10,000 balance, that means that you might end up paying $3,000 less in interest over the course of 12 months. That's a lot of money that could be redirected toward eliminating your balances.

The downside, of course, is that you now have a new credit card that you can run amok with. Instead of having one credit card to contend with, you may now have two. There's twice as much temptation, which can translate into twice as much potential for debt.

Additionally, balance transfers usually come with a one-time transfer fee that can start as low as 1% to 2% and can go as high as 10%. For example, a $10,000 balance transfer might cost anywhere from $100 to $1,000, which is usually added to your new balance.

If you do a balance transfer, consider doing the following:

◆ Cancel and cut up the credit card you are transferring the balance from.

◆ Don't activate the new credit card you receive. That way, even though the balance from your old card is now on the new card, you're not tempted to start using it to make purchases as well. That'll help you stick to keeping that one out of your wallet as well.

◆ Double-check the rules for your balance transfer. Oftentimes the rate automatically increases, and is applied retroactively, if your payment is even a day late.

Use Your Home Equity to Pay It Off

On the surface, this is a great theory. But below the surface, it is one of the main reasons that so many people find themselves in financial quicksand.

The theory is simple. You've got a home that is worth more than you owe. You've also got a credit card balance that you'd like to see paid off. So you go to the bank and request a home equity line of credit, or HELOC, where the bank loans you money against the net value of your home.

Why would you do this? Don't you still owe the same amount of money, even though you've moved it around? You do, but by shifting your debt from your credit card to your house, you've replaced a debt that might have charged you as high as 30% annually, to one that is charging you under 10%. To make it even better, the interest on your home equity line of credit may be deductible on your tax return, whereas your credit card interest is not.

So why might this be a bad idea? It's what I call the "snake and the cage" problem.

A few years ago, our seven-year-old son badgered us into buying him a corn snake. When I visited the pet store, the clerk asked me, "How large do you want the snake to grow to be?" This was a great question for me, because I'm not a huge fan of snakes. Given the option of having them be smaller than my arm (as opposed to large enough to swallow me), I'll choose smaller.

The trick, apparently, is to keep the snake in a smaller cage. If you put it in a larger cage, it will slowly grow to fit the cage. If you leave them in the smaller cage, their bodies instinctually stay smaller.

The same thing has been true with home equity loans, credit cards, and runaway real estate prices. Many of us grew as big as our "financial cages." Your house would go up in value, which would make you feel like you could keep running up the credit cards, paying them off every so often with your home equity. Too bad the real estate market doesn't go up forever …

Again, as with the balance transfer technique, if you borrow against your house to pay off your credit cards, you need to get rid of the credit cards that you pay off. If you don't, it's a matter of time and human nature until you run those things back up and have no more equity in your home to fall back on.

In the Red

Your home isn't the only long-term asset you can borrow against. Many of the large investment firms and brokerage houses now offer lines of credit against your investment accounts. In fact, many of them give these lines of credit to you automatically when you sign up for their "bells and whistles" cash management accounts. All you have to do is spend below your cash balance, and they'll automatically loan you money against your stocks, bonds, and mutual funds. The downside is that these are a lot more volatile day to day than the price of your house. This could force you to pony up funds on the spot if your investments go down in value too quickly. If you can, avoid these accounts like the plague!

Consider Balance Reduction and Debt Settlement

Credit card companies aren't as stubborn as you'd imagine. If anything, they're quite greedy, and that can work to your advantage if you're in over your head. While their preference is for you to faithfully carry a balance and pay interest on it, they also have a major fear of you completely walking away from your debts.

When credit card companies truly believe that you're on the verge of bankruptcy, they're usually happy to take whatever they can get from you before you disappear or declare bankruptcy. In other words, if they can get half of what you owe them now, as opposed to nothing later, they'll often take the half.

But don't just think you can call them up and offer to settle your debt for 50¢ on the dollar. Usually, credit card companies won't even consider a balance reduction unless you can prove that you're really in trouble. For many credit card issuers, that proof comes in the form of two to three months worth of missed (not late) payments, pending bankruptcy paperwork, or verification of unemployment.

To start this process in motion, you'll need to do the following:

1. **Speak to the Settlement Department.** While every credit card company might have a different name for this department, any customer service person will know exactly what you're talking about.

2. **Show no fear.** Really, this is one of the keys to settling a debt. The credit card company will only settle if they perceive you as truly unable to pay. To them, that doesn't look like someone who is stressed and begging for a break. It actually looks like someone who doesn't give a darn, and is making a last ditch effort before they go to bankruptcy.

3. **Give them a low-ball offer.** Your credit card company knows it's probably not the only one, and that you are making offers elsewhere. With that in mind, it'll try and get its hands on just a little more of that sweet cash by getting you to compromise. Start with 10% to 20% on the dollar, and negotiate from there.

4. **Negotiate some confidentiality.** Everything is open to negotiation. As part of accepting its compromise, ask to keep the debt negotiation off your credit report and report the account closed at your request (not theirs).

5. **Get everything in writing and save it all!** Credit card companies and collection agencies are notorious for saying whatever they can to get you to send in some money. Then, as soon as they get it, they keep asking for more. Make sure you have written correspondence (not an e-mail) agreeing to completely release you from the debt if a certain payment is made.

6. **Pay them—anonymously.** One of the classic mistakes you can make is sending a check from your personal bank account. Guess what info you just gave them? That's right, your bank account number. You just made it much easier for a collections department to go after your cash. Instead, send a cashier's check or money order by registered mail.

> **Dollars and Sense** _____
>
> How do you think it looks if you call and ask for a balance reduction, and the customer service person reviews your account history only to find recent visits to the spa, five-star restaurants, and the swankiest stores in the mall? They probably think you're living a better life than they are. Your best bet is to completely cut your high-dollar spending for about six months before you're daring enough to ask someone to forget about the debts you owe them.

Consolidate Your Credit Cards

We've all seen the commercials. Heck, even my kids have seen them. My seven-year-old can tell you that "if you're feeling stressed out by your bills, you can just call ACME Company, who will help you to combine everything into one low payment!"

On the surface, this may sound like a great idea. But there are some definite drawbacks that I'll talk about in Chapter 17. Suffice it to say that to get into this kind of program, you end up selling your financial soul. In one way or another, you're going to pay for the privilege of having your credit cards consolidated to a single payment.

Here are some important questions to ask before your open up your finances to a consolidation company. Even better, try to get these answers in writing:

◆ **What is my effective interest rate?** Many companies will simultaneously lower your monthly payment and raise your interest rate. They do this by extending the length of your loan, allowing you to pay less each month, but over a much longer period of time.

◆ **What fees are involved?** Just like a balance transfer, a debt consolidation can have substantial fees associated with setting it up or maintaining a program. Considering that surprise fees are the biggest complaint filed against debt consolidation programs, make sure you read the fine print.

◆ **Can my interest rate change for any reason?** If it can, you need to figure out the formula. Again, the best consolidation companies will give you one fixed rate for the life of your loan.

◆ **Are there prepayment penalties?** Avoid companies that will penalize you if you pay off your consolidated debt sooner than planned. A prepayment penalty is a definite red flag that a company is going to try to squeeze as much profit as possible out of you.

- ◆ **Can you sell my consolidated loan?**
  Oftentimes, a consumer's loan will
  get sold by a nice company to a not-
  so-nice company. Then everything
  changes. The interest rates go up,
  the harassing phone calls start again,
  and you're right back where you
  started.

- ◆ **How will this consolidation affect
  my credit score?** Different companies have different policies on what,
  how, and when they report to the
  credit bureaus. Find out your company's reporting policy for late payments, early payoffs, etc.

> **Debt in America**
>
> Peer-to-peer lending net-
> works are one of the hottest
> trends in debt consolidation.
> Instead of borrowing money from
> some fly-by-night operation, you
> can go through a number of
> websites that match up private
> borrowers and lenders. Through
> companies such as Prosper and
> The Lending Club, hundreds of
> thousands of individuals with
> extra money are able to loan it
> to other individuals at competitive
> rates with minimal fees.

Use Your Credit Insurance

Credit insurance is one of my big pet peeves in life. There are few things that waste
more money for the average person than insurance that promises to pay off your
credit card if you die. They sell it to you because most of the time, they'll never have
to pay on it.

As the economy continued to expand beyond reason in the last decade, and unemployment sank to nearly all-time lows, credit card companies began to expand this coverage to unemployment. In other words, if you get laid off and can't find a new job, the
credit card company will cover your minimum monthly payments.

While most people who know better passed on these policies, they were still unscru-
pulously added to many credit card accounts by overly ambitious telemarketers. Go
back and check your statements for a mysterious and regular recurring charge, usually
about $10 to $20 per month. If it's there, whether you chose it or not, it's time to cash
in on it.

Call your company and ask where you can get a copy of the fine print of that insurance policy. Then grab a cup of coffee and a highlighter, and go through and see if it's
supposed to cover your payments for one reason or another.

The Least You Need to Know

- There are only two true ingredients to eliminate credit card debt: stop using the card and pay an amount greater than the interest charged to the account for each month.

- It's a good idea to retain one credit card for special circumstances such as travel or emergencies.

- Attempting to negotiate your interest rates and fees is a must for all of your credit cards.

- Be careful with balance transfers, because new accounts create the opportunity to dig yourself even deeper in debt.

- Make sure you ask thorough questions and do your research before you sign up with a debt consolidation or settlement company.

- Check to see if you purchased credit insurance that protects against loss of employment or financial hardship.

Chapter 14

Mortgage Strategies

In This Chapter

◆ Asking the hard questions

◆ Refinancing: often the best solution

◆ When you can't refinance

◆ Facing foreclosure

◆ Speeding up your payments and avoiding unnecessary insurance costs

There are few things that represent the American dream as much as owning a house. There's something freeing about the idea of someday being able to live in a home that you don't have to make payments on and that no one can take away from you. To boot, it represents status and stability in our society; a sign that you've simultaneously arrived and are going somewhere.

All those things combined make for a good amount of pressure when it comes to buying a home. Mix in a mortgage industry and real estate market gone wild, and you've got a recipe for financial disaster. For many people in our country, two old sayings have come home to roost: "Their eyes were bigger than their stomachs," and "They bit off more than they could chew."

There's a good chance that you, or someone close to you, is staring down the barrel of a bad mortgage. It may be bad because it had features you weren't aware of or it may be bad because it flat out became unaffordable. Either way, considering that keeping a roof over your head is probably your largest expense, you've got to figure out what to do.

Getting to Know Your Mortgage

The first step in developing a specific strategy for your mortgage is to really understand how your mortgage works. Many mortgages from the last decade were done by two parties who were usually in quite a rush and didn't take the time to study the fine print.

You had a homebuyer who needed that new home, and they needed it yesterday. Forget for a second that it was the third home they had bought in five years, that it was a five-bedroom home for two people, or that they had to bid $50,000 over the asking price to get it. They needed it "now"—another thing that makes us truly American!

You also had mortgage brokers and loan officers who were having the time of their lives. They were making more money than they had ever made and people were lining up to hand them more commissions. While the creation of higher, riskier mortgage products should have caused them to take pause and wonder about their clients' best interest, they assumed that they'd always be able to refinance people out of bad mortgages into other bad mortgages. This assumption was based on the less than historical belief that real estate does nothing but go up in price.

Long story short, you had people on both sides who didn't take the time to ask the important "what if" questions. Sadly, many people with shaky mortgages are still avoiding those crucial "what if" questions, instead hoping that everything will work itself out.

So if you're in any kind of mortgage besides a 15- or 30-year fixed-rate mortgage, it's time to ask those questions. The answers will help you chart a course for your mortgage debt, which in turn will affect how you get everything else paid off.

Probably the hardest question to ask, but the one that you should ask first, is "Can I afford this?" In other words, does it make sense for me to still live here, even if I don't technically have the money to pay the mortgage or rent? Remember, just saving $200 per month on your lease or mortgage could save more than $10,000 over five years.

That'll go a long way toward getting you out of debt. After that, you can upgrade your living arrangements again.

"What If" #1: Interest Rates Adjust

The first thing you need to get a handle on is what your interest rate situation is. If it's going to adjust in the near future, you need to figure out what the damage will be. In other words, how much will your increased payment affect your ability to pay other expenses?

Start by digging out your mortgage paperwork and reading the fine print about your interest rates. Here are two important questions—write your answers in the margin, you'll need them in a minute:

◆ **When does it reset?** Some mortgages reset once and then never again and some reset on a recurring basis (monthly, semiannually, annually, etc.).

◆ **How is the rate calculated?** Sometimes the rate itself is determined in advance (8% after year 5, 8.5% after year 7, etc.), but more often it is tied to a formula. Most times, your rate will be "pegged" to a well-known interest rate index such as the rates on Treasury bills or the LIBOR rate.

Now that you have answers to these questions, grab a pad of paper and get on the Internet. Go to BankRate.com and find its "mortgage reset calculator." You can also do a search for that same phrase and find numerous calculators that'll do the trick.

Now plug in different interest rates and see what happens to your monthly payment amount. Try some small changes (.25–.75%) and some large changes (1–3%). Write down those different payment amounts.

Next, pull out your compromise budget you made in Chapter 8. Start plugging that payment into that budget. Are you still breaking even or better? Does it chew up so much of your discretionary income that there is nothing left to make more than the minimum payments on your other debts? If so, you're going to need to figure out a strategy to get your payment down and keep it in an acceptable range for your budget. More on that in a few pages.

"What If" #2: Balloon Payment Is Coming Due

One of the great failed promises of the last mortgage and real estate boom was that you'd always be able to refinance. Because of this overly optimistic belief, many home-owners took on mortgages with balloon payments. These loans often offered a lower

> **Debt in America**
>
> According to a January 2008 Federal Reserve study, states such as Nevada, California, and Florida led the country in the percentage of loans issued as adjustable-rate mortgages. In January 2008, these states were also among the leaders in the country in the number of mortgages in default.

payment, but required the loan to be refinanced or paid off at a certain point in the future (usually 7 to 10 years).

Of course, if your home goes significantly down in value or if the people loaning money begin running tight on funds, you may not be able to refinance. This leaves many people holding a ticking time bomb—the inability to refinance or pay off hundreds of thousands of dollars in debt. Ouch!

If you are not sure if or when you have a balloon payment due, you need to pull out that paperwork. If you have questions, all you need to do is pick up the phone and call your mortgage lender.

"What If" #3: Your Principal Isn't Shrinking

In the beginning of this book, I talked about how a mortgage is usually one of those "good debts." That statement was built around the idea that you are repaying a loan that was used to purchase something that increases in value. Ultimately, over time, this kind of loan will help you create net worth and wealth. But if the amount you actually owe on your home isn't decreasing or, even worse, is increasing, then you've got to figure out a new payment strategy ASAP!

Now before you panic, you need to realize that all mortgages, even 30-year fixed mortgages, don't show a lot of reduction in principal in the first few years. That's normal and okay. As long as your mortgage payments are consistently paying off a little more principal each month, then you're headed in the right direction.

If they're not, however, you probably have what is called an interest-only or "negative amortization" loan. If so, you're going to need to find a strategy to get you moving toward reducing this debt over time.

Refinancing: A Bad Mortgage's Best Friend

When it comes to mortgage solutions, there's one that trumps them all … refinancing. In other words, the best solution is a new mortgage with better terms and interest rate. However, knowing when to refinance and which loan option to choose can be daunting. It often amounts to comparing apples to oranges because the terms can be so different and there may be significant out-of-pocket costs associated with a refinance.

Let's look at each mortgage scenario one by one and see how a "re-fi" might ease the burden and keep your debt reduction plan on track.

> **In the Red** _____
>
> A trend that has led to skyrocketing debt is the "cash out" refinance. These transactions allow consumers to withdraw money from their house in the refinancing process. Whatever amount is withdrawn is added to the balance of the mortgage. Oftentimes, this money is used to pay bills or nonessential expenses, which erases years of paying down your principal overnight.

Refinancing an Adjustable Rate to a Fixed Rate

This is one of those moves that can often seem to defy common sense. You've got an adjustable-rate mortgage with a couple years left to go before it adjusts. You're just barely making the payments as it is. So why should you refinance to a fixed-rate mortgage with a slightly higher payment?

If it's likely your interest rate, and therefore your payment, will rise significantly, you may want to cut this one off at the pass. Your best bet may be to take the smaller hit now by refinancing to avoid a much larger one later. This is especially true if housing prices are falling and you won't be able to refinance in the future.

Refinancing a Shorter Term to a Longer Term

A shorter-term mortgage at a lower rate will always cost more each month than a longer-term mortgage at the same rate. For example, a $250,000 mortgage at 7% costs $2,247 per month on a 15-year loan. On a 30-year loan, the payment drops to $1,663. It drops another $100 on a 40-year loan.

Now remember, you don't want to carry debt your whole life, but you also don't want to lose your house. If your payments have become unaffordable, even in a shorter-term fixed-rate loan, consider refinancing to a longer-term fixed-rate loan.

Refinancing an Interest Only or NegAm to a Fixed

For the most part, I don't think your day-to-day homeowner should have anything to do with an interest-only or a negative amortization loan. In both of these scenarios your home loan is not shrinking and may in fact be growing. These are ticking time bombs as well.

Because you should eventually be eliminating all debt in your life (even a great mortgage), you've got to be paying down principal. If your mortgage doesn't force you to pay down principal, you should really consider refinancing. Ideally, you'd refinance to a fixed rate, but I'd even suggest a decent adjustable-rate mortgage over an interest only or NegAm.

Refinancing a HELOC into a Fixed Mortgage

If you have made use of a home equity line of credit (HELOC), or "residential ATMs" as I like to call them, you need to put a cork in it. If you're not careful, you'll slowly use up all the equity in your home, creating more debt that you'll have to figure out how to eliminate.

If there is any way you can get your lender to combine your first mortgage and this line of credit into one payment, while taking away the checkbook you used to dig yourself into the hole, it's probably a smart move.

Knowing When to Refinance

One of the questions that mortgage brokers get asked the most (and also don't have any real good answers to) is whether or not "now is a good time to refinance." By asking this, you're trying to figure out if interest rates are going to go up or down, which translates into whether you should wait or hurry.

The funny thing is, even the best mortgage brokers can't tell you what is going to happen day to day and week to week. That's not to say that they don't have an idea of whether or not rates, over the course of a couple of years, seem to be climbing or declining. But most people aren't asking about that broad of a time period.

The real answer is simple. The right time to refinance is when you're missing out by not doing it. If refinancing would significantly lower your payment or avoid painful future increases, then you should do it now if you can.

Whether or not you can is another question, and one that deserves a little thinking as well. If you are thinking you'll need to refinance and home prices are falling as you're thinking about it, you might want to think a little faster.

The problem comes when your home's value drops too close to the value of the mortgage you're trying to refinance. Even worse is when your house is worth less than your existing mortgage. In both of these situations, you become an increasingly risky proposition for a lender to loan new money to and your chances of a refinance will disappear.

Origination, Points, and Closing Costs ... Oh My!

One of the most difficult parts about refinancing is the out-of-pocket costs, which may include *closing costs*, *origination fees*, and *points*. In fact, refinancing a mortgage can easily cost you 2% to 3% of the total value of loan, which might easily amount to $5,000 to $10,000 up front. So how do you know if that's worth it when there are so many other good uses for that money, like paying off other debts?

My rule of thumb is that you should be able to recover all your upfront costs from the savings on your monthly payments within a short amount of time. For an adjustable-rate mortgage, you should be able to recoup your costs in less than one year. For a fixed-rate mortgage you should be able to recoup your upfront costs in less than five years. Any longer than that and there is a good chance you'll have moved or needed to refinance again, and that upfront money you paid is basically a loss.

To get an honest idea of what your refinance will cost, ask your lender for a good faith estimate, which will show a breakdown of your upfront closing costs associated with your refinance.

def•i•ni•tion

> **Closing costs** refers to all the various fees you may have to pay to finance or refinance a home. These fees can include points and origination fees, as well as paperwork, notary, and third-party fees. **Origination fees** are fees paid in part to the broker or officer who helps win your business for the lender, and can vary from under 1% to over 2%. **Points,** or discount points, are fees that you pay when you finance a mortgage to "buy a lower rate." For example, when you refinance, your mortgage rate might be 6%. But if you are willing to pay 1% of the total loan amount up front, the bank is willing to lower your interest rate to 5.75%.

Choosing a Lender You Can Trust

For most people, a trip to their local mortgage lender might as well be a trip to Timbuktu. Everyone seems to be speaking a foreign language and you're not sure if they're on your side or not.

It's crucial to work with someone you trust and who has a deep desire to serve their clients' interest over their own. Unfortunately, there's no directory of the "best mortgage brokers" around.

Most people don't realize that there is no formal education requirement to be a mortgage broker or loan officer. Oftentimes, the people in these positions do not hold any type of college degree in business and may have only been in the profession for a matter of a couple of years. The National Association of Mortgage Brokers (NAMB) has over 25,000 member brokers, many of whom have earned designations showing their experience and expertise. The top designation, something you should look for when seeking advice on your mortgage, is the Certified Mortgage Consultant (CMC).

I recommend asking around, because referrals from pleased customers are always the safest bets. Ask your mom, your barber, your butcher, and the guy sitting next to you at the traffic light. But don't just take a blind recommendation. Ask them why they liked them!

When You Can't Refinance

Perhaps one of the most terrifying and paralyzing situations is when your monthly mortgage payment is starting to climb or is actually past what you can afford, and no one will refinance you. What the heck do you do?

The most important thing is to not panic; instead, take immediate action. Deer in headlights get run over because they don't move—they just stand there staring at their problem. Don't let a change in your mortgage payment leave you standing there staring at oncoming traffic.

I would encourage you to work through this list over and over until someone comes to take your house away. Chances are, one of the following solutions will extricate you from this nasty situation relatively unscathed.

Debt in America _____

One of the perks of living in a civilized, taxed economy is that the government has the ability to rescue troubled industries and sectors of the economy. An example of this would be the Savings and Loan (S&L) bailouts of the 1980s. Recently, many people have hoped that the government would institute programs to help bail out over-stretched homeowners. While the government has created some programs that can help banks to help their customers, these programs are not mandatory and can be ignored by banks. With that in mind, you shouldn't hold out hope that Uncle Sam will rescue your mortgage.

- **Talk to your lender.** If you just call and tell them you want to refinance, without expressing the urgency of your situation, you're not giving the bank a fair chance to help you. You need to realize that the last thing the bank wants to do is repossess your house and have to sell it in a hurry. You should tell them the desperate nature of your situation and ask for ideas and solutions.

- **Try to sell your home.** Okay, I know you don't want to leave your home, but leaving it on your own terms is way better than on the bank's. Repossession will haunt you for years and is heartbreaking and traumatic. If talking to your bank does not provide an immediate solution, a sale or *short sale* may at least help you walk away from the home financially even. But keep in mind that while a short sale may be a good option for some people, it can also create a tax problem, since the amount the bank "forgives" may need to be included as income on your tax return.

def•i•ni•tion _____

A **short sale** is when a bank allows a homeowner to sell their house for less than the balance of the mortgage. The proceeds, even if they are less than what is owed, are considered payment in full for the loan, effectively erasing part of what is owed.

- **Find someone to assume your mortgage.** Assumable mortgages are increasingly rare, but there are still some out there. In an "assumed mortgage" someone else essentially takes over your payments. This can be a great deal for both a buyer (because they may not need a down payment) and a seller (because they avoid real estate agent fees). Before you just let someone else start making your mortgage payments, check with your lender to see if your loan is even assumable.

◆ **Start generating revenue from your home.** Wouldn't it seem a little easier solution to lose just one room of your house, or maybe your garage, than the whole thing? For many people, renting out a room or the use of their garage can bring in enough money to cover the increased mortgage payments. You don't need to plan on having tenants for the next 30 years, just long enough to get your feet back on the ground and get refinanced.

Dollars and Sense _____

The U.S. Department of Housing and Urban Development (HUD) offers low-cost mortgage counseling at various offices around the country. In addition to helping you understand your options, they can provide you with prescreened referrals to other professionals in your area. Visit www.HUD.gov for more information.

Foreclosure: The Final Frontier

If you've fought the good fight, and done everything you can to save your mortgage or get yourself out of the house, it may be time to pull the plug. Sometimes you just can't make it work, and that's part of life. Don't worry about the bank, they're big boys and they know that all lending has some risk to it.

So what does foreclosure look like? For starters, it doesn't mean that you're filing for bankruptcy. It really means that you didn't make the payments (the reason is irrelevant) and the bank wants to sell the home to get back the money they loaned you.

Typically, foreclosure starts with a string of written notices and phone calls from your lender following your failure to pay one or more mortgage payments. Remember, they want to try to avoid foreclosure because it costs them a lot of time and money, so they're hounding you hoping for a positive solution. Talk to them when they call!

If you are unable to make any progress after another month or two, the lender will typically "accelerate" your loan. This means they demand the whole mortgage (not just your missed monthly payments) paid off within a short period of time. If you cannot do that (most people can't), then they ask you to vacate the house and begin the process of selling it.

Depending on the state where you live, the property may revert to ownership by the bank, which then sticks a "for sale" sign on the front lawn, or it may be sold by court order in an auction format. If the proceeds the bank receives from the sale are less than what you owe them, they may or may not come after your other assets.

Hopefully, your mortgage is the nonrecourse type, which means the bank leaves you alone after they take the house back. For more information on the foreclosure process and your options, visit the website for the Federal Housing Administration (FHA) at www.FHA.gov.

While foreclosure is something people usually imagine happening to a homeowner who is kicking, screaming, and begging for it to not to happen, it actually may be a good strategy for some. It's what I like to refer to as "financial triage."

There's a scene in the film *Saving Private Ryan* that helps many people to understand this strategy. It was the scene where a medic is going up and down the beach full of wounded soldiers. He had to decide where he would spend his limited time, efforts, and medicine. If someone was near death, he sadly decided to move on to someone who had more of a chance. That's the concept of triage.

If your finances are coming unraveled at the seams thanks to a mountain of debt, you may have to decide which battles are worth fighting. If your adjustable mortgage goes up by $1,000 per month, which is all you can scrape together if you tighten your budget all the way down, you're going to have to choose.

You've got to decide if you should use all that money to keep your mortgage alive, or use that money to take care of numerous other goals simultaneously (a couple of credit cards, a medical bill, and your car payment). It's not an easy decision for many, but it's a necessary one nonetheless. Just remember, everything has an opportunity cost. Letting the bank foreclose on your home may substantially ease your load, but it will also show on your credit report for seven years, which may make it very hard to find a new place to live!

Strategies for Not So Rainy Days

I chose to start this chapter by dealing with mortgage situations that require immediate attention, but that doesn't mean that you shouldn't be strategic if everything is going okay. With a debt lasting 15 to 30 years that costs you hundreds of thousands of dollars in interest, there are plenty of opportunities to lower your long-term costs as well.

The primary places you can cut down your costs and save money are by speeding up your payments and avoiding unnecessary insurance costs.

The Biweekly Payment

This is honestly one of my favorite financial planning strategies across all topics. This technique can put as much money in your pocket as funding a Roth IRA every year and picking great investments. This strategy works especially well for people who get paid every two weeks instead of once per month.

The idea behind the biweekly mortgage payment is that you pay half your mortgage payment every two weeks. Now, on the surface that doesn't seem like anything different than you're already doing. There are about four weeks in a month and I'm paying half my mortgage every two weeks.

Right? Sort of. Think about it this way: There are 52 weeks in a year. If you paid half of your mortgage payment every two weeks, you'd actually make 26 half payments throughout the year. And, class, how many full payments does 26 half payments equal? That's right—13!

How's that for weird? It seems like some kind of math trick, doesn't it? But by making a half payment every two weeks, you effectively make 13 monthly payments a year, instead of the 12 you'd normally make. And that makes a huge difference.

By making extra payments early, the balance your interest is calculated on is smaller, sooner. On a 30-year fixed-rate loan, this means your loan would typically be paid off in 22 to 24 years and you would save $50,000 to $100,000 in interest!

> **Dollars and Sense**
>
> Biweekly payment programs are so easy to put into place that you should never pay someone else to do it for you. You can either contact your lender directly about getting set up to make biweekly payments, or simply send in checks yourself every two weeks. Just be sure that you don't send half of your next payment when a full payment is due. Otherwise, your bank will consider the other half of your payment as late. Always be two weeks ahead on your biweekly payments, not two weeks behind.

PMI: Insurance You Don't Need

Primary Mortgage Insurance (PMI) is a monthly insurance premium charged by your lender when your loan is greater than 80% of your home's value. The purpose of PMI is to protect lenders against losing money on low-down-payment loans.

PMI is a necessary evil that you may want to consider getting rid of as soon as possible. While it's not ridiculously expensive, it is still about 1% of your loan's value each year. That translates into a couple hundred dollars a month for many of us.

The way to get rid of PMI is to get your loan value under 80% of your home's price. You can accomplish this by either wishing really hard that your home goes up in value or working really hard to pay off a little extra each month.

Make sure you notify lenders when you think you get below that 80% threshold. Taking PMI off your payment is not at the top of their list of priorities (the insurance makes them feel safe), and they don't do it automatically until you get below 77% to 78%.

The Least You Need to Know

- You've got to figure out exactly what your mortgage holds in store for you.

- Refinancing into a fixed-rate mortgage is usually one of the best options if you have an adjustable-rate, interest-only, or NegAm loan.

- If you can't refinance, be proactive in seeking out ways to keep your mortgage afloat.

- Foreclosure may be a good strategy if you're managing multiple, overwhelming debts.

- A biweekly mortgage payment can shave 5 to 10 years and thousands of dollars off your mortgage repayment.

Chapter **15**

Student Loan Strategies

In This Chapter

- Student loans: the last debt to eliminate?
- Student loan repayment options
- Consolidation, deferment, and forbearance
- Loan forgiveness programs
- Dealing with student loan default

Spending a few years at college is one of life's most valuable experiences. Not only do you deepen your academic knowledge, but you also learn about so many other aspects of life. You learn who you are and who you want to be. You learn how much junk food a body can tolerate. Perhaps most importantly, you learn that it's a lot easier to borrow money than it is to pay it back.

Due to the rapidly rising costs of a college education, many students and parents are left with no choice but to borrow money. As with mortgages, people don't question the practice too much, because the money helps them build the life they've always dreamt of.

But for many young adults, the payoff of even the best of student loans can seem to drag on forever. Of course, the situation is much worse for students or parents who have utilized one of the private student loan companies that seem to be springing up like weeds.

The Student Loan Stew

One thing that always seems to stay the same is how different each person's student loan situation is! It's what I like to call the "the stew." Some students have a little bit of this loan and a lot of that one. Others have equal amounts of three or four different kinds of loans.

In fact, there are so many different variables to keep track of that it's worth taking a little bit of time to make sure you understand what your unique loans are. Having a strong working knowledge of each ingredient in your "stew" will help you arrive at the most efficient debt elimination strategy for you.

> ### Debt in America
>
> One of the biggest problems with student loans is that a large portion of the money goes straight to the student. Many times, if a student loan amount that is larger than what is needed is sent to a student's school, it gets refunded to the student. Sadly, college road trips and happy hour can eat up a lot of these funds before they get spent on tuition. My recommendation is to make a request with your school, before the first check ever arrives, that your or your child's excess loan disbursement be held by the college for future tuition.

Let's first look at the primary different types of loans and their unique characteristics.

Stafford Loans

Stafford Loans are the bread and butter of the student loan world. If you have student loans, it is very likely that you have some Staffords mixed in there.

The Stafford Loan program is a government-based program that essentially guarantees lenders they will not lose money by loaning to students. The responsibility of repaying these Stafford Loans falls on the student, not their parents.

Stafford Loans are either subsidized or unsubsidized. Subsidized loans, available to students demonstrating certain levels of financial need, get a slightly better rate of interest, which the government actually pays until six months after graduation.

Loans issued prior to June 30, 2006, have a variable rate that cannot exceed 8.25%. New Stafford Loan interest rates are locked in for the life of the loan, depending on when they're issued, as shown in the following table.

Loan Date	Undergraduate Subsidized Rate	Undergraduate Unsubsidized Rate	All Grad Students
07/01/2008– 06/30/2009	6.00%	6.80%	6.80%
07/01/2009– 06/30/2010	5.60%	6.80%	6.80%
07/01/2010– 06/30/2011	4.50%	6.80%	6.80%
07/01/2011– 06/30/2012	3.40%	6.80%	6.80%

Perkins Loans

Perkins Loans are also loans made available through government programs, but are reserved for undergraduate students with the greatest of financial need. Their rates and terms are even more generous than the Stafford Loans.

At the time of this book's publication, interest rates on Perkins Loans are 5%, with all interest being paid until nine months after a student leaves college.

Because the maximum loan amount on Perkins Loans is a fraction of the Stafford limits, it's very common for a student to have both Perkins and subsidized Stafford Loans. It's even possible that they'd have unsubsidized Stafford Loans on top of all those.

Dollars and Sense

Grants are different than student loans and are not something that you are required to repay. Federal Pell grants, the most common program, are reserved for students showing the greatest financial need.

PLUS Loans

PLUS Loans are the only federal government undergraduate loan program that parents are truly responsible for repaying (although independent graduate students also have access to this program). These loans are meant to absorb any remaining costs of education not met by other financial aid sources.

For many parents, these loans are lifesavers. Even if their son or daughter receives close to 100% of their financial aid, just a few thousand dollars in leftover costs can strain many families' budgets to the breaking point.

PLUS Loans are the least generous of all federal loan programs, but are still well in the range of "good debt." PLUS Loans currently have an annual interest rate ranging from 7.90% to 8.50%, and must begin being repaid within 60 days of their issuance.

Dollars and Sense

Did you know that the vast majority of families in America could qualify for federally backed student loans? While many people think that their income or assets are too high, this only keeps them from getting things like scholarships, grants, subsidized Stafford Loans, and Perkins Loans. Virtually everyone has access to unsubsidized Stafford Loans and PLUS Loans. To get an official estimate of how much federal financial aid you're eligible for, visit the Department of Education's financial aid calculator at www.fafsa4caster.ed.gov.

Private (for Profit) Lenders

Government-backed student loans are a sweet deal when you stop and think about it. Based on what you know of credit, where else can an 18-year-old with no credit history go out and borrow over $100,000 for under 8.50% per year? Nowhere!

Let me repeat that ... nowhere!

I'm trying to make the point because "private" student loan lenders are popping up all over the map. These companies prey on students and parents who don't understand the financial aid process, don't know about the government programs, or don't think they'd qualify for federal financial aid.

The problem with these companies is that they, by their very nature, are most interested in turning a profit. As such, their rates are much higher (10–20% per year) and their repayment terms are not as generous with regards to length or rules if you encounter a financial hardship.

The Standard Repayment Options

While there are as many private loan repayment options as there are companies, for the main federal loan programs there are four general repayment options. You must choose one fairly quickly after you graduate or your loan defaults to the quickest repayment plan.

Perkins Loans must be repaid over 10 years, and may allow for a "graduated" payment option, depending on your school's policies.

Stafford and PLUS loans, on the other hand, have four repayment options:

1. **10-year level repayments.** Under this repayment method, you must make the same payment for 10 years (120 months) in order to completely pay off your loan.

2. **10-year graduated repayments.** With a graduated payment program, your monthly payment starts at less than the level repayment amount and gradually increases to a larger amount. This repayment plan is designed with the idea that as students you make the least in your early years and more as you progress.

3. **25-year extended repayments.** This plan, available to students with over $30,000 in loans, allows you to spread out your payments over a maximum of 25 years, depending on the size of the loan.

4. **Income-based plans.** This option bases your monthly payment on your income, and can provide a significant savings for lower-income or larger families. After 25 years, whatever amount has not been repaid is forgiven. Income-based plans actually refer to a grouping of programs (such as income-sensitive or income-contingent), each with minor nuances on how your monthly payment amount is calculated. Any of these programs accomplishes virtually the same thing, and are great choices if you qualify.

So how do you choose between the four main repayment options? Well, when it comes down to it, I'm not sure why they actually give you four options. Considering that your interest rate stays the same regardless of what option you pick, and the fact that there is no prepayment penalty for paying extra early, you should take the smallest payment possible.

Now, don't get me wrong. I'm not arguing for you to drag out your loans as long as possible. Rather, I'm arguing for the maximum amount of flexibility. With a rate that stays the same regardless of the length of your repayment period, it would be in your favor to be as least committed as possible. I'd rather be committed to paying $100 a month with the option of paying more if I have it, than being committed to $250 per month.

This is especially true if you're managing other higher-cost loans and credit cards. Because your student loan is probably one of the cheapest loans you'll have, with the bonus of having deductible interest, you'll usually want to pay off other things first. The only time I'd caution against this is if you don't have the willpower to pay more than your minimums. In this case, you might as well do yourself a favor and commit to a higher monthly payment!

Dollars and Sense

You'll often hear of people "paying the interest" on their unsubsidized student loans while they're still in school. While this is not required, I'm all for it because it keeps your debt from growing too much while you're still a student. However, if you have other higher-cost loans (such as credit cards or an auto loan), it would make more sense to pay those first.

This means you'd choose the income-contingent repayment plan first, because it minimizes your payment and spreads it over a time period up to 25 years. If you can't qualify for that option based on your income, you should take the 25-year level option if your student loan balance is large enough. If you're carrying a smaller balance, you should consider choosing the graduated payment option, because it costs you nothing to start with lower payments (adding more if you have it each month).

If you decide at some point that your federal student loan repayment plan isn't right for you, switches are permitted. However, you may not switch more than once per year and may not use a switch to reduce your balance in any way (such as the 25-year limit on an income-contingent plan).

Reducing Your Student Loan Payments

Even at the great rates offered through the Department of Education, you may have at least temporary trouble making your student loan payments. And, despite the fact that these loans are made under government programs, they can be sent to collections and harm your credit score.

Just like with every other kind of loan, there are certain strategies that can help reduce your monthly payments. But just like everything else, there are also pitfalls and scams that you need to watch out for.

Student Loan Consolidation

Student loan consolidation gets a lot of press, so I thought I'd tackle that first. When it comes to reducing your student loan payment, a consolidation loan doesn't actually do much besides allowing you to make one easy payment instead of paying on multiple loans.

Unlike refinancing a house, where you are given a brand-new mortgage with a brand-new rate, student loan consolidations typically average together all your previous rates and then round up to the nearest one eighth of a percent. This technique is called a weighted average, and basically preserves the nature of your previous loans.

For example, let's say you have a $10,000 subsidized Stafford Loan at 6.00% and a $20,000 unsubsidized Stafford Loan at 6.80%. You new rate if you consolidated would be comprised of ⅓ ($10,000 out of $30,000 total) of your subsidized rate, and ⅔ of your unsubsidized rate ($20,000 out of $30,000 total). In other words, your blended rate would be 6.488%, which would get rounded up to 6.50%. Because this rate is comprised proportionately of your two previous rates, it only changes your overall payment by a small amount.

The only time that a federal consolidation loan would actually save you money is if you had a PLUS Loan that was charging 8.50%. The wrinkle here is that federal consolidation loans have a maximum "blended" rate of 8.25%. So by consolidating, you'll save one fourth of a percent. It's not a lot, but every bit helps.

In a nutshell, you should probably consolidate if you have more than one loan, just to simplify your paperwork. Outside of that, though, there are not a whole lot of advantages to the process.

> **Dollars and Sense**
>
> Are you interested in a free .25% to .50% reduction in your student loan rate? Many lenders offer discounts for making your payment on time for 24 to 48 months, as well as for using automatic withdrawal to make your payments. Check with your lender for more details.

Here are a few other points to keep in mind if you're considering a student loan consolidation:

◆ Parent and student loans, as well as the loans of individual spouses, cannot be consolidated together into one loan.

◆ Federal loan consolidations are free. Don't get suckered into paying someone to consolidate your loans.

◆ There are plenty of companies out there whose loan consolidations don't have anything to do with the federal programs. Check directly with your lender about your loan consolidation options.

Deferment

Deferment refers to a period of time granted by your lender, usually lasting 6 to 12 months, during which no payments are due. If your loan is unsubsidized, interest will still be added to the loan, however.

A deferment can be requested for minor financial hardships, unemployment, childbirth, and disabilities. Deferments may also be allowed if someone with student loans re-enrolls in school or goes to graduate school. If granted, you would be allowed to postpone your payments, which would be added back to the loan balance, to be repaid later.

As with a forbearance, which I'll discuss next, you need to request paperwork before you ever start skipping payments. Even if you've had a conversation with a customer service representative at your lender, you still need to wait until you receive your deferment letter before you skip payments.

Dollars and Sense _____

Unlike many other government programs and agencies that are virtually impossible to get someone on the phone or find information on the net, the Department of Education provides great resources for borrowers and families. For helpful repayment calculators and guides to student loan programs, visit www.StudentAid.Ed.Gov. If you can't find answers there, call the Student Aid Division at 800-4FED-AID.

Forbearance

Forbearance may be a great option for many people reading this book who have found themselves in very tight times. Forbearance is when your student loan lender actually lets you miss payments without ever needing to make them up.

Now, obviously, they don't just hand out forbearances to everyone who asks, every time they ask. Otherwise, everyone would be talking their way out of ever having to make student loan payments. To get a forbearance, you have to show (not just claim) significant financial hardship, a major disability, or other extenuating circumstances. More significant paperwork is required than for a deferment.

Loan Forgiveness Programs

In my opinion, one of the greatest missed opportunities for many graduates (even those who graduated years ago) are loan forgiveness programs. These programs reward your service with a certain agency, program, or community by paying off a significant portion of your student loan for every year of service. In fact, some of these programs can completely eliminate $50,000 or more in student loans in four to five years.

These loan forgiveness programs are typically an employee benefit in addition to your normal salary and benefits. In other words, working somewhere with a student loan forgiveness program can be the equivalent of receiving a $10,000 to $20,000 bonus each year for your first few years. Of course, after your loan is paid off, you can leave your employment there and go work somewhere else.

I've provided an extended list of these programs in Appendix D, but here are some of the largest programs out there:

- **Programs for teachers.** There are numerous federal and state loan forgiveness programs for credentialed teachers. Under the federal programs, teachers can get 100% of their Perkins Loans forgiven, as well as up to $17,500 in Stafford Loans. For a comprehensive listing of state and federal programs, visit the American Federation of Teachers website at www.aft.org/tools4teachers/loan-forgiveness.htm.

- **Programs for medical professionals.** Substantial loan repayment programs are offered for individuals who choose a professional career in medicine, nursing, mental health, and related professions. The National Health Services Corp. (http://nhsc.bhpr.hrsa.gov) offers up to $50,000 in loan repayments for qualified medical professionals. The Health Resources and Services Administration (http://bhpr.hrsa.gov) offers to pay up to 60% of qualified nurses' loan balances.

- **Military benefits.** Many graduates assume that they've missed the boat on the military funding their college education because they enrolled after college was paid for. Thankfully, this is untrue. Though you missed an opportunity to use the *Montgomery GI Bill*, the U.S. Army, Navy, and Air Force all offer loan repayment as an enlistment bonus. In fact, the army and navy offer to repay up to $65,000 in student

def•i•ni•tion

The **Montgomery GI Bill** is a program offered to all full-time service people and offers to pay over $39,000 for qualified education expenses. In some instances, it can even be used to fund the education of a service person's child. Visit www.gibill.va.gov for more info.

loans, and the air force offers up to $10,000. Check out www.Military.com for easy-to-read info on this and the Montgomery GI Bill.

◆ **Peace Corps.** People with a Perkins Loan can get 15% of their loan forgiven for every year of service, up to 70% of their total Perkins Loan Balance. Join the Peace Corps, see world, and come home with less debt! You can find more info at www.peacecorps.gov.

◆ **AmeriCorps.** Maybe going overseas isn't your cup of tea. AmeriCorps employees provide the backbone for many nonprofit and social programs located in the United States. In addition to an annual stipend of over $7,000, employees also receive loan forgiveness of $4,725 in return for 12 months of full-time service. Partial amounts are available for part-time employment. Visit www.americorps.org for more info.

◆ **Private companies and corporations.** Many companies, especially large corporations, offer loan forgiveness programs for their employees. Oftentimes, however, these programs are underpublicized to employees. Check with your Human Resources department to see if such a program is available.

If you are thinking about going back to school, consider getting a job at a school that offers free tuition for their employees. Some large national programs like National University in the western United States, the University of Phoenix (nationwide), and many community college districts offer free or discounted tuition for employees after a certain length of employment.

What to Do If You're in Default

Because it is impossible to foreclose on a degree you've earned (what would they do—make you give your diploma back?), missed payments on a student loan actually cause a default. While the immediate consequences of defaulting on your student loans may not seem as serious, the long-term consequences to your credit score and ongoing finances are.

In fact, most lenders refuse to negotiate the amount owed and are fairly quick to turn your balance over to a collection agency. The lousy part about this is that the actual collection costs are usually added to your student loan balance. Depending on state laws and program restrictions, this can be as high as 30% to 40% of your total loan balance!

Loan Rehabilitation

Though these practices may seem harsh (especially for students getting their feet on the ground after years of college), you need to remember how easy they made it to get your loan. If they didn't follow up aggressively with borrowers in default, they'd lose the ability to loan money so freely.

With that in mind, just as with your mortgage, your lender would much rather see you make good on your loan than to have to start collections. To help this process, they offer a program called loan rehabilitation.

There are a couple of levels to rehabbing your defaulted student loan. After you make six consecutive and voluntary payments (not a garnishment taken from your wages), you become eligible to again receive future financial aid. After you make 9 out of 10 consecutive and on-time payments, your lender reports to the credit agencies that you are no longer in default.

It is extremely important that you are communicating with your lender during this process. If you just make a mental commitment to get out of default, without ever talking to them, they'll have no way of knowing that they should stop collection actions. Even more so, they'll often temporarily lower your payment to as little as $50 per month to help you get back on your feet. But again, you've got to communicate with your lender instead of hiding from them.

Consolidation to Fix Your Default

Consolidating your student loans is the student loan version of a credit card balance transfer. By using a consolidation loan, you are paying off your old defaulted loan with a new consolidated loan. This is a temporary solution, however, because your next payment is due right around the corner. If you are struggling to make your payment on a month-to-month basis, all this would do is buy you one month. In this case, you'd probably be better off to have a discussion with your current lender about your options with them.

Consolidating would make sense if you got behind, but now have a more stable income and can meet your required monthly payments. It this case, consolidation would help pay off the amount you are behind on, shifting it to a new loan that is current by its payments.

The Least You Need to Know

◆ Federal student loans are some of the best loans you'll ever hold—pay them off last.

◆ Choose the longest repayment schedule possible; you can always pay more, earlier.

◆ Federal loan consolidations make your paperwork easier, but don't save you a ton of money.

◆ Beware of private companies offering student loans or consolidations.

◆ Request a deferment or forbearance if you are struggling with your payments.

◆ The costs of default are very high, so talk to your lender about rehabilitating your loan.

16

Strategies for Other Types of Debt

In This Chapter

◆ Payday loans have got to go!

◆ Keep car loans from driving you crazy

◆ Making nice with your doctor, lawyer, and the ex

◆ Standing up to the IRS

As a kid growing up in California, I spent a lot of time playing in the waves. We'd spend every summer day bobbing up and down in the ocean at places like Laguna and Newport beaches. Early on, we figured out how to tell who was a tourist and who was a local. When a big wave would come, everyone in the know would just hold their breath, sink to the bottom, and let the wave roll right over them. The out-of-towners, who didn't know how to duck under the waves, would get tossed around like rag dolls. By the time they'd finally regain their footing, there was another wave just behind, about to break on them.

Owing money to a bunch of different businesses, people, and government agencies can feel a lot like that. Just when you think you're about to regain control, something else comes rolling in on top of you, leaving you gasping for air!

Just like sinking to the bottom and letting the wave roll over you, there are tricks to surviving every one of these random types of debt.

Payday Loans

If there is one type of loan that can make you feel like you're drowning, it's payday loans. On the surface, they seem like a life preserver because they help your finances stay afloat in a month when money is tight. But thanks to the ridiculous rate of interest these loans charge (anywhere from 250% to 1,000% per year), you quickly figure out that your life preserver is made out of concrete.

Payday loans are so dangerous because they rob from next month to pay for this month. By the time next month's paycheck rolls around, it's already less than what you had this month when you couldn't make ends meet. It's a dreadful cycle that only snowballs because of the exorbitant interest rates.

If, in the course of eliminating your debts, you're tempted to use a payday loan, *don't*. There's a good chance that you'll never recover from the cycle of borrowing from the future to pay for today.

Breaking the Payday Loan Cycle

If you're already caught in the payday cycle, you've got to figure out how to get out—now. Eliminating this loan is more important than any other loan you have.

So how do you get out of the payday cycle? The answer is both simple and frustrating at the same time. You need to find cash, wherever you can, as soon as you can. In fact, I'd rather you get behind on paying your other bills (as long as it won't result in a repossession of your car or home), and divert all your available cash to ridding yourself of this financial parasite.

If you don't have the funds to divert into paying off your payday loan, here are some quick ways to raise some cash:

◆ **Check with your bank.** Many banks, especially *credit unions*, share my hatred of payday lenders, even though theirs is more of a financial motivation. When you are caught in the payday loan cycle, it will slowly drain away all your other assets and eventually cause you to be late on your bank's loans. To help avoid this situation, many banks and credit unions offer short-term "swing" loans to help you get out of this cycle.

> # def•i•ni•tion
>
> A **credit union** is basically a bank that is owned by its customers. When you join a credit union and deposit money, you become a member of a group of people pooling their money and acting as their own bank. Often, because these banks are run by the members for the members, you can earn higher rates of interest on your deposits while also paying less for your loans.

- **Borrow from family or friends.** Normally, I'm not a huge fan of borrowing money from family members or friends. Besides the fact that it puts them on the spot when you ask for help, it can severely damage your relationship if you aren't timely with your repayments. But in the case of payday loans, the amount is usually fairly small and the benefit is huge. Consider asking them for a loan and offering to repay them over three to six months, with a fair rate of interest. Then, make sure you follow through on your commitment to ensure money doesn't become a barrier between the two of you.

- **Sell some stuff.** Two websites, eBay (www.ebay.com) and CraigsList (www.craigslist.org), may be some of your best friends as you battle to get out of debt. Whether it is that video game system you shouldn't have bought or that extra bike you've got sitting in the garage, the sale of a few key items can bring in hundreds of dollars.

- **If the tag is still on it, return it.** If you have any purchases sitting around that can still be returned (clothes, electronics, etc.), take them back. You can always buy the stuff again later if you really need it. The reality is, by the time you pay the interest on that payday loan for another six months, you probably could have bought two or three of that item!

- **Put it on your credit card.** I know this recommendation sounds insane ... and it is. But truthfully, paying 25% per *year* is better than paying 25% per *month*. If it comes down to it, I'd rather see you get a cash advance from your credit card than continue to lose perpetually more from each paycheck as the payday loan cycle continues.

Getting Help with Food Costs

If you are using payday loans and struggling to end that cycle, you'll want to take assistance wherever you can get it. One way to cut back significantly is through the use of food stamp programs. Unfortunately, the idea of receiving government assistance for groceries may cut deeply into your pride. However, if you're in this situation, I'd encourage you to remember that you've paid into the system with your tax dollars. There is no shame in relying on it when necessary.

Food assistance is based on income and has surprisingly high limits on who can receive it. For example, a family of four can earn over $2,200 per month and still receive assistance buying groceries. The benefits can be substantial and provide a huge boost as you try to eliminate debt. An individual may qualify for approximately $150 per month. A family of four may receive close to $550 per month. And amazingly, a family of eight earning $3,700 or less can receive up to $975 per month. Check out www.fns.usda.gov for more information.

Car Loan Strategies

Outside of your housing costs, paying off a car loan (or more than one) can be one of your biggest expenses. To make matters worse, the need for a car (and therefore, the need to borrow) reappears at least once per decade. Minimizing the amount of money that flows out to pay for the privilege of driving is crucial to getting your other debts eliminated and achieving your financial goals.

As with other things, controlling your auto payments must start with the essential questions of "Do I really need this?" and "Can I really afford this?" If the answer is no, then it is time to consider selling your ride.

Even if you only break even on selling your car, this still may offer you a huge advantage over continuing the payments. While you'd eventually own that car if you kept making your pricey payments, you may save thousands by starting all over with an economy car. Remember, you can always go back and buy a nicer car later. Right now, you need to get out of debt and get into a sane existence.

If you are not going to sell your car, you still have a number of options for bringing down your payments to a more manageable level. You'll also want to take a long-term look at how you acquire cars and see if you can get out of the loan cycle once and for all.

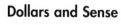

Dollars and Sense _____

Most people dispose of their old car by trading it in at the dealer toward the purchase of a new one. Unfortunately, many people don't know that they are literally throwing money away. Most dealers buy your trade-in at significantly below market value because they hope to also make a profit reselling it. Often dealers offer 25% to 50% of what you could sell it for to a "private party." That extra money could go a long way toward eliminating some of your debt. Visit www.AutoTrader.com for tips on selling your used car for more than a dealer will give you. You can also get a low-pressure, trade-in quote by taking your car to any CarMax location.

Pay More Than the Minimum

The great truth of debt reduction, pay more than your minimum, applies to auto loans as much as any other loan. If you pay more each month than you're required to pay, you will shave months off your repayment period and save hundreds, perhaps thousands of dollars in interest.

For example, a five-year auto loan for $20,000 at 8% would cost approximately $405 per month. That is a total of approximately $24,331 out of pocket, or $4,331 in interest on top of your $20,000 loan.

If you increase your payment to $500 per month, your five-year loan suddenly gets paid off in 46 months, or less than four years. Even better, your total cash out-of-pocket drops to $22,839. That's a whole lot of green that can be used to enjoy life, pay off other debts, or save toward your other financial goals.

Refinance Your Auto Loan

Believe it or not, refinancing is not just for mortgages. Many banks are now offering the ability to refinance an auto loan, which may allow you to lower your payments through a better interest rate or a longer loan term. This can provide a huge savings if you purchased a car when your credit was less than stellar, but has since cleaned up your credit score.

For example, someone who purchased a $15,000 car on a 60-month loan at a (brutal) rate of 15% would have monthly payments in the ballpark of $356 per month. Their total of all their payments by the time that car was paid off would be $21,411. That's over $6,000 in interest to buy a $15,000 car!

But after two years and some hard work, let's say they get their credit significantly cleaned up and can now refinance their loan. At this point, their remaining balance is $12,993. If they refinanced this over four years at 8%, their new payment would be $317.

The refinancing would drop the total of their remaining payments to $15,225. If they kept their old loan at 15%, the total of their remaining payments would be $17,088. That's a savings of over $1,800, which could be used to help speed the elimination of auto loans or other balances.

Set a Goal
There's no doubt that you need to at least consider refinancing your car if your interest rate is higher than 10%. If, after checking your credit score and talking to your bank, you find out that you cannot refinance, you should try again every six months. Because your credit score can change significantly in that period of time, you may qualify for something then that you can't now. Although you've been writing in your Debt Journal up to this point, I want you to pull out your calendar right now instead. Flip to six months from today and write "Try to refinance car loan!"

Pay Off Your Car with a HELOC

If you own a home and can get a home equity line of credit (HELOC), it may make mathematical sense to use this to pay off your loan. But using a HELOC can also set you up for failure if you're not disciplined about how you pay it off.

The good news about your HELOC is that it's easy to qualify for and will usually have a fairly low (and deductible) rate associated with it. The bad news with the HELOC is that they don't force you to pay it off as fast as your auto loan. For many people, it takes them 5 to 10 years to pay off the HELOC they used to finance their car, because sizeable payments aren't mandatory.

If you do choose to use your HELOC, commit yourself to paying it off in equal payments over your original loan period. In other words, if you used your HELOC to pay off a car that had 36 months left on the loan, divide the balance by 36 and make that your new payment.

Other Expenses

These expenses can be some of the most frustrating, because there's very little control of when they pop up or how horrendous they'll be. This can be so disheartening when you've worked hard for a year or more to eliminate your debt, only to be body slammed by one of these surprises.

The truth is, if you need medical care or timely legal advice, you get it and sort out the details later, as you should. When a marriage or partnership comes to an end, you often have very little control over the timing or the other person's emotions.

To add insult to injury, these are never cheap events. Legal and medical services can easily run into the tens of thousands of dollars. Likewise, alimony and child support can easily run thousands of dollars every month.

In the Red

If you owe money because of medical expenses or a lawsuit judgment against you, you need to check your "other" insurance policies immediately. Many times, policies like your homeowner's policy or auto policy have additional types of coverage attached that cover these types of expenses, if they occurred under certain conditions. Be sure to speak to your insurance agent if you think there's even a slim chance a certain cost might be covered.

While there are a couple of unique strategies for each one of these situations, they all have a couple of steps in common. First, you should always try to negotiate. It's key to realize that all the parties involved have very little "real cost" associated with the money you owe them. They didn't carry much of an inventory, if any. Instead, they've decided that their time is worth a whole lot and charged you for it.

As time goes by and they haven't been paid, most people in these situations begin to give up some hope that they'll ever get money out of you. So when you wave an alternative amount in front of their faces, they often will jump on it and forgive the rest of your balance.

Second, they all rely heavily on collection agencies to collect their debts. Remember, doctors and lawyers make a lot of money per hour and won't generally waste their staffs' time calling to hound you. Similarly, a partner or ex-spouse has other obligations to attend to and very little ability on their own to force you to pay.

All this is important, because you want to stay out of collections if you can avoid it. Besides the fact that a collection agency hounding you is extremely stressful, most of the balances you owe to a lawyer, doctor, spouse, or someone who has sued you won't show on your credit report. A collection agency going after you most likely will.

If you can agree on any type of temporary payment plan to keep them from turning your balance over to a collection agency, you should do it. The $25 or $50 per month you pay them just to give them hope can save you a lot of heartache.

Curing Your Medical Bills

Past-due medical bills, especially those owed to a hospital, are some of the easiest to cut dramatically with a little effort. If you don't believe me, spend some time on the Internet reading up on the "negotiated rates" that are given to health-care plans when their customers use a hospital or doctor.

What you'll find is that the same procedure that costs someone without insurance $10,000 might only cost an insurance company 25% to 50% of that. Besides the fact that that is semi-disgusting, it tells you that hospitals are used to taking much less than the full price for procedures. This means that your bill may be seriously negotiable.

Dollars and Sense

Getting injured at work does a double-whammy on your personal finances. Not only can you no longer earn a paycheck, but you also experience major medical costs. That's where workers' compensation comes in. These programs are meant to protect the financial interests and livelihood of someone who has been injured on the job. They usually cover a significant portion of your medical bills from a work-related injury or illness. Even if your employer doesn't have a worker's policy, you may still be covered because most states require these policies of even small employers. Be sure to file your claim promptly, because your injury is your largest piece of evidence. As your body heals, your case will begin to lose steam!

Remember my friend from Chapter 3 who got charged close to $10,000 for a couple of kidney stones? By the time he was done arguing with the hospital, as well as tapping other resources, he paid just over $800. Here's how he did it, and how you can, too:

1. **Cry foul.** Now granted, my friend was in a lot of pain, but had he known that an MRI and a prescription to "take two Vicodin and call us in the morning" was going to cost nearly $10,000, he probably would have toughed it out. The truth

is, the hospital did not disclose to him that his emergency room visit was going to cost as much as a car. While I'm opposed to tantrums in children, I'd recommend them for adults in this case.

2. **Threaten legal action.** Find a friend who is a lawyer to write you up a letter threatening to take the hospital to small claims court over their unexpected and inflated charges. Go get the letter notarized just for the heck of it … it doesn't do anything, but it looks mighty official. By showing the hospital or the medical practice that you're not going to roll over and take their unexpected charges, you're going to raise their desire to close the case and move on.

3. **Find out the usual and customary rate.** As you bicker with your health-care provider, it would be helpful to know what insurance companies consider the usual and customary rate (UCR) for a procedure. Call your insurance company, or have friends call theirs if you aren't insured, and find out what the going rate for a procedure is. This will help you make a counteroffer they will accept as well as know when to stand your ground.

4. **Make a counteroffer.** Once you've told them you won't take being pushed around, threaten legal action, and find out what the customary rate is, then you make a counteroffer. I'd recommend offering about 25% above the usual and customary rate for a procedure. This will become increasingly attractive to a medical provider as the process drags out. If they come back asking for a small and reasonable amount more, you should consider taking the offer.

5. **Look into state and federal programs.** In addition to federal *Medicare* and *Medicaid* programs, many states have health-care programs that help lower-income people partially pay for medical care. These programs are especially generous toward adults over age 65 and families with children.

def•i•ni•tion

It's easy to confuse the **Medicare** and **Medicaid** programs. Medicare is the federal insurance program that covers individuals over age 65 or those who are permanently disabled. Medicaid may cover these individuals, but also covers younger, low-income individuals and families. Helpful to people struggling with medical debts, Medicaid may cover expenses three months prior to your actual application for assistance. To find out more about Medicare and Medicaid services, visit www.cms.hhs.gov.

6. **Look into medical assistance funds.** Many hospitals and medical groups have some type of fund set aside to help individuals who do not qualify for other types

of financial aid. Because you've probably butted heads with the Billing department, don't waste your time asking them. Hang up the phone, call the hospital again, and ask the receptionist for whoever handles financial assistance for patients. Tell this new person your story and ask them if any financial assistance is available.

Settling Legal Debts

Owing money to an attorney doesn't leave you many options besides those I've mentioned. But if you've been sued and a judge has decided that you owe money, there are some other options to consider.

By no means would I recommend trying to hide assets or put them in someone else's name, as this could ruin your credibility in an ongoing lawsuit as well as result in additional legal action. Do your best to work within the laws to minimize the effects of a lawsuit, including one or more of the following techniques:

- **Offer other assets in compromise.** If you own a plot of land, a share in a business, valued collectibles, or anything else that might be saleable, consider offering those in lieu of cash. The reasoning might go something like this: "If I have to pay cash, it might take years for me to pay you off. How about I give you this piece of artwork and we'll call it even."

- **Request a modified garnishment.** Many times, when you are unable to pay a judgment against you immediately, a judge will order your wages to be garnished. If this happens, your employer is sent a court order to send a portion of your wages to someone to help satisfy your debt. If you can prove that the garnishment as it was initially issued is going to provide an extreme hardship, a court may reduce it at least temporarily.

- **Keep an eye on the statute of limitations.** Many judgments must be collected within a certain amount of time, after which someone loses their ability to pursue your assets or garnish your wages. I'm not suggesting that you hold out as long as you can, but an expiring statute of limitations provides you with a strong bargaining chip.

Dealing with Alimony and Child Support

Dealing with past-due child support and alimony is a tough one. It's natural that parents and spouses who are struggling to manage a pile of other balances would also struggle to stay current on these obligations. I know there are plenty of selfish people out there, but I also know how hard it can be.

Not paying child support can have major repercussions on your finances. Not only might you get your wages garnished or be unable to register for certain basic services in your state, but you could actually end up getting jail time. Last time I checked, folks sitting in jail don't make too much money and their debts often fall even further behind.

Similar to payday loans, you need to do whatever is required to stay working and productive so you can eventually find the light at the end of the tunnel. If you need to let other bills slip to stay out of legal trouble with child support or alimony, it's generally worth doing.

As far as a unique strategy, there is one primary strategy I've seen work well for people who are behind on large amounts. The core of this strategy has to do with how alimony and child support are viewed for tax purposes.

Alimony is considered income to the spouse who receives it and a deduction (actually an "adjustment to income") for the spouse who pays it. This means that a spouse receiving $1,000 per month may only keep $800 after taxes.

Child support, on the other hand, is not taxed to the recipient and not tax-deductible to the donor. If you are behind on a combination of alimony and child support, it is worth thinking over the merits of raising your child support in order to erase some of your back alimony.

For example, if you're $20,000 behind on alimony, you might offer to increase child support payments $500 per month for the next two years if your ex-spouse agrees to release you from that overdue alimony. The smaller monthly amount may be doable for you, and also will avoid taxation to the spouse. It may be a win-win that keeps you out of trouble.

Dollars and Sense

What do you do if your ex-spouse owes you money but isn't following through on his or her obligations? One quick remedy is to go after his or her retirement plans using a Qualified Domestic Relations Order (or QDRO, pronounced "Quad-Row"). While a court may not be quick to act in your favor if he or she doesn't have sufficient income, your ex may be happy to give you a portion of his or her 401(k). Be sure to talk to your attorney about using a QDRO, especially if you live in one of the nine "community property" states in the United States.

Standing Up to the IRS

I'm not sure there is anything that will stop me in my tracks as much as an envelope with the IRS as the return address. It's not like they send you letters when everything is just fine. I have yet to receive a Happy Birthday card or a Christmas letter from my local auditor.

It's for good reason that the IRS freaks me out. No one else has the power like the IRS to collect on the money it's due. Remember, these are the people who bring in the money for virtually every other type of government program there is. As such, the IRS is given a lot of latitude and immense resources to do its job.

For the vast majority of people who owe money to the IRS, it comes down to some type of honest mistake. I mean, really, the tax code is so complex that many IRS agents have trouble understanding certain aspects. But these letters are scary even if they're about an honest mistake.

Even more frightening is when the letter they sent you says something more than "You forgot to sign your tax return." If you owe money, you are in for a heck of a fight and some serious interest and penalties if you don't act quickly.

The IRS Penalty System

There are three main penalties that taxpayers run into regarding their individual tax returns. Each has its own upfront penalty and unique interest calculation:

1. **Filing a fraudulent return.** Aside from the fact that willingly and knowingly filing a return in which you tried to cheat the IRS may land you in jail, it may also land you in the poorhouse. The penalty can run as high as 75% of the unpaid amount, in addition to the unpaid amount itself.

2. **Failure to file.** Surprisingly, the IRS comes down harder on people who fail to file a return than people who file a return but don't pay the amount due. The penalty for failing to file is 5% per month of the amount owed, up to 25%.

3. **Failing to pay.** If you file a valid return but do not pay the amount owed, the IRS charges you 12% a year, up to a maximum of 25%.

These amounts may be determined automatically with you being notified by mail or may be the result of an audit. Either way, it is crucial to communicate with the IRS and to make your case as soon as possible. If you and the IRS cannot see eye to eye, you will likely receive what is called a deficiency letter or a 90-day letter.

This letter basically gives you 90 days to appeal your balance due through the U.S. Tax Courts. If you do not make an appeal within 90 days, you are on the hook for whatever balance the IRS notified you about. Period.

Dollars and Sense _____

If you were formerly married and filed a joint tax return with a spouse, you may not be liable for criminal or irresponsible actions committed by your spouse that you didn't know about. The IRS calls this the "Innocent Spouse" rule and it exempts unknowing spouses from amounts and penalties owed. The IRS will not just take you at your word, though. Like other waivers of penalties, the IRS makes you endure a detailed process to establish your innocence. Talk to your tax advisor or refer to IRS Publication 971 for more information.

Installment Agreements and Offers in Compromise

The IRS is a world unto itself. This is not the place to prove that you could have gone to law school. I'd highly recommend hiring a certified public accountant, enrolled agent, or tax attorney to help you appeal your case, or use one of the following methods.

For taxpayers who cannot demonstrate extreme financial hardship, the IRS allows you to enter into an installment agreement. This is basically a payment plan that allows you to spread out your balance over an extended period of time, subject to some minor fees.

For taxpayers whose situation is extreme, the IRS may be willing to reduce the balance owed through what is called an "offer in compromise." This process is very similar to debt settlement with the IRS or a medical provider, but your ability to pay will be heavily researched by the IRS. To be considered for an offer in compromise, you must complete Form 656 and file it with the IRS.

The IRS has its own internal and independent organization, called the Taxpayer Advocate Service, to help taxpayers who cannot get their IRS issues resolved or feel the IRS is unfairly pursuing them. While the service and attention you get may not be as fast as hiring your own professional, it is still knowledgeable and impartial. To find out if you are eligible for their services, you can call 877-777-4778 or go to www.IRS. gov and type "advocate" in the search box.

The Least You Need to Know

◆ Beg, borrow, or scrimp—do whatever it takes—to get out of the payday loan cycle.

◆ Consider refinancing your auto loan if your current rate is over 10% and you have a couple of years of payments left.

◆ The best way to cut your medical, legal, alimony, and child support costs is by offering a smaller but immediate payment.

◆ Use government programs whenever you can to help reduce your monthly expenses and medical costs while getting your feet back on the ground.

◆ Don't delay responding to the IRS or seeking professional help to understand your situation.

◆ Seek out an installment agreement or an "offer in compromise" with the IRS.

Chapter 17

Strategies That Can Backfire

In This Chapter

- ◆ Three questions about any strategy
- ◆ 401(k) loans: easy access to a bad choice
- ◆ Signing away your life with debt consolidation
- ◆ No love for some debt settlements
- ◆ Don't mix family and finances

There comes a point when you're dealing with debt where you feel like you just can't take it anymore. It feels like another week of phone calls by angry lenders, surprise expenses, and disappointing paychecks will pretty much drive you to the brink of insanity. Those are the weeks when it's easy to grab for the most convenient and immediate solution, without really caring if it is the best for you in the long run.

Sometimes, the strategies you choose hastily end up robbing your future financial goals. Other times, they solve your immediate problem but immediately wreak havoc on your credit score. Worst of all, they end up being the equivalent of pushing a "financial self-destruct" button that nukes your finances come tax time.

In the midst of your anxiousness to eliminate debt, it's of the utmost importance that you know how some strategies can come back to haunt you. I'm not saying that you should always avoid them, but you should know the risks and costs up front.

Three Important Questions

When it comes to any debt reduction strategy, there are three questions you need to ask yourself. Even if the strategies you're considering are different than what I cover in this book, you'll still be able to evaluate them on your own with these basic questions:

1. **What is the long-term cost?** In other words, what will you think of this strategy a couple of years from now? Will you be angry that you're still making payments on some new debt or to a new lender? Will you have to do massive work to make up for a financial goal that you torpedoed to pay off your debt? Would you be able to say, "Yep. I'd totally use that strategy all over again!"

2. **What are the short-term costs?** Are you paying a lot up front to use this strategy? Will it cost you when tax time rolls around? Will this put you between a rock and a hard place if an emergency comes along?

3. **How does it affect your credit score?** Is this strategy going to hurt your credit score? If so, how much and for how long?

If you are unsure of the answers to these questions, you need to do more than take a friend or stranger's word for them. You need to do some research, buy a book, or pay for a professional opinion. Yet more old sayings come to mind: "An ounce of prevention is worth a pound of cure." Or, as an old carpenter friend used to chide me, "Measure twice so you have to only cut once."

Dollars and Sense _____

If you can't imagine a questionable debt strategy shaving at least six months off the elimination of any one balance, it's probably not worth the additional risk. As the saying goes, "If it ain't broke, don't fix it!"

Even if you are sure of the answers and comfortable with the costs and risks, I would still encourage you to sleep on it for a few weeks. If, after the initial sense of urgency passes, you still feel like it is a good call, then go for it. I'm proud of you for doing your homework and making an educated decision for yourself or your household.

With all that said, here are some of the main strategies to think through carefully before you dive in headfirst. I've touched on these in other chapters, but I want to give you the full dose here.

Taking a Loan from Your Retirement Plan

This strategy is so simple and so tempting, which is perhaps why it is used (and backfires) so often. On one hand, you've got some large balances you need to pay off. On the other hand, you've got a 401(k) with $10,000 to $20,000 sitting in it. One day at the water cooler, the office know-it-all tells you that you should just take a tax-free loan against your 401(k), pay off your debts, and get on with life. He or she also reminds you that you pay interest to yourself, so you're actually "making money" by doing this.

In the Red

While a 401(k) or retirement plan loan won't show up as a balance on your credit report, it can still hurt your ability to apply for certain other loans such as a mortgage. This is due to the fact that lenders will include your 401(k) loan payment in the front- and back-end ratios I talked about in Chapter 5. If you think you are going to use another strategy like an auto or home refinancing, you'll want to hold off doing your 401(k) loan until after those transactions are complete. Doing these loans first will not affect your ability to use a 401(k) loan, because no credit check is required for that.

Borrowing from your 401(k) is one of those strategies that can backfire in a huge way on many levels. Be careful before choosing this option. Here are some 401(k) loan pitfalls you need to consider:

◆ **Taxes.** If you quit or are fired while you are still repaying this balance, and you cannot repay it almost immediately, the loan becomes a distribution. This means that the unpaid balance is now added to your income for IRS purposes, which will cost you federal and state income tax plus a 10% early withdrawal penalty.

Unfortunately, because this was a loan originally, no withholding was ever done. This means you'll potentially need to come up with the entire tax due come April 15th. On a $10,000 loan, this can easily translate into $5,000 you'll pay out-of-pocket to the IRS!

◆ **Your retirement growth stalls.** Every 401(k) I've run into in my career freezes 100% to 200% of the amount you borrow. This means that an amount equal to your unpaid balance is removed from the investments of your choice and will now only earn the interest that you pay on the account. Of course, it is not really earning interest, but simply putting more of your own money into the account.

◆ **Decreased paychecks.** The repayments for your loan come directly from your paycheck and are based on a preset payment schedule. In other words, you have no wiggle room on how much or when your loan gets repaid each month. Your money disappears before it ever makes it into your bank account. For many people, this creates a new financial hardship that tempts them into using credit cards again.

Dollars and Sense

If your company or industry is going through downsizing and a layoff is more likely than in the past, you'll really want to reconsider that 401(k) loan. If your company gets bought out, however, and you retain your job, there should be no negative tax consequences associated with your 401(k) loan.

Debt Consolidation

While it may be tempting to combine all your debt payments into "one easy payment," it comes with some immediate and delayed consequences. Before you choose this option, especially with a company that only offers that service, you need to understand the effect on your ability to borrow and the potential for asset seizure:

◆ Debt consolidation makes a strong statement to the future lenders of your life. It'll likely raise the level of concern they'll have about collecting their potential loan payments from you. In essence, when a potential lender looks at your credit report and sees all your balances moving to a consolidation, it seems to prove that you can't handle the responsibility of a loan.

◆ For debt consolidation companies to justify the risk of taking on people who are not currently making their payments, they need to have some pretty strong resources as far as collecting their money. Hence, they'll often make you sign a paper giving them broad powers to seize your assets to pay off your debts if you fail to pay. By consolidating, you go from working with multiple lenders who have minimal collection powers, to one lender who can take the shirt off your back.

In the Red

Getting a car or other items repossessed can add to the weight of your debt load. Unlike a mortgage, which is often set up as nonrecourse debt, you are generally on the hook for the difference between what your bank sells a repossessed car for and what you owe. On top of that, the entire cost of a repossession action (usually $300–$500) is passed on to you the consumer. Think carefully before you enter into any agreements with debt consolidators that give them greater repossession rights than what your current lender has.

Debt Settlement

I've talked a lot about negotiating a debt settlement throughout the book. For many people on the brink of bankruptcy or collections, this is a great method to get a financial leg up. Unfortunately, not all debt settlements are created equal in terms of how they affect your credit report. Additionally, a debt settlement may suck up what little available cash you have to manage day-to-day expenses.

Many companies that are not in the full-time business of lending money (like hospitals or local businesses) don't even know how to begin reporting things to the credit reporting agencies. Credit card, mortgage, and auto lending companies, on the other hand, do.

Many times (but not always) a professional lender will report debt settlements on your credit report while other types of businesses do not. Again, looking through the eyes of a potential lender, a debt settlement makes you a scary prospect for a new or cheap loan.

The key concept behind a debt settlement is that you are waving cash in hand in front of your lender. You're not offering them a payment plan. You're actually offering them a final payment, albeit less than your balance. You need to ask yourself where that cash will come from and what the effects on your ongoing spending plan will be.

Borrowing from Friends or Family

I mentioned earlier that I'm not a huge fan of borrowing money from friends or family, unless the situation is beyond desperate or you are paying off a payday loan. While friends and family are not likely to gouge you on interest, borrowing money can create significant strain on relationships.

In fact, just recently I was speaking somewhere on personal finances and a woman came up to me with a helpless look on her face. She had loaned her best friend about $750 six months ago due to a financial hardship. Her friend made a couple payments to her and then stopped.

After a few months, the woman I was talking with called her friend to just see if everything was okay. In fact, she wasn't even worried about the money, but just her friend. Months, and dozens of calls later, it's clear that her friend can't bring herself to call her back. In the end, a friendship may have been destroyed over a relatively small loan and good intentions.

Here are some of the risks to consider in borrowing from a friend or family member:

◆ **You're putting them on the spot.** One of the most important lessons I learned from my mom (which made a big difference in keeping my wife from killing me over the years) was to never put her on the spot. In other words, if I wanted to go spend the night at Jimmy's house, it was really lousy to ask my mom right in front of Jimmy. Doing so made it harder for her to say no.

When you ask someone who cares about you to borrow money, they're going to have a hard time declining because you matter to them. In the grand scheme of things, that may be a pretty lousy thing to do and may cause someone to resent you for even asking. This may be especially true if you can't repay it when you promised.

◆ **You'll owe them.** Good friends and family would loan money to you just because they want to help, not because they think you'll help them out someday. But, realistically, you will owe them the same favor. If that time comes and you aren't ready to return the favor, it can create some major awkwardness and resentment.

◆ **You may be hurting their financial goals.** Borrowing $50 is one thing. Borrowing $5,000 is another. That large of a request may keep some people from making their IRA contribution for the year, taking their dream vacation, or paying down their own debts. If you are going to borrow, consider asking someone who has plenty of cash and has achieved the vast majority of his or her financial goals in life.

Other Strategies to Avoid

Over my years as a financial planner, I've pretty much seen it all. Every imaginable way that people can dream up to cut corners on the debt elimination process has been tried. Before you think you've discovered a loophole or trick I've missed, here are some of the more off-the-wall strategies that I'd recommend against.

Credit Card Checks

There are a number of credit card companies that actually send out two to three blank checks every few months to their account holders. If they are used, the amount you write them for is added to your account. These checks usually come with exorbitant fees and high interest rates, and continue your cycle of using debt. Try to avoid using these to pay off other debts, much less your regular bills.

Tax Refund Loans

Many of the low-cost tax preparation chains offer you the ability to get your tax refund immediately upon filing your return. In reality, they are making you a loan against the refund you'll receive in just four to six weeks, if you use direct deposit. While the fee may seem small, when you look at the interest rate on an annual basis, it is often over 100%.

Dollars and Sense _____

The earned income credit (EIC) is money paid to you by the IRS if you are over age 25 and earn less than a certain amount of income. It increases substantially if you have children under 18 years old. Sadly, the IRS doesn't automatically hand out the EIC, but requires you to file a form with your tax return. Unlike the private tax or refund-anticipation loans that charge exorbitant fees to get your money a few weeks early, you can get a monthly advance on your EIC from the IRS through your employer's paycheck. To learn more about this program, talk to a professional tax preparer or request IRS Publication 596 from www.irs.gov.

Loans from Pawnshops

Pawnshops are places that will loan you money in exchange for some type of collateral, such as that set of diamond earrings Grandma gave you. Quite simply, you give them the item and they give you some cash. If you don't repay them within a certain time period (usually 30, 60, or 90 days), they can sell your item. In short, pawnshops are a rip-off. The interest they charge can range from 20% a year to over 100%, not counting all their fees. You'd do better to sell your stuff on eBay, where you'll likely get a lot more without paying any interest.

Getting Paid Under the Table

It's hard to not get angry sometimes when you look at your pay stub. The amount of income, payroll, and employment taxes that come out makes it almost feel like work isn't worth the effort. So when someone gives you the opportunity to get paid "under the table" it's natural to want to take it.

Here's the problem. Getting paid in cash and not reporting it on your tax return isn't just a cool perk of working for some employers. It's tax fraud and it is a felony. While you might save some significant tax dollars for a few years, there is a good chance it will eventually catch up with you. As prehistoric as the IRS is in so many aspects, its computer system that identifies tax cheats is cutting edge. In addition to steep fines, you could face jail time for hiding even a portion of your income.

Before you report your employer to the IRS for paying you "under the table," double-check to make sure they aren't planning on issuing you a Form 1099 at the end of the year. A Form 1099 means your employer is actually reporting your wages, but considers you an independent contractor. This means that all the responsibility is on you to set aside money for taxes and Social Security. If this is your first year receiving a Form 1099, talk to a tax preparer as soon as possible, because the amount you owe can be substantial.

The Least You Need to Know

- If you're thinking of trying an innovative debt reduction strategy, be sure to consider the short- and long-term risks.
- 401(k) loans backfire on their users as often as not, and should be used with great caution.
- Debt consolidation and debt elimination can keep you from getting new loans and put your assets at risk.
- Borrowing from friends and family may save your finances but significantly damaging your relationships.
- Don't be hasty to cut corners in your debt elimination plan.

Bankruptcy

In This Chapter

◆ The types of bankruptcy

◆ What bankruptcy will and will not do for you

◆ Recent bankruptcy law changes

◆ The hidden cost of bankruptcy

If there is a dirty word in the financial planning world, it's bankruptcy. Utter it loud enough for people to hear and people will look up to see whose dealing with it. It's kind of like how people slow down to look at car accidents.

For some, filing for bankruptcy is the ultimate admission of financial failure. It can feel like saying, "I've acted irresponsibly, can't handle my bills, and now need a financial restraining order against my creditors." For other people, bankruptcy is a way of life. It's a get-out-of-jail-free card that they are more than happy to use every 5 to 10 years.

Either way, it is a huge decision that has lifelong ramifications. It is a strategy that should be saved for the most desperate and dire of situations, because though it may help you walk away from a financial car wreck, you'll probably walk with a limp the rest of your life.

Overview of Bankruptcy

There are probably more misconceptions out there about what bankruptcy is or isn't than any other debt topic. I hear people throw it around like you just flip a switch and your creditors leave you alone. I also hear people who truly should use bankruptcy talk themselves out of it because they think there's no way that a court would take pity on them. Both of these misconceptions lack a basic understanding of what bankruptcy is and its value to society.

Bankruptcy as a theory is built around the idea that sometimes a member of society can be more productive for society as a whole if they are given a fresh start. In other words, it is good for the economy and our society to help people who are beyond the point of no financial return.

Debt in America

Before you start thinking bankruptcy is unglamorous, here's a quick list of stars and celebrities who have filed for bankruptcy protection: Kim Basinger, Toni Braxton, Francis Ford Coppola, Walt Disney, Zsa Zsa Gabor, Dorothy Hamill, MC Hammer, Don Johnson, Larry King, Olivia Newton-John, Willie Nelson, Burt Reynolds, Mickey Rooney, Mike Tyson, and of course, Donald Trump!

Part of the way bankruptcy helps society is by helping certain lenders and creditors to receive at least some funds toward what they are owed. The settlement amounts or payment plans (depending on the type of bankruptcy) keep someone from sticking it to those who they owe money to.

A bankruptcy will generally involve court proceedings within a specialized bankruptcy court, where your ability to pay debts and level of hardship will be measured against established standards. If yours is worse than those standards, your petition for bankruptcy will likely be granted. If not, you'll have wasted a lot of time and money just to have a judge tell you to pay your bills.

There are different types of bankruptcy, often called *Chapters*, which each come with different privileges and obligations. You decide, before you submit your application, which type of bankruptcy you'd like to apply for. It usually takes the advice of a bankruptcy professional to help you decide which type is most appropriate for you.

Though you're going to court, it's unlikely that you'll have any extended interactions with the judge. Because the whole process is pretty formulated, the judge's role is to basically approve the application and confirm the declaration of bankruptcy. Once in a while, you may get a few stern words about this being a "second chance" and "not wasting it."

Depending on the type of bankruptcy, you may be required to close accounts, sell assets, agree to payment plans, and/or take classes educating you about personal financial management. You will generally not be excused from making payments on assets that you continue to use and derive benefit from, such as your house or car. Bankruptcy gives you a fresh start with old debts, but doesn't hand out free assets to anyone.

The two most frequent types of bankruptcy filed in the United States are Chapter 7 and Chapter 13 bankruptcies. But there's also Chapter 11, Chapter 12, and Chapter 15, each of which has a very specific use.

Chapter 7

Chapter 7 is the granddaddy of all bankruptcy filings. It is the one that generally provides the most relief from what you owe, but is also the most intrusive and has the highest loss of personal control. Chapter 7 may not be available to you if you have a larger amount of assets or higher income level.

Chapter 7 is also appropriately called liquidation, because that's in essence what happens. The court assigns a trusted third party, called a trustee, to come in and take control of the majority of your assets. That trustee then liquidates, or sells, those assets and begins distributing the money to your creditors based on a formula or court order.

Chapter 13

If your creditors got to pick a bankruptcy for you, this would be the one they'd opt for. While the name is quite confusing, "Adjustment of Debts of an Individual with Regular Income," the concept is simple. It's a payment plan.

Under Chapter 13, you usually get to keep all of your assets but you must propose a plan to pay off your debts. If the court approves of your repayment plan, then it's back to life as usual. Unlike a Chapter 7, in which your bankruptcy will be complete in a short period of time, a Chapter 13 filing continues during the entire repayment period.

A Chapter 13 bankruptcy is helpful because it gives you protection from lawsuits, collections, and garnishments during the repayment plan.

Dollars and Sense _____

Bankruptcy and a sense of guilt can be heavily intertwined. Some people even feel like filing a bankruptcy is morally and ethically wrong. If this is you and a bankruptcy seems imminent, try to opt for a Chapter 13 bankruptcy. Even though it is technically called a bankruptcy, it really entails you coming up with a workable plan to make sure your creditors get as much money as you can afford. That's something that is easy to feel good about!

Chapter 11

Yes you, too, can file the same kind of bankruptcy as the major airlines. Just don't expect any free seats in first class because you're both in Chapter 11.

Chapter 11 is actually intended for businesses that need to "reorganize" their financial affairs in order to stay afloat. But because you can run a business as a sole proprietor, this form of bankruptcy is available to and may benefit you if your assets and debts are primarily tied to your business.

Chapter 11 is much more complex and costly than a Chapter 7 or 13. Like a Chapter 13, your debts are not discharged when the judge approves your reorganization plan. Your bankruptcy will only be complete months or years from your filing date, when you meet all the obligations of your reorganization.

Chapter 12

If a Chapter 13 bankruptcy and a Chapter 11 bankruptcy got together and had a baby, it'd look a lot like a Chapter 12. In fact, a Chapter 12 bankruptcy is a hybrid between the two plans and is specifically aimed at family farmers and fishermen. Before you even ask, fishing with your buddies on the weekends does not qualify you for Chapter 12.

A Chapter 12 bankruptcy is meant to help professional farmers and fishermen stay in business by creating a three- to five-year repayment plan on their debts. A big reason for this special category of bankruptcy goes back to our original discussion of bankruptcy's value to society. Keeping farmers and fishermen in business helps us all.

A Chapter 12 also has what I like to call a "mini-Chapter-7" provision. If, at some point in the future payment plan, a fisherman or farmer runs into a severe hardship, the judge may completely dismiss the remaining obligations. However, creditors must have received at least what they would have received under a Chapter 7 bankruptcy.

Dollars and Sense _____

It's amazing how one person's or company's bankruptcy can ripple outward and force other companies into similar financial hardships. In fact, it's not uncommon for someone filing bankruptcy to actually be a creditor who is owed money in someone else's bankruptcy. If you own a business that provides skills or materials to create personal property or real estate, you can file what's known as a "mechanic's lien" if you haven't been paid. This lien basically states that you have a claim to the property because you have not yet been compensated for what you contributed. If your customer files for bankruptcy, you'll generally be given preferential treatment in collecting funds over other suppliers and contractors who don't have a mechanic's lien.

Chapter 15

While a Chapter 15 bankruptcy won't apply to most people reading this book, in today's global economy, it's worth mentioning. That's because a Chapter 15 helps to coordinate bankruptcy proceedings in multiple countries.

This may be of use to a foreign national living in the United States or a U.S. citizen whose business operates or has vendors in more than one country. If you think this might apply to you, be sure to seek out an attorney who specializes specifically in this area.

The Benefits and Limits of Bankruptcy

When it comes to what bankruptcy can actually accomplish for those overwhelmed with debt, there are as many misconceptions as accurate ones. What it doesn't do is let you walk away scot-free, without having to pay any of your debts. What it can do is give you a fresh start, but at a significant emotional and financial cost.

Before you decide if bankruptcy is right for you, you should stop to consider what it might or might not do in relation to your existing debt reduction plan.

What Bankruptcy Will Do

While it does have some major drawbacks, filing bankruptcy can cause a miserable situation to change into a bearable one. Here's a short list of the "pros" of filing for bankruptcy, along with some corresponding questions to ponder:

◆ **Give you some breathing room.** Probably the most guaranteed result of bankruptcy is that it creates some sense of order to your creditors trying to squeeze money out of you. They'll be ordered by the court to get in line and stop hounding and harassing you.

In the Red

While a bankruptcy might buy you a little bit of time with your lenders, don't rest on your heels. Most protections only last 20 to 30 days. If you haven't worked out a remedy by then, lenders can begin their collections actions again.

Question: Could you accomplish this simply by communicating with your existing creditors? If so, bankruptcy might be overkill.

♦ **Discharge some portion of your obligations.** Bankruptcy will inevitably reduce the amount you owe. How much it reduces it will depend on what type of debts you owe, how much you earn, what assets you have, and what type of bankruptcy you are eligible to file for. Additionally, the discharge of your debts can and will be challenged by your creditors.

Question: If you are on track to get your debts paid off in three to five years, that will likely be the length of time a Chapter 11, 12, or 13 will take to complete. Would you be better off sticking with your current plan and avoiding the major hassle of bankruptcy?

♦ **Make you eligible for new loans.** While the best lenders and the best rates will elude you, your ability to borrow may actually strengthen. This will come from the fact that those all-important ratios will drop significantly, signifying cash flow that can be used for new payments.

Question: Will you need new loans in the next 7 to 10 years? If not, in that amount of time, depending on the type of bankruptcy you file, the bankruptcy will completely disappear from your credit report.

♦ **Force you to deal with your finances.** Some people can exercise on their own and some people need a personal trainer. Well, bankruptcy will be the financial equivalent of having Arnold Schwarzenegger standing behind you, yelling at you to exercise. Bankruptcy requires you to get counseling, eliminates a significant amount of your ability to get and use credit, and forces you to begin operating on a cash basis. If you can't imagine yourself doing this on your own, then bankruptcy might be the boost you need.

Question: Do you really want Arnold breathing down your neck? Or do you think you can learn to do these things on your own?

What Bankruptcy Won't Do

Bankruptcy will only go so far in helping you get your feet back on the ground, protecting you from creditors, and jump-starting your finances. Aside from the limitations of bankruptcy itself, the process won't change who you are. Only you can do that. As another dear friend told me once, regarding the biggest risk in moving to escape your problems, "Wherever you go, you take *you* with you!"

Bankruptcy won't …

♦ **Wipe out all your debts.** While many types of unsecured debts like credit cards may be reduced or fully discharged, some debts are generally left intact. You can likely expect to still be responsible for IRS debts, alimony, child support, and student loans.

Debt in America

I've mentioned that some people make a lifestyle out of bankruptcy. As absurd as that sounds, it's not too hard of a cycle to fall into. In fact, you could hypothetically file for a Chapter 13 bankruptcy every two years! While that may seem like an unlimited stack of "get of jail free" cards, it will ultimately take its toll. As you build a reputation within a local community of being in "chronic bankruptcy," more and more financial doors will close to you, until you will not even be able to secure basic necessities such as an apartment.

♦ **Protect you from unnamed creditors.** In order for a balance to be subject to the ruling of a bankruptcy court, you must list it in your bankruptcy filing. If you do not list it, that creditor can still theoretically pursue you as if you never filed for bankruptcy.

♦ **Protect you from future debts.** If you incur new debts during or shortly after your bankruptcy proceedings, these are fair game from a collections point of view. These lenders are not bound by the court's bankruptcy order.

♦ **Affect just you.** If anyone has co-signed on your loans or credit cards, and you file for Chapter 7 bankruptcy, creditors can (and will) pursue the co-signer. Further, if you own assets jointly with someone else, it could either keep you from declaring bankruptcy or force the sale of the asset to meet your obligations.

Recent Changes in Bankruptcy Laws

In late 2005, President Bush signed a set of new bankruptcy laws that make it harder to file for a bankruptcy, as well as limit what kind of bankruptcy you can file for. It also took away some of the protections you received from filing your bankruptcy.

The Bankruptcy Abuse Prevention and Consumer Protection Act of 2005 was not put in place to keep honest consumers from filing bankruptcy. Rather, it was put in place to protect businesses and creditors from people who can pay, as well as people who've made bankruptcy a way of life. It's important to understand these changes, especially if your idea of bankruptcy is based on the previous laws.

The "Means" Test

A Chapter 7 bankruptcy, which provides the most generous debt relief, is now reserved only for those with income below a certain level. This rule, known as the "means test," actually involves a semicomplex three-step formula. If you fail the means test, you cannot file for Chapter 7 bankruptcy, only Chapter 13.

> **Dollars and Sense**
>
> Interested to know what the median income is for your state for purposes of doing the means test? Visit the Department of Justice website at www.USDOJ.gov and type "census median income" into the search box.

Step 1: You must determine whether or not your average monthly income for the last six months is less than the median for your state. For example, if the median monthly income for your state was $2,000 per month and you earned $1,500 on average, you can file for Chapter 7. If your income is greater than the median, you need to move on to Step 2.

Step 2: You must multiply your "income available" for debt repayment (income minus all expenses but your monthly debt payments) by 60. If the total exceeds $10,000, you cannot file for Chapter 7.

For example, let's say your income is $1,500 per month and your living expenses (not counting debt payments) are $1,300. That would leave you with $200 in "income available" in the eyes of the court. Since $200 multiplied by 60 equals $12,000, which is over the $10,000 limit, you cannot file for Chapter 7.

Step 3: If your monthly available income from Step 2 is less than $100 per month, you can file for Chapter 7. If it is more than $100 but less than $166.67 per month, you may be able to file for Chapter 7, but have to pass one last test.

If your monthly available income multiplied by 60 is less than 25% of your total debt, you can still file for Chapter 7. If it is over 25%, you must file a Chapter 13 bankruptcy.

For example, if your monthly available income was $130, 60 times that would be $7,800. If your total debts were $35,000, 25% of that would be $8,750. Since your 60-month total is below that, you can still file for Chapter 7.

Debt Counseling

One of the hopes of the new laws was that people considering bankruptcy would be both educated on the process, as well as educated on how to stay out of future bankruptcies. With that in mind, new counseling requirements were put in place to both start and end bankruptcy.

At least six months before you file your bankruptcy paperwork, you must complete a "pre-petition" course. Your bankruptcy cannot proceed until you've completed this course and waited six months. These pre-petition courses can be done on the Internet, over the phone, or in person. They can range in cost from free to over $100, and generally last about 45 minutes to an hour.

Before your bankruptcy is officially closed or "discharged," you must also complete another round of counseling. This too can be taken over the phone, on the Internet, or in person. It lasts roughly two hours and also ranges in cost from free to a couple hundred dollars.

Dollars and Sense

To find out more about these counseling services in your area, which are available to you even if you don't file for bankruptcy, you can visit the Department of Justice website. Go to www.USDOJ.gov and type "bankruptcy approved providers" in the search box.

Automatic Stays

Under the old bankruptcy laws, a filing of bankruptcy would put an immediate halt to certain actions against you or your finances. For example, an automatic stay can keep your utilities from being shut off for a short period of time. It can also temporarily suspend foreclosure on your home.

However, the new bankruptcy laws removed certain protections of the automatic stay. Primarily, filing bankruptcy now will not protect you from your landlord evicting you for not paying rent. It may slow him or her down, but courts will generally side with the landlord and lift the stay.

Not Filing Your Tax Returns

When it comes to stuff going wrong with your finances, the IRS and bankruptcy probably top the list of most people's fears. Ironically, filing bankruptcy can start a domino effect that leads you straight from bankruptcy court to dealing with the IRS.

Under the new bankruptcy laws, you must be able to provide your most recent tax return before your first court-ordered meeting with your creditors, as well as any future returns if your bankruptcy is still open in subsequent years. If you don't have these returns, your bankruptcy cannot move forward. Thus, if you are thinking of filing bankruptcy, you've got to go back and catch up your tax returns. Who knows … you might actually find a refund in there somewhere!

Dollars and Sense _____

If you or your spouse is in the military, there are special legal provisions to protect you before, during, and after a bankruptcy. The heart of these provisions is built around the idea that someone who is off serving or protecting our country needs to focus wholly on that. While legal, eviction, and collections actions are not erased, they can be postponed until a more appropriate time. These protections fall under the Servicemembers' Civil Relief Act (SCRA). Be sure to talk to the legal personnel at your base or installation for more details.

How to File for Bankruptcy

There are really only two choices when it comes to filing for bankruptcy. You can do it yourself or you can hire a lawyer to help you with it. Without a doubt, I'd advise you (I'll even beg you) to use a lawyer. A screwup anywhere in the process could set you back a significant amount of time, which could in turn allow collection actions and foreclosures to continue.

When it comes to selecting a good bankruptcy lawyer, I think the old axiom holds true: you get what you pay for. The local lawyer who advertises "$599 Bankruptcies!" on your town's billboards will probably leave you so frustrated that you'll wish you did it yourself. Realistically, you should expect to pay $1,000 to $2,000 from start to finish, with Chapter 13's costing you a little more than Chapter 7's.

As always, try to find someone through a referral from someone else you know who has gone through the same thing. If you don't know anyone who has, or feel a little shy about e-mailing everyone you know and announcing your bankruptcy, go on the web and check your state's Bar Association. Many of these state websites will allow you to search the credentials of attorneys in your area.

The Hidden Costs of Bankruptcy

I've tried hard to give you a balanced view of bankruptcy, without making it sound like it's this horrible choice. Truthfully, I don't think you should feel bad about filing for bankruptcy if it is the best choice for your situation.

But I do think you also need to realize that there are some hidden costs associated with bankruptcy. You should weigh these carefully before you proceed with a filing.

Your Credit Score Will Plummet

Despite what anyone may tell you, a bankruptcy is worse than any other credit choice you can make. It hurts your credit score more than late payments, debt settlement, consolidations, or a lender closing your account.

If you file for bankruptcy, it will likely cost you a couple thousand dollars up front. But it may also cost you thousands through higher interest rates and increased loan payments. If you hope to buy a home in the next 7 to 10 years, a bankruptcy will be something you'll want to avoid at all costs.

> **In the Red**
>
> Giving away your assets to another friend or family member prior to filing bankruptcy may seem like a good way to make sure your most important assets don't get liquidated. But doing so can also constitute fraud and can land you in hot water. If you are going to file bankruptcy, do it honestly and right. That way, you can get it over with and move on with your life!

You're Going to Get Asked

Each Chapter 13 bankruptcy (the payment plan type) remains on your credit report for up to seven years, so you could hypothetically show multiple bankruptcies on one credit report if you filed every two years. All other kinds, including a Chapter 7, can remain for up to 10 years.

But even after a bankruptcy has been dropped from your credit report, potential lenders still have the right to ask, which obligates you to tell. In other words, for the rest of your life, you will be on the hook to be honest about your bankruptcy if asked by a lender. Lying on an application about a bankruptcy constitutes fraud and can have serious penalties.

Jobs and Apartments May Become Harder to Get

Both employers and landlords are allowed to review your credit report if they give you notice and you give consent. If you don't want to give consent, they do not have to offer you the job or the rental.

To a landlord, a bankruptcy raises the risk that you'll cost them money at some point. To an employer, it makes you look irresponsible and potentially unqualified, especially for jobs dealing with money.

Your Ego and Reputation May Take a Beating

For many people, the idea of filing bankruptcy is equivalent to admitting you've really blown it and you've given up to trying to fix it. I don't necessarily see it that way, but many people feel that way once they do it.

To add insult to injury, you may end up feeling embarrassed and humiliated by your choice or need to file bankruptcy. In addition to your family usually knowing about it, there is a good possibility that others may find out, too. This is because bankruptcy filings usually require some type of public notification so all your creditors have a fair chance to make a claim. In my community, that means that your filing ends up on the back page of our community paper!

The Least You Need to Know

- There are two real types of bankruptcy—one wipes out some of your debts while the other establishes payment plans.

- A bankruptcy can give you breathing room and a fresh start, but will not let you off the hook without a cost.

◆ Recent changes in the bankruptcy law have made it harder to get debts discharged and removed some of the automatic protection a filing use to provide.

◆ If you are going to file for bankruptcy, you are taking your financial life in your own hands by not using a lawyer.

◆ Even after a bankruptcy falls off your credit report, it may haunt you for the rest of your life.

Part 4

Protecting Yourself

As the saying goes, "the best defense is a good offense." In other words, to truly protect yourself, you should be proactive and get the upper hand on the things that can cause you harm.

When it comes to your finances, it's crucial that you are both looking down the road and watching your own back. Sadly, the road to financial freedom is full of booby traps and unsavory people hiding in the shadows, trying to do your finances harm.

In this part, you'll learn how to fend off the angry mob of creditors, safeguard your identity, nurture your credit score, and stay out of the sights of scam artists.

Getting Your Creditors Off Your Back

In This Chapter

- ◆ Sympathy for the devil
- ◆ Understanding your rights under the law
- ◆ Steps to stop the harassment
- ◆ If a creditor steps over the line
- ◆ Steps to take when facing auto repossession, eviction, or utility shutoffs
- ◆ Reporting a violation of your rights

Being in debt is stressful enough by itself. But, when your creditors start bombarding you with letters, harassing you with phone calls, and even making threats, it can be downright terrifying. Worst of all, you feel completely helpless because you know your creditors have a legal right to get paid.

But it doesn't have to be that way. Thanks to legal protections put in place by the federal and state governments, you are entitled to a minimum level of courtesy and professionalism. In fact, if the people to whom you owe money fail to operate within the legal limits given to them, you can actually sue them for damages!

It's crucial that you know your rights, take quick action to assert them, and communicate to your creditors the unacceptable nature of their collection practices.

Understanding Your Creditors

There's an old Rolling Stones song called "Sympathy for the Devil." That title always struck me in terms of the position your creditors are stuck in. In fact, I think you should take a moment to stop and try to sympathize with their predicament. It'll go a long way toward smoothing over your relationship with them.

> **Debt in America**
>
> According to the American Banker's Association, in the fourth quarter of 2007, overall delinquencies on loans and credit cards reached their highest levels in 15 years. There's no doubt that this is putting pressure on the payrolls and profits of companies that loan money for a living, whether they're banks, credit card issuers, or mortgage companies.

Ultimately, your creditors loaned you money because you promised to pay it back. Truthfully, no one forced you to borrow money from them, but it was a choice you made. Now that you're not repaying, it's affecting them.

That may seem like a little bit of a stretch to say your late payments are affecting some gigantic credit card corporation, but they do. Someone's head is always on the block over whether or not they can collect the money they're entitled to. Whether it is the people who decided to originally loan you the money, the people who try to collect it from you, or even the CEO, they all have to answer to somebody. If it is not a boss or supervisor, then it is the shareholders of the company who want a fair return on their investment.

I'm not trying to send you on a guilt trip, but I am trying to get you to see that everyone is just trying to do their job. That's an important thing to realize, because if you can help them do their job even just a little bit, there's a good chance they'll stay friendly with you. If you become standoffish, difficult, and unsympathetic, then they'll return the favor.

Stop for a minute and imagine the "morning briefing" in the Collections department at your credit card company. The boss is deciding which accounts to assign to which collectors. In one corner, you've got Daisy. She's a wife and a mom, who works at the credit card company because she needs a job to make ends meet. While she's on phone calls with customers, she doodles rainbows and flowers on her notepad.

In another corner is Bruno. The folks in the office refer to him as "The Enforcer." He once broke a co-worker's arm for accidentally touching his lunch bag, which consisted of raw meat and spoiled milk. Bruno works here because his parole officer said it would be a good way to get out his aggression without having to be in the same room as other human beings.

If you've been difficult to deal with, who do you think gets your case, Mrs. Sunshine or The Enforcer?

The point is, you can bring aggressive collections on yourself by being difficult to people who are just trying to do their jobs. As you talk on the phone or respond in writing, an expression of sympathy and understanding for them goes a long way toward a peaceful resolution.

Your Rights Under the Consumer Credit Protection Act

While your creditors do have a right to their money, there are also limits placed on how they can go about trying to get it. These limits have been put in place to help you make healthy progress toward paying off your debts, but not avoiding paying them off. If that's what you're aiming for, you need to consider bankruptcy (see Chapter 18).

> **Debt in America** _____
>
> As the time of this book's publishing, there are numerous versions of a "Credit Card Bill of Rights" being circulated around Congress. It won't likely be long before a new set of laws is put into place to protect credit card users from some of the more dangerous and costly features of these cards. Be sure to keep an eye on the papers as new laws may be put in place in the middle of your journey to eliminate debt. Understanding the benefits of these laws may give your debt reduction plan a huge boost.

A big part of the reason that aggressive collections exist is because most consumers don't have the slightest clue as to their rights, much less how to begin asserting them. But as you'll find, the moment you start waving these around, you'll realize that collection agencies fear these things like Superman fears kryptonite.

The Consumer Credit Protection Act (CCPA) is one of the most sweeping pieces of legislation to be enacted to protect consumers, and Congress continues to add to it as time goes by. It is the biggest and most multiuse weapon in your arsenal. I kind of consider it the Swiss army knife of creditor protection. Let's look at some of the sub-chapters and acts of the Consumer Credit Protection Act.

The Fair Debt Collection Practices Act (FDCPA)

This is your atomic bomb in your war of words with collection agencies. Just by mentioning the "FDCPA," you'll often hear an immediate change in the tone of a collection agent's voice. It's important to note that this act does not apply to the company that originally loaned you the money, but only an outside company or person it turns the account over to for collections.

> **In the Red**
>
> Before you agree to (much less begin paying on) any payment plans or settlements with a collection agency, make sure you get your agreement in writing. Collection agencies are notorious for changing the rules on payment plans midway through, especially if you are late on even a single payment.

The most impressive part of the FDCPA is that it actually gives you the legal power to stop collection agencies from contacting you altogether. Yes, you read that right. You can force the collection agency to cease all communications with you.

To wield this mystical power, all you need to do is send a simple *cease and desist letter* to the collection agency stating that you no longer wish to be contacted about this debt. If you have hired an attorney for bankruptcy proceedings or a lawsuit regarding the debt, you can instruct the collection agency to contact them. A sample letter is included in Appendix B.

In addition to this important and effective tool, the FDCPA outlines a number of other rules that collection agencies must live by or they become open to a lawsuit:

1. In their efforts to collect a debt you owe, a collection agency may not contact your family, friends, neighbors, or employer.

2. Collection agencies are not permitted to call before 8 A.M. or after 9 P.M. in your time zone.

3. Use of racial slurs, obscenities, insults, or unreasonable threats is out of the question.

4. No collection agency or its employee can pretend to be an attorney or court employee, or create any communication that would look like it came from one.

5. No collection agency can threaten you with arrest for an unpaid debt.

The Fair Credit Billing Act (FCBA)

This set of laws protects users of credit cards and department store charge cards from bogus charges, double charges, math errors on their statements, and changes of addresses that caused your payment to be late. It's an important act to be aware of because it gives you the right to be late on a payment, without any penalty or negative credit reporting, if you believe one of these situations has occurred.

Once you provide your credit card company with a written *billing dispute letter* (see the sample in Appendix B), you may withhold payment on the amount in dispute, until the dispute is resolved. You must, however, pay all the other charges that are not in dispute.

To receive protection under the FCBA, you must mail the written dispute to your credit card company's billing inquiry address, which is usually different than where you send your payments. Additionally, your dispute letter must reach them (not just be mailed) within 60 days of receiving the bill with questionable charges. With that in mind, I'd definitely recommend sending your dispute letter by registered mail or some type of traceable service like FedEx or UPS.

def•i•ni•tion

A **cease and desist letter** is the official name of the letter you send instructing third-party collection agencies not to contact you anymore. A **billing dispute letter** goes directly to your creditor, disputes a charge, and actually invites them to contact you.

Your credit card company must then acknowledge your dispute within 30 days, and completely resolve the dispute within two billing cycles (about 60 days). If they fail to abide by the FCBA, you can sue your creditor for damages, twice the finance charge you paid, and your legal fees.

In addition to providing a process for disputing charges, the FCBA provides the following protections:

1. If your company charges late fees on payments, they must send you your statement at least 14 days before your payment is due. If not, you can dispute the late fees associated with that payment cycle.

2. Your credit card company must credit your payment on the business day it is received. In other words, they would violate the FCBA if they received your payment on the 30th, a day before your payment is due, but do not credit you until the 2nd.

3. If your credit card ever has a positive cash balance, usually caused by you over-paying, your credit card company must promptly refund the balance if it is greater than $1.

Restriction on Garnishment Act

While certain creditors can take action to collect on debts directly from your pay-check, there are also limits on the process meant to protect you. The Restriction on Garnishment Act comes in quite handy when creditors come after your paycheck.

The biggest protection provided by this act has to do with how much of your pay-check can be garnished. In other words, the government protects your right to work and earn enough money to provide for you and your loved ones. While many large companies are aware of these guidelines, smaller employers may not have a clue, requiring you to assert your rights.

The maximum amount that can come out of each paycheck is the lesser of 25% of your disposable earnings or the amount by which your wages exceed 30 times the federal minimum wage. This limit is increased to 50% to 65% in certain child support and alimony cases. The maximum is decreased to 10% for certain federal student loans in default. IRS and bankruptcy garnishments are not subject to these limits.

> **Dollars and Sense**
>
> Garnishments are one of the more confusing debt collection procedures out there. Because many employers, especially the smaller ones, do not have extensive knowledge of your rights under the Restriction on Garnishment Act, the Department of Labor has established a toll-free number for assistance. Their Wage and Hour Division can be reached for assistance at 866-4USWAGE.

Another protection, with an odd wrinkle, is that your employer is not allowed to fire you because of a garnishment action as long as the action only results from one debt. However, and here's the odd wrinkle, if garnishments are ordered because of two or more debts, the Restriction on Garnishment Act doesn't prohibit your employer from firing you. Yet another reason to communicate with your creditors and work hard to keep your debts out of collections and garnishment.

Truth in Lending Act (TILA)

The Truth in Lending Act, also known as Regulation Z, hasn't received much press until recent years. Years ago, when it was created, it was welcomed by consumers. This was because it forced lenders to begin using a standardized way of expressing interest costs called the annual percentage rate (APR). Because that has become semistandard terminology for most people now, the Truth in Lending Act has faded into the background.

But you can expect that to change, as many borrowers, especially people with mortgages, rediscover the other provisions of the act. Namely, those borrowers who were not given the proper disclosure paperwork can actually rescind or reclassify their mortgages into unsecured debt.

In other words, if you were sold a mortgage that was not properly explained and now has a payment spiraling out of control, you may be able to undo your bank's claim on your house. It's still a creditor you owe money to, but the bank has to get in line with all the rest of your unsecured creditors.

Since the subprime mortgage meltdown, many borrowers have sued and won the right to remove their bank's claim on their house. Many have also won the right to collect monetary damages, because their lender didn't adequately disclose the risks of their adjustable-rate mortgages.

Debt in America

In mid-2007, a class action lawsuit against Citibank and its affiliate, Associate First Capital Corporation, yielded a $215 million settlement in favor of homeowners under the Truth in Lending Act. That's almost a quarter of a billion dollars in damages awarded for failing to adequately disclose facts about mortgages it sold to people like you and me.

Can we all say "wow" together?

If you think that this might be you, you'll need to gather all your original paperwork for your mortgage and contact a lawyer specializing in litigating these kinds of cases. But if you had a mortgage pushed on you by a slick broker, a few phone calls may well be worth your time!

Predatory Lending Laws

It has been argued, and I truly believe, that there are people and companies within the lending industry that prey on certain populations of consumers. Their goal is to offer a high-rate or high-fee product to people who might not otherwise know better or have other options.

For example, certain credit card companies choosing to offer credit cards to college freshmen, who have no clue about the true risks and responsibilities of having a credit card. Or mortgage lenders who charge exorbitant (not just higher) interest rates to lower-income individuals who would not otherwise be able to qualify for a loan. Even retail stores get in on the act, offering the sale of simple products with ridiculous payment plans and hard-to-understand paperwork.

In response to this trend of excessively greedy people and companies that take extreme advantage of unaware consumers, many states have enacted predatory lending laws. In fact, 25 states now have some kind of laws on the books to prevent predatory lending.

Dollars and Sense

One of the organizations that is leading the way in fighting predatory lending and other harmful lending industry practices is the Association of Community Organizations for Reform Now (ACORN). By visiting the ACORN website (www.acorn. org), you can sign up for a free (donation optional) newsletter that will keep you informed about programs in your area that are fighting unethical lenders as well as helping financial victims.

While many of these laws may not place an immediate stop to your debt crisis, balances you owe that were loaned to you in violation of your state's laws can result in successful lawsuits for damages. While I'm not recommending you start suing every one of your creditors, I am suggesting that the loan that dug you into the hole may also offer you a ladder out.

I'd suggest that you spend some time online researching your state's predatory lending laws, as well as visiting the website for Housing and Urban Development (HUD). As always, seek legal advice if you think there has been a gross violation of your rights.

Usury Laws

Virtually every state provides a legal maximum on the different types of interest that may be charged. Interest rates that exceed these rates are called usury, and may entitle you to seek damages and refunds.

Oftentimes, there will be a maximum rate for personal loans, another for car loans, and yet another for mortgages. Some states will place caps on certain types of loans while not placing any on other types.

Face-to-Face Encounters

If things get bad enough, you may find yourself face-to-face with someone representing one of your lenders. This is especially true if you are in possession of collateral that backs up your loan, such as a car or a house. In these cases, you need to be both cautious and quick when it comes to seeking a solution.

My biggest piece of advice is to drop the baseball bat or the pepper spray. While I know it may feel like someone is stealing your car or house, they in fact represent a company that owns it until you pay it off in full. In reality, they are reclaiming the assets that you have failed to pay off. Taking a baseball bat to the repo man will only land you in cuffs.

Important Steps in an Auto Repossession

For many of us, life would grind to a halt without our vehicle. Naturally, it's a terrifying feeling to watch your car get hooked up to a tow truck by a burly repo guy. While it's pointless (and might land you in jail) to put up a fight, there are a few steps you can take to make the process as quick and painless as possible:

1. **Ask for paperwork.** Most of the time, the person repossessing your car will have copies of paperwork that will be very useful to you in getting your car back. Make a polite request for a copy of this paperwork and it's very likely they'll give it to you.

2. **Ask to grab your possessions.** I've heard about it time and again, where a car gets repossessed with someone's purse, Aunt Mable's birthday gift, and your kid's favorite action figure all locked inside. Again, if you ask politely to grab your important possessions, many repossessors will be happy to oblige. For what it's worth, if you think repossession may be part of your near future, don't leave any important items in the car. Many repossessions happen in the middle of the night to avoid conflict, and you'll never get a chance to grab your stuff.

3. **Offer them the keys.** If you are hoping to get the car back, do yourself a favor and offer the repossessor the keys. If you don't, they'll have to try to jimmy the door, potentially damaging your car.

4. **Snap some pictures.** Repossessed cars can definitely get a little banged up in the process. Because most of them end up being auctioned off "as is," your repossessor probably isn't too worried about the paint job. If you can snap a few pictures on your camera phone before they drive away, there is a good chance

you can get those damages repaired at no cost to you if you end up getting your car back in time.

5. **Call your lender immediately.** If you are able to make even a partial payment, there's a good chance you can get your car back within the first 7 to 10 days. After that, it's probably destined for the auction block. If your car is repossessed, your first call should always be to your lender.

> **Dollars and Sense** _____
>
> Unfortunately, just turning your car over to your lender because you can't make the payments still shows the same as a repossession on your credit report. If you think you can't afford the payments, consider trying to sell it yourself. However, if you are sure it's only a matter of time before your car gets repossessed, do it on your terms. Dropping the car and the keys off may be a lot less inconvenient or embarrassing than having your car repossessed right in front of your house or from your employer's parking lot.

Important Steps in an Eviction

There are few things as paralyzing as being evicted. For many people, their worst fears of being "out on the street" just materialized. It literally can leave you fending off an anxiety attack on your own front porch.

As unsettling as it is, though, you need to take a step back and consider your options and necessary next steps:

1. **Read the notice.** Evicting someone in the United States is not supposed to happen without warning. Your lender or your landlord can't just throw you out, in the middle of the night, with no forewarning. Whether you rent or own, you will be given written notice of what is coming. This is your chance to stop it dead in its tracks by negotiating, scraping together funds, or filing for bankruptcy.

   There are two main types of notices to be aware of when it comes to evictions. A "Notice to Pay or Quit" is used by landlords and basically says "pay up or move out." It doesn't mean you're evicted, but rather that you will be if you don't pay within the period allowed by your state. If you are paying a mortgage on your home, you'll see a lot more paperwork, and have a much greater heads up than with a rental. Aside from all the late notices, you'll eventually see a "Notice to Vacate." Unlike the Notice to Pay or Quit, this is usually in response to a court order. Your best bet for stopping it will probably be to file for bankruptcy.

2. **Make temporary living arrangements.** Don't worry about finding a new long-term place the same day an eviction happens. Just work on where you'll sleep that night. For the sake of any kids in the house, try your best to all end up at the same location. When asking if you can stay with someone, always ask for a little longer period of time than you expect to need. It's a lot easier to leave early than it is to stay longer.

3. **Make temporary storage arrangements.** If you have a significant amount of possessions or furniture, call your local storage unit location and get a month-to-month rental agreement. In most parts of the country, you can fit a good amount of furniture into a $50-to-$100-per-month unit.

4. **Get your mail forwarded.** Run down to the post office or go online and get your mail forwarded to a new address. The last thing you need is for bills and paychecks to start going to the wrong location. Consider using a family member with a stable address or getting a post office box.

5. **Fill out a new rental application ASAP.** While I'd never encourage you to lie to a potential landlord, many don't ever ask about evictions. If anything, they just pull your credit report to see if there have been any prior problems. The sooner you apply to rent elsewhere, the less likely it is that your recent eviction will show on your credit report.

Important Steps to Keep Your Utilities On

Utilities have some of the strongest leverage of all the people you might owe money to. If you don't pay your bill, they simply shut off your service. There's not a whole lot you can do and they know it.

It's crucial that you respond to utilities in a timely manner, because a shutoff can end up being very costly. Many utilities charge some kind of reconnection fee as well as require a mandatory deposit for future service. It's not uncommon for an electrical shutoff to cost over $300 in fees and deposits, in addition to the past-due bill itself!

Many times, a shutoff notice comes after a couple of months of missed payments. While the total past-due bill may be staggering, you can often talk your utility into leaving your service on by paying just the most past-due month's bill. As always, communicating with the people you owe money to will often buy you some significant time and flexibility to figure out other solutions.

Dollars and Sense _____

Many residents don't realize that most of the major utilities providers have programs that help lower-income wage earners with past-due bills. In fact, many of these programs will also qualify you for lower rates going forward. To find out more, call each one of your utility providers and ask about discounts for services based on certain income levels.

Reporting Violations of Your Rights

While reporting violations of your rights is unlikely to result in as much immediate action as contacting the company directly or getting a lawyer involved, the phone call may help point you toward other resources for dealing with the same company.

Any violations of the Fair Debt Collection Practices Act should be reported to the Federal Trade Commission at 877-382-4357.

If you feel like you've been the victim of predatory lending practices, usury, or an unfair repossession action, contact the attorney general's office for your state.

The Least You Need to Know

- If you show sympathy to your creditors' situation, you'll likely get some in return.

- You have a ton of rights under the Consumer Credit Protection Act. Know what they are, and don't be afraid to assert yourself.

- Consider pursuing legal action against creditors who overstep their rights and privileges.

- Be proactive in dealing with repossessions, evictions, and utility shutoffs.

- If you feel as though your rights have been violated, take necessary action.

Chapter 20

Salvaging Your Credit Score

In This Chapter

- What is a credit score, really?
- Understanding the credit score formula
- The biggest credit score mistakes
- How long does something stay on a credit report?
- Tips to raise your score

There are very few times as a grown man, with children of my own, that I feel busted, caught red handed, and scolded. But when someone pulls my credit report, it takes me right back to seventh grade and my parents opening my report card right in front of me. Back then, my social life hung in the balance. Good grades meant a summer of frolicking in the sun. Bad grades meant a summer confined to the house watching game shows and babysitting my sisters.

Now as an adult, a good credit score means that I get the loan, get the car or the house, and live the life I want to provide. A not-so-good credit score means the "walk of shame" out of the dealership or mortgage office. As much as anything else, a good credit score is the passing grade for financial adulthood.

If you plan on borrowing money, renting an apartment, or even applying for a job at some employers, you're going to want to spend some time salvaging your credit score. It's not that hard, but as they say, time heals all wounds. Change won't happen overnight, but it must start today!

Credit Score Basics

Before we go much further, we need to clarify what a *credit score* is and what purpose it serves. As with many things, once you understand the basic mechanics of something, you'll learn how to exploit it.

Going back to our grade analogy, our credit score is actually more of our overall grade point average (GPA) than it is a grade from any one class. It's an averaging together of how well you stack up in a number of different areas of financial responsibility. Just like a GPA is a good overall measure of the kind of student you are, a credit score is a good overall measure of your financial responsibility. From a lender's point of view, it gives them an "at a glance" way of evaluating whether or not they should loan money to you. It helps them cut through the façade that a borrower may try and put up.

def•i•ni•tion

People often confuse **credit score** and credit report. While the terms may sound similar, one is actually built upon the other. Your credit report is a history of your employment, residences, accounts, and borrowing/ payment habits. Your credit score is a value assigned to you, based on this history, that helps a lender estimate how likely it is that you'll pay back future amounts you borrow.

It comes as a surprise to most consumers to realize that there is not just one credit score, but dozens upon dozens. In fact, there is no legal requirement to use one credit score method over another.

However, when you think of credit scores, you think of the number generated based on your stats, as provided by one of the three major credit-reporting agencies (Experian, Equifax, and TransUnion). While any lender can take your credit history and calculate a score however they want, many lenders opt to save themselves the work and go with one of the scores provided by these outside companies.

Your Fair Isaac Corporation (FICO) Score

The best known and most well used of all credit scores is the FICO score. In fact, it is so widely used that many people mistakenly refer to all credit scores as a FICO.

The FICO score is produced by the Fair Isaac Corporation for businesses who need help assessing the risk of a potential borrower. Scores range from 300 to 850, with higher scores being better than lower scores. A score in the high 600s tends to be the cutoff for "good" credit in most lenders' eyes.

If you haven't requested your FICO score yet, you should. My preference is to get it straight from the Fair Isaac Corporation through its MyFICO.com website. Depending on if you catch any specials, a one-time credit score for one of the three major credit-reporting agencies will cost you between $10 and $20. If you want your score from all three agencies, it usually costs $40 to $50.

You don't need to waste the money on buying your FICO from all three agencies. But because there are usually some slight variances in your FICO, depending what each agency has on its records, some people are curious to see all three. Many times, lenders will average your three FICO's together when evaluating your safety as a borrower.

Other Major Credit Scores

While FICO might be the biggest game in town, it's definitely not the only. In fact, each of the three major credit-reporting agencies also offers their own version of a credit score. Within the financial planning industry, we jokingly refer to these scores as FAKOs because they are all seemingly knockoffs of the FICO scores. Ultimately, they all communicate roughly the same result—whether or not you're a good risk.

> **Debt in America**
>
> The median Experian Plus score in America hovers around 690, which means half of the country is above this line and half are below it. Interestingly enough, certain states and regions of the country vary widely in their credit scores. New England has the highest average score for a region, but Minnesota takes the cake with an average Plus score of 722. The southern United States checks in with the worst scores, with Texas coming in last at 668. For more fascinating geographic breakdowns of credit scores (including your zip code), visit Experian's website at www.NationalScoreIndex. com.

Just don't expect to have a lender who uses FICO scores take you seriously when you argue for an approval or a lower rate based on a higher score from one of these other services. The main types of other scores are:

- ◆ The **VantageScore** is a joint attempt by the three credit agencies to come up with a scoring system that rivals the FICO. This score ranges from 501 to 990 and also includes a letter grade. I personally feel like the VantageScore uses a range with a higher ending point to help consumers feel like they're getting a better score with VantageScore than FICO. Unfortunately, lenders don't fall for the trick. They know that a higher VantageScore translates into a lower FICO score.

◆ Equifax's **Beacon Score** is basically a streamlined version of the FICO score. The scoring range is a little narrower than the traditional FICO score, but doesn't usually translate into any major variation between these two.

◆ The **Plus Score** is calculated by Experian and is often sold as part of its credit monitoring and identity theft packages. I've had this service for a few years and it consistently seems to be lower than my actual FICO score. I wouldn't recommend buying it, but it's interesting to look at if it comes with another service or product.

◆ The **Empirica Score** is offered through TransUnion, and is also based on your Fair Isaac Score with some larger adjustments. Empirica scores typically range from the mid-100s to the low-900s. Again, I don't think you need to worry about this score and would advise you to opt for your true FICO score.

The Credit Score Formula

If you put 10 different people in a room and ask them to explain how the credit score is actually calculated, you'll get 10 different answers. Some will manage to guess a few of the key components, but not realize that they each affect your credit score to a different degree. Others will have no clue, guessing that your credit score has something to do with crop circles, the Bermuda Triangle, and your SAT scores from high school.

> **In the Red**
>
> It is against the law for your age, race, gender, sexual preference, location of residence, marital status, or the receipt of public assistance programs like welfare to affect your credit score.

While the actual credit calculation, or algorithm as it is called, is a closely guarded secret, the Fair Isaac Corporation publishes a rough breakdown of the factors. Understanding these factors will help you to understand where you can boost your credit score the most, as well as where you need to be the most vigilant about protecting it.

As I go through this list, I'm also going to dispel some of the myths surrounding these different factors. In fact, by the end of the chapter, the rest of the folks at work will think you are a regular genius when it comes to credit scores.

Here are the basic categories your credit score is calculated on:

35%	Payment History
30%	Credit Utilization
15%	Length of Credit History
10%	Credit Inquiries
10%	Types of Credit Used

Payment History

Before I even begin to explain what "payment history" is, you should realize what it *isn't*. Take a look at the second to last item on the breakdown of your credit score above. You'll notice that it's "length of credit history." So if that's there and payment history is elsewhere, then they must be different!

Payment history, which is the single largest factor of your credit score, is primarily a reflection of whether or not you've paid your bills on time. This category considers the last 12 to 24 months of your payment history as heavily as months 36 to 72 combined! In fact, someone who has had credit cards for 4 years should theoretically score the same in this category as someone who has had credit cards for 40 years, assuming they've both paid their bills on time.

What does this tell you about your credit score? It tells you that the single largest factor that is looked at is payment history. In terms of actual techniques for salvaging your credit score, which I'll talk more about shortly, your payment history will also be the biggest factor.

Dollars and Sense

While it doesn't carry the same weight, job and residential history do contribute to you being approved for loans and credit. If you change jobs or residences every 6 to 12 months, you have a higher probability of not being able to pay your bills. You may also be viewed as increasingly hard to track down for collections actions. To help ensure that you get the credit you want, try to stay put at a job or residence for at least one year at a time.

Credit Utilization

This category, which represents the next biggest factor in your credit score, goes by a lot of different names. Some people also call it the "Amounts Owed" or "Balance to Limit" ratio. Essentially, it is a measure of how maxed out you are.

In the old days, your credit score just took into account how much you owed. Someone who owed $5,000 was viewed as more risky than someone who owed $2,000. Of course, when you realize that the person who owes $2,000 only had a $1,000 limit, while the person who owes $5,000 has a $30,000 limit, you get a different picture of these two borrowers.

I know the wheels are turning for some of you (those who did well in high school algebra) as you read about credit utilization. Wouldn't you be able to make your credit utilization look better by opening a bunch of accounts and "diluting" how maxed out you are? While it might make your credit utilization look slightly better, it will probably end up hurting you more in the end. Rapidly applying for credit, opening a bunch of accounts, and raising your overall limits are negative items on your report, especially if done in a short period of time.

Credit scores ultimately try to predict the potential that a lender will not get its money back. With this in mind, things that indicate impulsivity, lack of control, and poor decision making naturally reflect worse on your score. Your credit utilization ratio measures a key part of a borrower's psychology … how maxed out you are as you apply for even more credit.

Your credit score in this category is ultimately judged based on a percentage. The higher the percentage, the more risky you look. The lower the percentage, even if you have a high limit available to you, the better you look.

For example, a consumer who is carrying $2,000 in balances and has $10,000 available to them would be carrying a 20% utilization ratio. Someone with a $10,000 balance and a $100,000 limit would be carrying a 10% ratio. Based on this, there's a good chance that the person with the larger balance but lower ratio would end up with a better score.

Length of Credit History

The first thing I want you to notice about the length of credit history category is how relatively little it contributes to your overall credit score—just 15%. This is in contrast to everything I hear about how college students and young couples need to begin building credit. The reality is, most young people who set off on a mission to build credit end up destroying it. Why, you might ask? Because they probably weren't financially stable or mature enough to borrow in the first place!

Dollars and Sense _____

Before you run out and try to open some company's "Double-Decker Diamond Platinum Members Only" card to try to build credit, consider starting with a gas card. A charge card for your local gas station is usually one of the easiest cards to obtain without any other credit history. It'll also keep you out of trouble because their limits are low, usually $250 or less, and you can only buy gas and Twinkies with them. After 6 to 12 months of paying your gas card regularly and on time, you'll have built enough credit to move on to other types of borrowing when the time comes.

The reality, as demonstrated by the fact that your credit score doesn't count this category very heavily, is that loans are not given based primarily on credit scores. While a good credit score might qualify you for a better rate on a loan, it will not get you a loan if you do not have a solid income.

Truthfully, if you were considering loaning $10,000 to someone, which fact would you be more interested in knowing—how long he had a credit card or whether or not he is making enough each month to make his payments? Having a long credit history may raise your score from good to great, but you'll still need the income to back it up.

Credit Inquiries

While it is one of the smallest contributors to your credit score—just 10%—the frequency with which your "credit is run" is enough to knock you from one credit score bracket to another. Unfortunately, many people don't even know their credit is being checked half of the times it is.

It's estimated that every credit inquiry someone makes about you knocks anywhere from 2 to 10 points off your FICO score for approximately six months. Checking your own credit, though, no matter how often you do it, does not harm your credit score in any way.

Dollars and Sense _____

Don't let the fear of too many inquiries keep you from shopping around for the best rate when it really is time to buy a car or a house. Just make sure you do your entire rate shopping in as short of a period as possible. Most credit checks within a week, but often up to a month, are lumped together as only one inquiry if they are for the same kind of lenders.

Because random inquiries can hurt your score, it's essential that you check your credit report to see if your lenders, credit card company, or landlord are running them excessively (more than once per year). If they are, you can make a written request that your credit history not be reviewed anymore without your written consent. If a company violates this request, or some company you've never given permission runs your credit, they can be on the hook for some very stiff fines.

Types of Credit Used

The last component of the typical credit score calculation is the types of credit used. In other words, certain types of credit and loans count more heavily against you than others. This is because these different kinds of credit both affect your ability to pay, as well as making statements about your habits as a borrower.

If you stop and think about it, a good home mortgage is probably one of the least risky types of loans to have on your credit report. The loan itself is backed by the bank's ability to sell the house.

After that, student loans are typically the next best type of loans to have on your credit report. While they are not backed by any physical collateral, they usually have great terms and represent you investing in your own ability to earn a living.

Cars are the next loan down on the food chain. While auto loans can definitely get you into trouble, they are still backed by an asset, force you to repay them over a specified period of time, and have no ability to "max out." From a lender's point of view, your car loan will only shrink, not spiral out of control.

Once you get into heavy use of credit cards, though, your credit score can get significantly bruised up. Credit cards represent a semi-unchecked ability to spend money and show that you borrow for nonessential purposes.

The worst of the credit cards are the "mall" credit cards. You know the ones I'm talking about ... when you're at the register with your pile of relaxed-fit khaki's and they offer you 15% off your purchase if you sign up for their store's credit card. What this ultimately says to other lenders, and your credit score reflects this, is that you are impulsive. Someone offered you additional credit, and in the space of 10 seconds, you said yes.

In the Red

I tend to imagine debt like that food pyramid you find on the side of your cereal box in the morning. At the bottom of that food pyramid, which is also the biggest piece proportionately, you have the stuff that is least likely to kill you—grains and vegetables. At the top of the pyramid, the smallest piece, you've got the stuff that can cause your heart to explode—oils, sugars, etc. Debt is no different. You should strive to have far less of the bad stuff than the good stuff. When your "debt pyramid" is inverted (more bad stuff than good stuff), lenders will want nothing to do with you. If you want to raise your credit score, work on shifting the distribution of your debt to a healthier mix.

So What Really Screws Up Credit Reports?

Now that you understand the things that weigh the most on your credit score, it's not a huge leap to deduce what things need to be avoided if at all possible. One of the great truths of credit repair is that if you keep an eye on these things, everything else will eventually fix itself. Here's what to avoid:

- **Bankruptcies and bank actions.** A bankruptcy, repossession, or foreclosure will take your credit score from hero to zero in one shot. IRS, state income tax, and property tax liens carry nearly the same weight as these other actions. Long story short, avoid these at all costs if you're going to need to rely on your credit score in the next decade.

- **Late payments.** Because payment history is the single largest contributor to your credit score, hiccups in your history will affect your score more per incident than anything else. But before you start sweating that payment that was a week late, most lenders only report payments that are 30, 60, 90, or 120 days late.

- **Debt settlements and consolidations.** Both of these actions indicate an inability to meet your obligations. While they may often be the best choice from a debt reduction point of view, you need to remember that they'll hammer away at your credit score. Use them if you have to, but use them sparingly.

- **Going over your limits.** Your credit report shows your limit as well as your highest balance on each account for the last seven years. So even if you accidentally go over your credit limit by a couple hundred dollars just once, paying it off the next day, you now show a history of exceeding your limits.

◆ **Lenders closing your accounts.** If an account is going to get closed, make sure you do it on your terms. If your credit report shows "closed at grantor request," it means that your lender pulled the plug on you. This label will ripple through your credit report and scare future lenders.

◆ **Letting your accounts go to collections.** When a collection action makes it onto your credit report, your score is going to be affected in a big way.

◆ **Getting preapproved too often.** While many people have better things to do than go down to the dealership or bank and fill out applications for loans, searching online for rates can have the same effect on your credit scores. Many times, when you search online banking sites or get preapproved for a loan, the owners of the website run your credit. More than a couple of these every six months and it can start to eat away at your score.

> **Dollars and Sense** _____
>
> Did you know that if a lender chose to, they could completely ignore even the worst FICO score and give you a loan with whatever rate they wanted? They can—just don't count on it. The point is, FICO scores are just one tool that lenders use to decide if they want to work with you. Because lenders are all so different, you should consider visiting or calling them 6 to 12 months before you will need credit or a loan. Take the time to ask them what they'd like to see changed on your credit report to get approved or get the best rate. You'd be surprised at how helpful they are!

How Long Does Stuff Stay on Your Report?

The general rule is that most types of credit mistakes and missteps stay on your credit report for seven years. Sometimes, though, they can drop off after a shorter amount of time without any real explanation.

Items that stay on for seven years:

◆ Payments that are 30, 60, 90, or 120 days late

◆ Debt settlements

◆ Debt consolidations

◆ Accounts closed by the lender

◆ Foreclosures and repossessions

◆ Lawsuits

In addition, bankruptcies can stay on for 10 years and tax liens can stay on up to 15 years.

Steps to Raise Your Score

Unlike eliminating debt, there are a few more tips and tricks to raising your credit score. Don't get me wrong, the best way is still hard work and time. But there are plenty of little things you can do to raise your credit score here and there:

- **Pay your bills on time.** I always say in my workshops that everyone is no further away than seven years from having a near perfect credit score. The reality is, if the only thing you do is get current and stay current on your bills, the worst credit scores in the world will likely rank "average to good" within five to seven years.

- **Decrease your credit utilization by keeping cards open.** This technique can give you a significant pop in your score in a short period of time. The theory is, if you start paying off your credit cards and cancelling them, your utilization ratio will look worse, even though you are reducing your debts!

  For example, if you have two credit cards, one with a maxed-out $5,000 limit, and the other with an unused $5,000 limit, your utilization ratio shows as 50% ($5,000 used out of $10,000 possible). But if you close the unused card, your utilization now jumps to 100% ($5,000 used out of $5,000 possible). Shred the cards, but don't close your account.

- **Contest your errors.** A ridiculously high percentage of credit reports have some errors on them that have nothing to do with the individual. You will definitely want to request a copy of your entire credit report (not just your score) and contest every item that you think might be reported inaccurately. Even getting one late payment removed will boost your score noticeably.

- **Use rapid rescoring.** While this sounds like some kind of too-good-to-be-true technique, it's legit. The bummer is that you cannot access it on your own. How it works is that a lender you're working with documents an error you've found, and requests the credit bureau to immediately rescore your report. This can cut six months off getting your credit score adjusted for legitimate errors. Lenders usually charge between $50 and $100 for this service.

- **Remember that variety is key.** The credit score computation and lenders are increasingly interested in your ability to juggle multiple types of payments at one time. While it might be tempting to use your home equity to buy a car, your credit score will probably benefit from the variety of having two different types of loans.

Piggybacking is officially dead. Over the last few years, hundreds of thousands of consumers have used piggybacking to raise their credit scores. In piggybacking, someone with a low credit score would be added to someone with a higher-score account as an authorized user. Some of that higher credit score would then rub off on the person with the lower credit score. That was until 2008, when the Fair Isaac Corporation stopped including being an authorized user in the computation of your FICO score. Now, if you are an authorized user on someone else's account, there is no effect (negative or positive) on your score going forward.

Set a Goal

Before you leave this chapter, I want you to set a goal for what your credit score will be 12 months from today. Because you are not a credit expert and the secret formula is well guarded, you'll need to visit a "Credit Score Estimator" website and play with the numbers a little. One of my favorite websites, BankRate.com, has a great FICO Estimator in their calculator section. Plug in some different changes that you know you could make, and see how much it changes your score. Then open your Debt Journal and write "Credit score of ___ by ____ of next year."

The Least You Need to Know

◆ Credit scores help lenders predict whether or not you're likely to repay future loans they might make to you.

◆ Your FICO score is the most widely used credit score and can be calculated on the credit report from any of the three major credit reporting agencies.

◆ Over 50% of your credit score comes from making your payments on time and not being too maxed out on your existing debts.

◆ Most bad stuff like late payments stays on your credit report for a maximum of seven years, but bankruptcies and tax liens stay on for much longer.

◆ One of the quickest credit card fixes is contesting errors and using a rapid rescoring.

Chapter 21

Guarding Against Identity Theft

In This Chapter

- ◆ Why everyone's at risk
- ◆ What identify theft will cost you
- ◆ Identity theft in the twenty-first century
- ◆ How to protect yourself
- ◆ What to do if you're a victim

According to the Federal Trade Commission (FTC), identity theft is the fastest-growing crime in the United States. Millions of people will be victimized this year alone, at an ever-increasing cost.

It is not uncommon for identity theft victims to now have tens of thousands of dollars in loans and credit cards issued in their name, over the space of months, before they ever discover the crime. This is a far cry from getting your wallet or purse snatched a few decades ago.

Knowing how to prevent, identify, and respond to identity theft is crucial for all people, but especially those battling their way out of debt. On an already tight and stressed-out budget, having everything grind to a halt while you sort out the details of an identity theft situation will put you firmly back at square one.

Are You at Risk?

Whenever I do workshops on identity theft, I'll always have one or two people who are excited to inform me right off the bat that they are not at risk. They tell me how they shred all their statements and receipts, have a locking mailbox, never shop on the Internet, and don't sign the back of their credit cards. They're diligent and they don't foresee a problem.

What these people don't realize is that they have a 1980s view of identity theft. One where the criminals grabbed your purse as you walked down a crowded city street and proceeded to run up a few hundred dollars at gas stations around town, before the card got shut off. That's not how it works anymore. Not only have the criminals gotten far more sophisticated, but your data is everywhere! It's on other people's laptops, computer servers, and even floating around the Internet.

Consider the following incidents from the early part of 2008, and how they have nothing to do with how vigilant you are with your own personal info:

- The Bank of New York Mellon lost a computer tape containing the data of 4.5 million customers including names and Social Security numbers.

- Over 11,000 current and former students at the University of Florida Gainesville accidentally had their names, addresses, and Social Security numbers posted on the school's website.

- A laptop computer owned by the Harley Davidson Owners Group, called HOG for short, was stolen. The laptop contained the names, addresses, credit card numbers, and driver's license numbers of approximately 88,000 members.

> **In the Red**
>
> Just like with many other types of crime, a noticeable percentage of identity thefts are committed by people who know the victim in one capacity or another. They might be coworkers, employees, customers, or sadly, even friends or family. There is an especially high percentage of this crime against older family members being cared for by a younger son, daughter, or grandchild.

Still think you can be vigilant enough to keep it from happening to you? Unfortunately, you just can't. But that doesn't mean that you shouldn't give it your best try. While such incidents are outside of your control, there is still so much within your ability that can keep you from being an easy target.

> **Debt in America**
>
> The list of large companies and organizations who've had their information com-
> promised grows daily. In fact, if you visit the website www.PrivacyRights.org, you'll
> see that there are approximately 20 to 30 major incidents per month, with anywhere
> from hundreds to millions of people's information being compromised. Since it started
> tracking such incidents in 2005, it has estimated that there have been over 200 million
> pieces of private data breached. Make sure to visit www.IDTheftCenter.org and sign up
> for its free news feeds that will help you stay on top of companies that you work for or
> with.

The High Cost of Identity Theft

One of the other false beliefs many people have about identity theft is that if it does
happen to them, it won't cost them anything. They believe, correctly, that their legal
rights will make the banks or institutions absorb the bulk of any loss associated with
identity theft. While this is true, people who think this way are failing to take into
account the invisible and ongoing costs of identity theft, namely their time.

For more serious identity theft cases, the initial resolution of the case will usually cost
someone $1,000 to $2,000 out of pocket. Now, I'm not talking about the money you
lose to thieves here. I'm talking about the time you have to take off work, the money
you spend on gas driving around, notary fees, etc.

That's just for the first time. Remember, just because you get an identity theft wiped
off the books doesn't mean the thieves won't turn around and begin doing it all over
again. There's no way that I know of that you can track down the identity thief's
records, and "delete" your info. Even worse, identity thieves make a secondary business out of reselling your info to other unsavory types. Chances are, once you've been
hit, you'll continue to be picked on for years to come.

One of the scariest trends in identity theft is that thieves will actually use your identity
if they are arrested for minor crimes. Then, because they (who gave your name and
information) don't show up for their court case, warrants are actually issued for your
arrest. If you think that this may have happened to you, contact the FBI and your local
law enforcement agencies as soon as possible to begin clearing this up.

How Identity Theft Happens

Identity theft is usually a multistep process that involves a lot more than people making a fake ID and using your credit card at the mall. In fact, only amateur identity thieves would do something so stupid.

Here's how it usually goes down in the twenty-first century:

1. **They get your info.** I'll talk more about this in a second, but it is so unbelievably easy that it'll make you sick. Just to give you a short example, when I was in college a law enforcement buddy of mine wanted to prove people's gullibility to me while we were staying at a hotel. He went over to one of those house phones in the lobby, picked it up, and dialed a random room number. When they answered, this is all he said: "Hi, this is Mr. Johnson down at the front desk, we had trouble processing your credit card. Could you please read me your information so we could process it again?" He held up the phone where I could hear it, and sure enough, someone was reading his or her card number to a complete stranger standing in the hotel lobby.

2. **They get a fake address.** With a little bit of info and a $25 fake ID, an identity thief can walk into your local PO Box rental store and get a mailbox with your name on it. Now they've got a safe place to send all your mail to. How would you ever know?

3. **They start opening accounts online.** It's pretty amazing to me that you can open a bank account online, without ever having to see a human face-to-face. There's absolutely nothing to prevent an impostor with your information from opening bank, credit card, and loan accounts in your name online.

4. **They create a mountain of paperwork.** This is one of the key things that is causing the damages in identity theft cases to escalate. By maintaining those accounts for 6 to 12 months in your name, keeping them paid up and current, they now have a paper trail making them look even more like you. They can then make bigger and bolder thefts that they could not make without your last six months' bank statements.

> **Dollars and Sense**
>
> If you've lost your driver's license or had it stolen, contact your state's Department of Motor Vehicles as soon as possible. Just like with credit card agencies, many states' DMV departments can place an alert on your card, which would keep someone from getting duplicates issued or getting a new picture taken.

5. **They go for the gold.** Once they've got a mountain of paperwork, some big credit lines or loans, they take you to town. They buy cars, take vacations, take large cash advances—all with no intent of paying the bills when they come due in a month or two.

6. **They disappear.** With $100,000 or more in false charges in your name, they close the mailbox, close the accounts, and effectively disappear. By the time you discover it, they're on to using someone else's identity here in the United States, and probably have sold your info to someone overseas.

That's sickening, isn't it? The worst part is it all happens and is finished before you have even the slightest clue.

Protecting Your Vital Information

In the old days, when you couldn't fit file cabinets full of information on something the size of your TV remote control, all you really had to do was keep your stuff locked up. But with the advent of the Internet and computer storage, there are many more opportunities for people to get what they need to do serious damage to your financial life.

But before you start living your life in day-to-day fear, I want to give you some hope. I think it is best illustrated by a joke about two guys and grizzly bear.

As it goes, there were these two hikers on a day hike through the local mountains. As they turn a bend in the trail, they come face-to-face with the largest grizzly bear they've ever seen. One of the guys turns around and starts running. His buddy, the nature expert, says, "Don't run. You can't outrun a grizzly. Just play dead." To this, his buddy yells back, "I don't need to outrun the bear, I just need to outrun you!"

The point is, thieves will go after the easiest target they can find. They don't want to work any harder or expose themselves to any more risk than they have to. While you can't make yourself invisible to identity thieves, you can make yourself a lot more difficult to take advantage of than the next person. For example, when I tell people how identity thieves love to go through the recycle bins in front of people's houses on trash night, they all get a look of panic on their face. Then I tell them, though, that a fresh "dirty" diaper from their toddler, strategically placed right on top of the pile of papers, is enough to make most thieves move on to their neighbor's bin.

In the Red _____

We don't think much about how our "personal trash" is cared for by other people, but it's worth asking. Most of us fill out numerous applications with our personal information throughout the year, for everything from jobs to rentals to loans. So what happens to all those applications? Do they just get wadded up and thrown in a company's dumpster? I hope not, but I know they often do. As you're filing out your next application, try to remember to ask "Where does this go when we're all done with it?" If you don't get a satisfactory answer, consider taking your business elsewhere.

You just have to make yourself a less attractive target than the next guy. With that in mind, here are some of my favorite techniques (don't worry, that was the only one that required a dirty diaper):

- **Get a locking mailbox.** It's hard to believe, with identity theft as rampant as it is, that people still have unlocked mailboxes at the end of their driveway. It only takes a criminal a little bit of observation to figure out exactly when you're not home and to swing by and sift through your mail. If possible, get a locking mailbox or put a mail slot in your garage or front door.

- **Shred everything.** As I've mentioned, thieves love paper. If they can find bank statements, order forms, tax returns, anything, they'll find a way to use it. Just like the dirty diaper, though, if your trash is filled with shredded paper, they're going to move on to the next person who doesn't make them work so hard.

- **Be careful what you carry.** Whenever I do classes, I ask how many people carry their Social Security card in their purse or wallet. Usually, about half the hands in the room go up. I know it may seem like a wise idea, but if your wallet gets lost, they've got your ID, credit cards, blank checks with your account number, and your Social Security number—think they can do some damage with that? The same goes for birth certificates, which have that absolutely invaluable piece of information on it—your mother's maiden name!

- **Secure your network.** One of the coolest tech innovations of the last decade is wireless Internet. Now, instead of having to sit at a desk to use your computer, you can surf the net during family dinner nights, while you simultaneously watch TV, or from the hammock in your yard. As cool as that is, though, it's also a magnet for high-tech thieves. If you stand at the end of my driveway and boot up your laptop, you're able to log on to four of my neighbors' networks without a password. I can't begin to tell you how to exploit that, but I could probably grab a 12-year-old who'd be able to explain it to us both.

◆ **Don't "autosave" your passwords.** As I listed all those major cases of identity theft in the beginning of the chapter, you probably cringed in disgust at the carelessness of some of these folks. Yet so many of these computers that are stolen are laptops in public places. It only takes a split second in the local coffee shop, while you go to grab some creamer, for someone to walk by and discretely snatch your laptop. Now, while you probably don't have 4.5 million Social Security numbers on there, you may have your bank account login "saved" so you don't have to key it every time. Considering that the vast majority of us use the same password for everything, it doesn't take long before a thief is off to the races.

◆ **Take care when taking vacations.** Okay, vacations by themselves don't lead to identity theft, but the pile of newspapers at the end of your driveway do! It's a sign that you're not there and no one is grabbing your mail for you. While you're enjoying the sunset and a tropical drink somewhere, con artists are enjoying your mail. You should always get the post office and your newspapers to hold your mail, or have a friend drop by daily to collect everything.

In the Red

Depending on whom you talk to, shopping online is either the scariest thing in the world or the greatest convenience known to man. But few fans of online shopping know how to tell if a website is secure or not. One of the most basic ways is to look for the "padlock" and "https." Pages that use industry standard security features will cause a small padlock symbol to appear somewhere in your browser's information bar. This is usually accompanied by the beginning of a website's address changing to "https" from "http" when you go to an order page. Avoid shopping on any unsecure website to truly minimize your risk.

I could write a whole other book of all the different ways people expose themselves to identity theft, but I'm hoping that you get the idea. Thieves are looking for any little way they can find to get your info. You've got to be one step ahead of them and make yourself a difficult target.

Phishing

I want to take a moment and highlight phishing (pronounced "fishing"). Because it is one of those identity theft techniques that can cause the most damage, phishing deserves special attention. Avoiding it is as simple as pie, because you are the "piece of information" they are trying to tap into. If you just keep your lips zipped, you won't get phished.

Remember the story about my friend calling the hotel guest and asking for his or her credit card number? That's phishing. It is someone trying to get you to reveal information about yourself, so that they can take it and exploit it.

Phishing is usually employed by someone who has a little bit of information about you and can use "perceived authority" to get a lot more. Perceived authority is the ability to convince us that they are someone official and that we need to submit to their requests; kind of like my friend saying he was the front desk manager at the hotel.

> **Dollars and Sense**
>
> In recent years, there have been a number of cases of unscrupulous waiters "skimming" your credit card when they take it up to process your bill. Many times, they use high-tech devices that look like a pager, which allows them to quickly swipe your card and record its information. To be truly safe, consider walking your bill up to the register at more casual restaurants.

The way phishing usually starts is someone will "shoulder surf" you at the gas pump or the ATM. They'll literally watch over your shoulder, in person or with binoculars, as you input your PIN. Then they'll jot down your license plate number and go through the trash to find your receipt (which typically only has the last four digits of your account number). After a quick trip to the DMV or by using an online records search, they've got your name and address and can probably find your phone number using a reverse directory.

Then, during dinnertime, you get a call like this:

Them: Hi Mrs. Jones, this is Jay Bell, I'm a fraud investigator with ABC Bank where you have your account.

You: Um, okay.

Them: Sorry to bother you, but we think there has been some fraud on your account, last four digits 1234, PIN 9999.

(Remember, they got that information by pulling your receipt out of the trash and looking over your shoulder.)

You: Oh my.

Them: Before we go any further, we need to verify that we are speaking to the right person. Is that account we mentioned yours?

You: Yep.

Them: Okay, thank you. Can you please verify your Social Security number …

That's it. They've got you singing like a canary. They might even throw in the purchase they know you made (because they have the receipt) to make it sound even more official. At this point, you'll tell them anything they want to know.

Avoiding phishing is simple. If you get a call like that, just tell them you'll call them right back and hang up the phone. Grab your credit or debit card, flip it over, and call the number on the back. If it was a legitimate call to begin with, they'll have an open file on it and you can get cracking. If not, you know someone's trying to scam you.

Spoofing

Spoofing is the computer equivalent of phishing and can be just as easy to fall for. Instead of an incoming phone call, you get a really official-looking e-mail about your account. It's got all the disclosures at the bottom, links (or so you think) to your bank's website, and even a few offers for banking products.

Of course, when you click on the link, it takes you to a website that looks identical to your real bank's website, including a place to input your username and password. Of course, when you input that info, it gets sent to the criminal who then turns around, logs on to your account, and drains it as quick as you can say "ouch!"

The same advice holds true as for phishing. Delete the e-mail and call your bank or credit card company as soon as possible.

Dollars and Sense

Did you know that a deleted e-mail isn't really deleted, even after you empty the "Recycle Bin" on your computer? In fact, unless your computer's memory is completely maxed out, it's likely that that e-mail is still floating around on there somewhere. To truly delete private files, especially if you use any financial software like Quicken or TurboTax, you should consider a "Wipe" program. A wipe program is the equivalent of taking a black marker and crossing the information out. But instead of a marker, your computer actually overwrites the deleted file with nonsensical information. These Wipe programs usually come bundled with other programs such as Anti-Virus or Firewall programs.

Monitoring Your Identity

As I've mentioned, even the most vigilant and secretive person can still get his or her identity stolen because of the carelessness of others. Because of this, you have to be proactive about reviewing your financial information on a regular basis. By doing so, you may catch something in the very early stages of happening, which will not only cover your tail, but also give the authorities a good chance at catching the thief.

Checking Your Credit Report

You can get your free credit report once per year from each agency at www. annualcreditreport.com. While you can get all three credit reports at once, I'd recommend spacing them out to receive one every four months. This would allow you to keep a more regular eye on things.

In addition to this free service, many banks offer free credit reports as one of their account features. You can also request a copy of your credit report from your lender anytime you apply for a loan.

Credit Monitoring Services

The jury is still out for me on these things. I think for most people who are vigilant, the chances of a crime are low enough that they shouldn't waste $100 to $200 per year on credit monitoring services. But then again, the costs and frustrations are great enough that it's arguably worth it. I personally use a service, but then again, I've had fraud committed against me already, so I need it to cut more fraud off at the pass.

If you do decide to go with one of these services, I'd buy it straight from one of the big three credit agencies. Their basic service is more than sufficient, and you shouldn't be paying more than $10 to $15 per month.

Review Every Statement

I've already encouraged you to review every credit card and bank statement with a highlighter each month as part of growing your own financial consciousness. But it also serves to keep you aware of the beginnings of suspicious activity.

Many times, the lazier identity thieves who are going to charge stuff on your existing cards will start by testing the account. They'll charge $10 here and there, to see if you pick up on it and cut that card number off. After a few months, if you haven't caught on, they'll take you to town.

The Next Steps If You've Been a Victim

If you've been an identity theft victim, you've got to be proactive. In fact, your protection under the law is in part based on how quickly you report identity theft after it has been discovered. The Fair Credit Billing Act limits your liability on fraudulent credit card charges to $50 per card. However, if you fail to act in a timely manner you could be held responsible for additional charges that a company might have to absorb, which may set your debt reduction plan back significantly.

If you've been a victim, take the following steps immediately:

1. **Contact your compromised account's institution.** First and foremost, you need to work to limit your and your lender's losses on the compromised account. Before you even bother calling the police, call your company's 24-hour fraud prevention line. Be sure to keep a list of your account numbers and each company's contact number (found on the back of each card) in a secure place. This will keep you from wasting valuable time looking for that information in the event of a theft or loss.

2. **Contact your other lenders and companies.** If you haven't actually had your other companies' cards or account numbers compromised, you won't likely need to go through the hassle of having the account numbers changed. But these companies will put a "fraud alert" on your account that helps them watch for suspicious activity.

3. **Contact the credit agencies.** Just like you placed a fraud alert on your existing accounts, you'll want to get one placed on your whole identity. Thankfully, by just calling any one of the agencies, they'll pass the word on to the others. There are two types of alerts you can place through the credit agencies. An Initial Alert, which can be put in place with a phone call, stays active for 90 days. An Extended Alert, which requires a police report as well, stays active for seven years.

   If you are not expecting to apply for credit anytime soon and the theft was part of a more complex scam, you can also request a freeze on your credit report, which keeps anyone from even looking at your credit report. That will effectively keep anyone from getting a loan in your name, because lenders can't even look at your credit report without your permission.

4. **Contact the authorities.** Yes, after contacting all three of those other parties first, you should now contact the authorities. The reason I place this one fourth is that the police really don't do a whole lot. I can promise you it's not the first identity theft report they've received that day, and they aren't going to send a team from the crime lab over to start dusting for prints. In fact, you should

realize that the police departments are so overwhelmed that you probably won't ever hear anything from them after you file the initial report. However, you do need that initial report to assert your rights with your creditors.

5. **Report the crime to the FTC.** The Federal Trade Commission doesn't actually pursue identity thieves themselves, but they do share information with law enforcement nationwide. You can reach the FTC Identity Theft Line at 877-IDTHEFT.

6. **Tell debt collectors if an account is from ID theft.** If an account that has gone to collections is an account that was fraudulently opened by someone else, collection agencies have to cease collections, cannot sell the debt to anyone else, and must notify the original creditor.

7. **Sign up for a credit monitoring service.** Once you've been the victim of identity theft, I'd go ahead and sign up for one of the credit monitoring services. Don't get too enthralled with fancy features like "E-mail Alerts" or financial guarantees. The biggest reason to sign up is that you can look at your credit report as often as you want to see if there have been any new inquiries, residences, or accounts reported on your histories. With any new discoveries, repeat this process from Step 1.

> **Dollars and Sense**
>
> Under new laws that went into effect as part of the Fair and Accurate Credit Transaction Act (FACTA), a debt collection agency must provide you with statements and applications from fraudulent accounts if they're available. Once you've requested these (because the police won't do it for you), be sure to forward copies on to law enforcement.

The Least You Need to Know

- Identity theft can happen to anyone because of another person's or company's carelessness.

- Identity theft can cost you hundreds of hours and thousands of dollars getting it straightened out, even after your loss is reimbursed.

- The biggest key to avoiding identity theft is to make yourself more difficult than the average victim.

- You should monitor your credit report and statements regularly for suspicious activity.

- Always contact your bank or credit card company immediately to ensure they absorb the entire loss.

Chapter 22

Avoiding Scams and Rip-Offs

In This Chapter

- ◆ Ten rules to live by
- ◆ Services that are the biggest wastes of money
- ◆ The top scams to watch out for
- ◆ What to do if you've been scammed

There's an old saying that reminds me of how many people feel when they're trapped at the bottom of the pit of debt. "Desperate times call for desperate measures," or so the saying goes.

The endless onslaught of calls and bills, the ease with which progress seems to be erased, and the ongoing anxiety of not knowing when it will all end leaves many people open to just about any solution. While that openness often can lead people to adopt radical lifestyle and spending changes which truly do get them out of debt, it can also lead people to believe just about anything.

Whether it is online moneymaking scams, too-good-to-be-true debt relief techniques, or methods with questionable ethics, people deep in debt are prone to believe the outlandish promises of others.

Back to the Basics

I want you to dog-ear or bookmark this page. You are going to want to come back and reread it before you make any major decisions about innovative debt reduction techniques, get-rich-quick schemes, and ideas with legal gray areas.

Here are 10 things you need to remind yourself of over and over again, as well as some thoughts to keep you on the straight and narrow:

1. Getting out of debt doesn't happen overnight, but it is inevitable if you change your money habits and attitudes.

2. If a technique sounds too good to be true, it is.

3. No for-profit company truly cares about you as much as they care about making a profit off of you.

4. Just because someone claims that they're a nonprofit doesn't mean they are.

5. If a get-rich scheme really worked, they wouldn't be trying to sell it to other people!

6. Nobody gives away free money!

7. Cutting a little bit of time off your debt reduction plan with a legally questionable technique isn't worth a fine or jail time.

8. Most "free" things have a catch or a cost.

9. You will survive your debt—there's no need for reckless solutions!

10. Your creditors don't hate you; they just want their money back.

> **Dollars and Sense**
>
> One of my favorite sites for detecting different scams is www.ScamBusters.org. You can sign up for a free e-mail newsletter that keeps you informed on the latest versions of the classic scams.

The Biggest Wastes of Money

In the debt reduction industry, there are a lot of people promising a lot of things. Unfortunately, most of those services are a big waste of money in that they either accomplish something you could have done for free, or they don't accomplish anything at all.

Before you sign up for anyone's services, you need to ask yourself if it is possible to get the same benefits elsewhere for free. If you cannot, or if you are too overwhelmed to handle this piece of your debt reduction plan yourself, you need to get a company's guarantees and promises in writing.

From the start, I'd remind you that a reputable attorney is the one place that I'd always opt for professional help, especially in matters of bankruptcy (see Chapter 18). These issues are so complex that their expertise will ensure a speedy and accurate processing of your case.

Debt Elimination

When someone promises to "eliminate your debt" I can only guess that they are one of three things: a bankruptcy attorney, a sugar daddy, or someone who is convinced they have magical powers. The reality is, people who are owed money aren't really that keen on having their "balances" eliminated.

In the Red

One of the classic scams associated with debt settlement companies is that you make monthly payments to them while they are busy negotiating with your creditors. Of course, the fact that money is not going to your creditors only angers them more and causes them to pursue you harder than ever. To add insult to injury, the debt settlement companies will often charge a handling fee ranging from 10% to 30% of whatever payments they negotiate. In essence, you are paying a company to delay your payments even further, shrinking them in the process with their service fees.

No amount of yelling, screaming, letter writing, or phone calls to their "internal contact" at your company will get a debt erased. A debt is what it is and can only be eliminated by one of the following methods:

- Paying it off
- Proving it is not yours
- Filing for bankruptcy
- Negotiating a portion of it away
- A natural disaster that destroys your lender (actually, they'd still probably find a way to collect!)

The only things on the list that you can't do yourself involve legal matters and acts of God, both of which I recommend outside help on.

Debt Negotiation

The only real difference between you and a "debt negotiator" is that you don't have your own late-night infomercial. The truth is, you are absolutely entitled to deal on your own behalf with your lender or credit card company. The company cannot deny you the right to contact them and try to negotiate your debt.

By paying someone to do this for you, you are only going to add to your costs and time associated with getting out of debt. Even if you don't believe me, you might as well at least give it a try before you sink the money into a hired gun. Copy the debt settlement offer letter out of Appendix B and make an offer that's 10% to 30% of what you owe.

Free Credit Reports

Signing up for a "free" credit report will likely cost you a lot more than nothing, which is my definition of free. A lot of times, these companies have slick, even funny commercials that offer to provide you with a free credit report or score.

But, as always seems to happen, you start seeing a mysterious charge on your bank statement for $12.95 per month. When you finally make sense of who is charging you, and call that company offering the "free" credit report to find out why you're being charged, you get the world's greatest run around.

As I've mentioned before, there is only one truly free source for a free credit report, and that is the credit reporting agencies themselves. You can access that report at www.annualcreditreport.com.

The classic free credit report red flag that unfortunately hooks person after person is a company's requirement that you enter your credit card number to verify your ID. Of course, somewhere in the fine print, it also says that they're going to bill the credit card from here to eternity for some service you never wanted in the first place.

Credit Protection

When a company offers to protect your credit, backing it with a million dollar guarantee, you need to realize that it's all smoke and mirrors. Besides an occasional e-mail telling you that something has changed on your credit report, most of these companies don't do anything to justify a fee that may be $20 to $50 per month.

In fact, their bold promise to protect you for up to a million dollars worth of damage is a load of marketing manure. By law, your lenders cannot hold you responsible above minimal amounts for charges and loans you did not authorize. Its million-dollar promise does nothing more than refer you to the legal protections already in place for every consumer.

Remember, you can check one of your three credit reports for free every three to four months by visiting www.AnnualCreditReport.com.

Credit Repair

As I mentioned in Chapter 20, the only cure for a lousy credit score is time. Everything except bankruptcies and government liens drops off your credit report after seven years. Someone who promises that he or she can get these things to drop off earlier is selling you a promise he or she can't deliver.

Additionally, any errors or discrepancies you find on your credit report can easily be handled by you over a couple of lunch breaks. Under the new laws of the last few years, both lenders and the credit agencies have made it much easier for you to contact them and dispute how something was reported or fraudulent activity.

There is no real way to repair your credit overnight, and only a few proven ways to boost your score in a short period of time. Stick to what is in this book, and you'll have done all you can do.

> **Dollars and Sense**
>
> Before you ever waste money on credit repair services, contact the Better Business Bureau in your town and the company's town to see if there are complaints regarding their services. Visit them at www.BBB.org for a contact in your local area.

Seminars and Workshops

My guess is that many seminars and workshops you might attend on dealing with debt problems actually provide you with some great information. The problem is, 99% of it will be the information I've already covered in this book.

Before you shell out $99 or more for a workshop, see if you can get a breakdown of the topics. If there isn't new subject matter mentioned above and beyond this book's contents, consider putting that money toward one of your balances.

The same is true for additional books about managing your debt. It's very likely that there are other good ones out there, but they won't really provide you with any new information beyond what you've read here.

I would recommend, however, picking up books on the more broad topics of personal finance, investing, and planning for retirement or your children's college education. Each one of those topics is complex in and of itself, and deserves your full attention at some point. The *Complete Idiot's Guide* series offers some outstanding books on these topics.

In case you're wondering about the books that have meant the most to me in my own financial journey, there are three that I'd highly recommend. *The Millionaire Next Door* by Thomas Stanley is a demographic study of wealth in the United States. *The Richest Man in Babylon* by George Clason is a fun and short piece of historical fiction based around personal finance topics in ancient Babylon. Last but not least, *Extraordinary Popular Delusions and the Madness of Crowds* by Charles McKay takes a look at financial fads over the last 500 years. See Appendix C for details on these and other books.

Get-Rich Schemes That Don't Work

Before we close the books on things to watch out for, I do want to give you some quick thoughts on the different get-rich-quick schemes I've seen over the years. Suffice it to say, most of these don't work, and the only people getting rich are the ones who are trying to get you to say yes.

Multilevel Marketing

Whether it is makeup, vitamins, kids' toys, candles, or cookware, most multilevel marketing businesses fail miserably. These programs ultimately rely on you to market their amazing products to your friends and family, who usually buy one or two things to be supportive and then never buy anything again.

Because the companies do not teach you how to truly sell and market, and aside from the fact that direct sales is brutally hard for even seasoned professionals, it is an almost guaranteed matter of time before you have a garage full of inventory that no one wants. Since these programs usually require you to buy some inventory on the front end or pay an enrollment fee, you end up losing that money, setting you farther behind.

Easy Money in Real Estate

Yet another one of my favorite late-night infomercials … it's the guy who was making no money in his dead-end job, until he signed up for this great program that lets him buy real estate for no money down. Now he's got so many checks coming in that he can't find the time to cash them!

Really, if you could buy real estate for no money down, it'd be snapped up by people with a lot more money, resources, and smarts in real estate than you or me. Of course, by the time you figure that out, your initial fee and their money-back period are long gone. Send that money to your credit card instead of the guy on TV in the nice suit.

Dollars and Sense _____

I think they run those infomercials so late at night because the only people watching them are too tired to think clearly about what is being pitched. There's a whole website devoted to debunking these late-night infomercial scams called www. InfomercialScams.com. Next time you can't sleep, spend a few hours reading this site instead of watching the infomercials themselves.

Day-Trading and Currency Transactions

I'll be blunt. I'm a former stockbroker and I'm not sure I could day-trade stocks, currency options, or pork bellies to save my life. But if you believe the commercials, anyone who knows how to use a computer can makes thousands each week.

Unfortunately, it's just not true. Financial institutions with their supercomputers, trading programs, and huge trading staffs will almost always beat the little guy in the day-trading arena. Don't get me wrong, I think the stock market is the way to go for long-term investments. But I wouldn't consider buying a stock and selling it five minutes later a long-term investment.

Scams That Are Also Illegal

I think it's worth mentioning the moneymaking scams and schemes I often see people get duped into that are both foolish and illegal. Some of them are downright dangerous.

While you may find it hard to believe that people fall for some of these, it happens every day. In fact, some demographic groups like teenagers and seniors are continually being scammed because they are both relatively new to the Internet.

Nigerian 419 Scams

These e-mails border on absurd once you've seen a few of them, but if you've never seen one before, it sends your imagination running wild. What a dream come true this would be for someone who was eyeballs deep in debt!

The e-mail, which tends to originate from a foreign country on the African continent, seems to be sent from someone with a problem you can help solve. You see, they've got $20 million sitting in a bank account in a country that's in the midst of a civil war or unrest. They're afraid that if they don't get it out soon, it'll be lost due to the corrupt government. But, for one reason or another, they can't withdraw the money themselves. However, they can transfer it to someone else's bank account. If you would be willing to accept the transfer, they'd be willing to give you $5 million of the money. You'll then transfer the rest to their Swiss Bank account. What a deal!

This is actually a scam that has not only ripped off Americans, but also gotten them killed. Once they've got you hooked, then all sorts of problems start, such as you needing to pay certain transfer fees, etc. Eventually, they ask you to fly to their country to pick up the check; they've even been known to hold some people for ransom.

As I listed in the rules at the beginning of the chapter, if it sounds too good to be true, it is.

> **In the Red**
>
> Nigerian 419 scams (a.k.a. "advance-fee" scams) are a major concern of the U.S. government due to the high level of losses being experienced by trusting Americans. If you receive an offer for one of these, or other versions of the scam that claim you've won a foreign lottery, report it immediately to the Federal Trade Commission at www.FTC.org.

Chain Letters

Chain letters are one of the oldest scams out there and have experienced a resurgence thanks to e-mail. Chain letters are essentially pyramid schemes, where the people at the top of the program make more money as more lower-level people are duped into participating.

What happens is you receive an e-mail inviting you to participate in this money-making program. To participate, you send $50 to the person who sent you the e-mail and then send an e-mail instructing 8 to 12 other people to do the same. When they send you $50 each (that's $600), you keep most of it, but also send a percentage to the person who invited you to participate. All your people do the same as well, and everyone makes a whole bunch of money.

> **Debt in America** _____
>
> College students are one of the largest targeted groups for certain moneymaking schemes like chain letters and other types of pyramid schemes. If you have a child or relative in college, take a few minutes to warn them about both the rip-off and the illegality of these scams and schemes.

Unfortunately, someone always gets the short end of the stick in this deal, because it is always relying on new participants. A bunch of people always end up losing their money in these deals, which is perhaps why you can get fined and jailed for participating in one.

If You've Been Scammed or Duped

If you or your family member has been scammed or duped, you should take immediate action to protect yourself and recover whatever funds possible. The sooner you act, the more likely it is that you'll protect yourself and be able to get your money back.

For legitimate businesses and so-called nonprofits offering debt-related services or moneymaking scams, your best bet is bad publicity. You can call and yell all you want, but they're used to that. You'll eventually get over it. But if you show that you're serious about hurting their ability to make more money, they usually pay you off so they can get on scamming other folks.

In these situations, what I'll usually have a client do is write up a nasty letter addressed to a local newspaper, outlining the scam or rip-off that occurred. Make sure you are completely truthful, so as not to be legally liable for falsely bad-mouthing a company or person. The letter will usually say something like "I would recommend that you avoid this company and tell everyone you know to do the same."

Then, fax a copy of it to the company that ripped you off, with instructions where to send your refund. Inform them that, if they do not promptly give you a full refund, you will make sure every newspaper, TV station, and Better Business Bureau within a 100-mile radius gets this letter.

If this does not bring action, do as you promised, as well as contacting your state's attorney general and the Federal Trade Commission.

Report illegal scams that you are invited to participate in to the FBI (www.FBI.gov), the U.S. Treasury Department (www.USTreas.gov), and the U.S. Postal Inspector (http://postalinspectors.uspis.gov).

Dollars and Sense _____

Just because someone has an .org after their website's name doesn't mean they're a nonprofit. Before you work with any nonprofit organization, I recommend taking a glance at their records and tax returns, which you can find online. By looking at an organization's Form 990 tax return, you can get a better understanding of what exactly the organization does with its money. Visit www.GuideStar.com to do a free nonprofit organization search.

The Least You Need to Know

- Stick to your debt reduction goals and plans. Don't get distracted with fancy solutions that sound too good to be true.

- Most "miracles" that companies promise to work on your behalf are things you can do easily and for free.

- If you want to earn extra money, get a weekend job. Stay away from get-rich-quick ideas.

- Before you respond to an e-mail promising vast riches for a few minutes of your time, do a little bit of Internet research.

- If you have been scammed or duped, threaten to make a public scene and create negative publicity if you don't get an immediate refund.

Part 5

Life After Debt

In the classic 1960s TV show *Gilligan's Island*, those seven unlucky cast-aways were eventually rescued from that uncharted desert isle. What did they do to celebrate? They took a reunion cruise, of course. Then, as fate would have it, they got shipwrecked again on the exact same island they had recently escaped from!

Like the castaways, perhaps the only thing worse than being in debt is getting back into it once you've worked so hard to get out. In this last part, you'll identify the best ways to use credit and loans properly in the future, tools to keep from accidentally slipping back into debt, and methods for passing on healthy financial habits to your family.

Chapter 23

You and Debt: Is It Really Over?

In This Chapter

- ◆ Adjusting your financial attitude
- ◆ Dealing with existing commitments
- ◆ Using credit in the future
- ◆ Shopping around for the best rates
- ◆ Money talks: yours, mine, and ours

Ever since middle school, I've been a sucker for movies and TV shows about romances that just weren't meant to be. You know, those couples who kind of had that love/hate relationship with each other. They couldn't stand each other, but then again they couldn't stand to be apart, either.

You and credit have that kind of relationship. In fact, I think most of us have that relationship with borrowing money. We hate it when we're stuck in it, but it feels like there are times we can't live without it. We are suckers for it, and it's always there for us.

But I think it is time to grow up. To call it for what it is … an unhealthy relationship. It's time to say "Girlfriend, you need to be moving on! You deserve better!"

A Shift in Attitude

You picked up this book because you wanted things to change. You've worked hard throughout it to put these changes into place. But, as with all things, the biggest change that needs to occur is within your own attitude about the use of borrowed money. If this doesn't change, things will inevitably drift back to where they were before you started on this journey.

How has your attitude about money changed since you started the book? What is the biggest thing that has changed in how you view the use of borrowed money? What's the single biggest piece of advice you'd pass on to someone if you had 30 seconds to talk about debt?

In cognitive behavioral therapy, which has been proven to be one of the most effective methods of changing unwanted behaviors, you're forced to deal with your irrational thoughts. These thoughts, if allowed to continue to reside within you, will eventually turn into attitudes. And of course, these attitudes affect your actions.

To solidify and make permanent all your hard work, let's start by looking at and disarming some of these irrational thoughts about your use of credit and debt. If we don't, these separate attitudes, temporarily defeated by your hard work throughout this book, might reunite for a victory tour.

You Can't Live Without Borrowing

Of course you can. A statistically significant portion of the country does. But living without it may mean living without certain other things. It may mean having to delay getting what you want or enjoy. It may mean you have to say no even when saying yes would be so fun. It means you'll have to budget and think about what gets spent and when.

You *can* live without it. In fact, the vast majority of people who have wealth in this country got there without a whole lot of borrowing. Rather, they did it by minimizing their spending until they could save enough to buy the things they really wanted.

> **Debt in America**
>
> People use the word *wealthy* to describe someone who seems to have money dripping off them. Their clothes, watch, car, sunglasses all seem to advertise the fact that they've made it. As a financial planner, though, I'm always curious to know people's *net worth*. It's neat that they have all those things, but when you subtract out what they owe, are they really worth anything? A few years ago, there was a TV show called *Who Wants to Marry a Millionaire?* Well, it turns out that the millionaire wasn't quite worth a million bucks when someone finally did the math and subtracted out what he owed on all his real estate.

Budgeting Is Impossible Without a Credit Card

Of course it's not. It might be easier to use a credit card than having to think about your spending as you go, but then again a solid budget and spending plan takes care of that for you.

What has been impossible, or felt like it at least, was getting out of this state of debt that you've been in. The use of credit, which was supposed to make your life easier, has really made it substantially harder.

Using Credit for Life's Big Purchases

Borrowing money is often necessary for life's big purchases, especially if you haven't planned ahead at all. It's a little too black and white to say that you either borrow money or you don't ever enjoy a car, house, or college education.

The reality is, there's plenty of middle ground in there. By saving money toward these goals and keeping your use of loans to a minimum, you may end up having to borrow far less to enjoy certain things than if you did nothing.

It Pays to Have Debt

I'll often hear people argue that credit card usage and certain types of borrowing are a wise choice because the interest is deductible, they get airlines miles, or their card gives them cash back. But the truth is that all these things are more discounts than they are rewards. They make borrowing money slightly cheaper, but don't even come close to making it a good investment.

By all means, you should use the best lenders and types of loans when you have to. But don't just use them because you can. This kind of debt attitude helps to blind you to the damaging effects of debt as you spend and borrow.

> **Dollars and Sense** _____
>
> If you can't imagine living without rewards as you move to a cash-only spending plan, there's good news for you! A growing number of banks are offering debit cards (which subtract money directly from your existing balance) that pay a reward for their usage. While the rewards are not quite as big as your credit card, it's a nice compromise for many!

You Need to Borrow to Build Credit

Besides the fact that this is at least partially untrue, the reality is that you probably end up hurting your credit scores more than helping them. Most people do more damage mismanaging their first credit accounts than they ever gain by having them.

You Won't Be Able to Handle Emergencies Without Debt

I think you are really selling yourself short on this one. The reality is, in this day and age, few people go from the desk job to being homeless because they get laid off or have a medical emergency. If they do, it's because they couldn't keep up with their monthly payments on all their existing loans and cards when one of those things happened.

What is more likely is most of us know that we'd have to buckle down if an emergency came along. Being able to borrow helps ensure that the effects of an emergency on your lifestyle are minimal. Sadly, those rainy-day credit cards and home equity lines of credit (HELOCs) sit there, beckoning you to use them to help you enjoy the sunny days as well.

Getting Your Last Hurrah

One of the hardest parts for many people working through a debt elimination plan is the future plans they had that were based on the use of a credit card. Maybe it was a trip next summer with the family, a major update to the wardrobe, or that special occasion with the person they adore.

Whatever it is, you now face a tough question. You've resolved to avoid debt, but you had previously planned something that you and maybe others were counting on, which will require the use of debt. What do you do? Do you make an exception this one time and then get back to doing what you're supposed to?

Before you answer, you need to consider the risk you are facing. There's a good chance, based on my experience working with people trying to eliminate debt, that if you use a credit card once, you'll rationalize it and use it a bunch of times. Chances are, your expenditures won't just be limited to that event, but you'll use borrowed money to make other purchases a couple weeks before and a couple weeks after. From there, you find yourself on the slippery slope saying, "Ah, screw it. I'll get back on track next month," but then never do.

Even if you do use your available credit only for that event, people tend to use it with a vengeance. It's almost like they're saying to themselves, "This is my last hurrah before I've got to get serious about my debts, let's go out in style!"

Of course, either of these leaves a mess for you to clean up when the party is all over. Thus, my unpopular advice is pay cash or change your plans. Sorry.

> **In the Red**
>
> The longer that you wait to change your plans, the more costly it's going to be. Whether it's a vacation, a night at the theater, or that catalog item you purchased, a call today or tomorrow may catch it in time to cancel with little or no fees.

Here are some tips for dealing with the emotional and social ramifications on changing that family vacation from Kauai to Kansas, or that girls' night out from sushi to Subway:

- **Talk honestly about why.** People who really care for you will not be angry that you're making the right choices for your own financial health. They may be bummed just like you, to not spend a week lying on the beach. But, especially when they see how sad you are to change plans, they'll likely step up and assure you that it's okay.

- **Think creatively.** One of the things I learned early on about my wife is that the gift itself took a distant second place to how much effort I put into dreaming it up. My wife doesn't need me to buy her $500 shoes (though I don't think she'd complain). What she needs is to know that I think enough of her to spend a Saturday secretly driving all over town to find her favorite candy. In truth, I'm no different!

◆ **Invite them to help plan.** Whatever plans you need to change, ask your friends and family to help you think creatively about what else you and the group can do to enjoy each other's company.

◆ **Postpone it.** As my wife and I were battling to get rid of debt years ago, there were a number of times when we had to make the frustrating decision to cancel or postpone something. After we did it, though, we almost always felt a deep sense of peace and even relief that we didn't just dig ourselves deeper into debt.

Dollars and Sense _____

For the vacation that needs to be toned down in the cost department, visit www. ReserveAmerica.com, which rents campsites, cabins, and other cool lodgings at the country's most scenic locations. For example, a beachfront cottage in Laguna Beach, California, rents for $174 per night for up to four people, compared with over $500 for some local hotel rooms!

Rules of Thumb for Future Use of Credit

My hope for you and everyone else is that borrowing money would cease to be part of your lives once and for all. That's something you should aspire to, even if it takes you until age 60 or 70 to completely rid yourself of mortgages and car loans. Until then, though, some debt usage may actually have to be part of your plan to eventually be debt-free.

But before you get all excited, and start trying to glue your credit card back together, I'm not telling you that all debt is a necessary part of life. Specifically, once the following types of debts are paid off, I'd recommend that you never allow them to be part of your life again:

◆ Payday loans

◆ Credit cards

◆ Installment purchase (such as for furniture or electronic equipment)

◆ Retirement plan loans

◆ IRS and government balances

This leaves mortgages, student loans, and car loans as the three types of loans you may need to use until you can do otherwise. In using these, I want to give you some rules of thumb to keep them from holding you back over the long run.

Rules of Thumb for Mortgages

In Chapter 2, I talked at length about the right and wrong kind of mortgages to have, so now I want to focus on how much mortgage to have. As with the other two rules of thumb I'm going to provide you here, these are relative to your monthly pretax income.

If you are considering buying a home and taking on a mortgage, or even getting a larger existing mortgage, there are two rules:

1. Your "adjusted" mortgage payment is less than one third (33%) of your monthly pretax income.

2. Your "adjusted" mortgage payment plus all your other debt payments is less than 50% of your household's pretax monthly income.

Both of these calculations allow room for the other expenses of life, from food to emergencies to fun. If you have no other debt expenses, I know it'll be tempting to allow your mortgage payment to take up that whole 50%, but don't. That doesn't leave any room to buy a car or absorb a student loan if you need to later.

You'll notice that I refer to an "adjusted" mortgage payment. What this calculation does is help you calculate the effects of a tax deduction on your net mortgage payment. To calculate your adjusted mortgage payment, multiply your actual payment by 80%. So a mortgage payment of $2,000 per month would result in a $1,600 adjusted payment to be used in the adjusted mortgage calculations discussed earlier.

Rules of Thumb for Student Loans

Student loans are a significant commitment for any student or parent trying to finance a college education. To make matters worse, they feel relatively painless as you commit to them, because payments aren't required until after college ends.

With a car loan or a mortgage, you can't go more than a month without having to face the reality of your payments. With student loans, the size of the payments doesn't really hit home until years after you take out the first loan.

As a rule of thumb, your student loan payments after you graduate shouldn't exceed 10% of a conservative estimate of your starting monthly salary. This payment level leaves room for a car payment, rent, and a little bit of an enjoyable lifestyle after you graduate. In other words, if you think you are going to make $3,000 per month, your student loan payments shouldn't exceed $300. While that may not seem like a whole lot of loans, you have to remember that that is a monthly payment on a 10-year loan.

That equates to a borrowed amount of $26,000, which would finance a large portion of a state school education.

I don't use an "adjusted amount" with student loans like I do with mortgages, because the amount of deductible interest is not usually big enough to make a substantial difference in your taxes.

Debt in America

Many students are finding themselves saddled with an impossible amount of student loan debt from post-graduate studies. In fact, it's not uncommon for a Ph.D. or M.D. to graduate with over $150,000 in loans. Even with a 30-year extended repayment plan, the monthly payments on a loan that size are at least $1,000 per month. Even for a freshly minted doctor, that can be more than he or she can afford.

Rules of Thumb for Car Loans

Because cars are a non-negotiable expense for many people, you need to establish a rule of thumb for your loans until you can get to the point of buying your cars for cash (more on this in Chapter 24). My rule of thumb for car loans is that your payment should not exceed 15% of your monthly income, assuming the loan is six years in length or less.

With car loans especially, use the rule of thumb as an "upper limit" and try to get as far under it as you can. The higher your payment on this depreciating asset, the longer it will take to reach your other financial goals.

Taking Your Time

With any loans that you take on in the future, take your time and really shop your loans for the best rates and terms. If you are going to use debt, use it wisely and efficiently.

A big part of shopping around means planning ahead on your major purchase decisions, especially housing and cars. The worst way to select a mortgage is to not even be in the market for a house, see one you like that is for sale, and then scramble to find a mortgage before someone else buys it out from underneath you.

This is even truer when you go to buy a car. You walk onto the lot, fall in love with a test drive, and then can't imagine not driving that car home to show your jealous neighbors. So when it comes time to get a loan, you are at the mercy of the dealership's finance department, which they're well aware of.

If you are going to buy a car, check with four to five banks and credit unions to see what their rates are. Then when you walk into the dealership, you'll be armed with a preapproval that the dealer might happily try to beat.

In the Red

A growing number of websites allow multiple lenders to bid for your loan business. This can be great for you, because they'll often keep knocking their rates downward to try to get you to choose their company over someone else. However, many of these sites are also the source of numerous customer complaints. Most often, they stem from mounds of hidden fees that erased any value received from getting a lower rate. If you're considering using one of these lenders, do a quick search of the company's name followed by the word *complaints*.

How much of a difference does doing your homework make? Let's look at the purchase of a $25,000 car, using a 60-month loan, at some slightly different rates.

Interest Rate	Monthly Payment	Total Payments
6.00%	$483.32	$28,999.20
6.50%	$489.15	$29,349.00
7.00%	$495.03	$29,701.80
7.50%	$500.95	$30,057.00
8.00%	$506.91	$30,414.60

Doing your homework and finding someone who will give you a 6.00% loan instead of the 6.50% saves you about $350 over the course of your loan. That's an airline ticket to somewhere tropical.

Going from an 8.00% auto loan to a 6.00% loan would save even more. In fact, it would save about $1,400—that's a ticket to somewhere tropical, a hotel room, and a whole lot of drinks by the pool! Further, you can imagine how shopping your rates on mortgages, which take 30 years to pay off, would save you tens of thousands of dollars if not more.

Be sure to always read the fine print on auto loans. Lower-interest-rate loans may charge a prepayment penalty if you pay off the car before the loan ends. This is a company's way of ensuring that it earns its expected profit from your loan.

Debt and Love: Yours, Mine, and Ours

One of the most frustrating things for me as a planner is to watch someone fight a two-year battle with debt, finally making it out of the quicksand, only to fall in love with someone with horrific debt problems and attitudes. Don't get me wrong, I'm glad for anyone who finds that special person. But when that special person undoes everything you've worked hard to accomplish, it's maddening.

Love-related debt problems can arise from a number of sources. By you thinking through them ahead of time, you'll be a lot more likely to be wise about the use of debt as your relationship progresses:

◆ Money-related fights are one of the biggest sources of discord in relationships. And yet when you fall for that special person, you tend to overlook this critical topic. Now, I'm not advocating you only fall in love with rich people, but I am encouraging to think twice about a relationship with people who use credit to act rich.

◆ When you're in love, especially if you've waited a long time for it, it's like being on a merry-go-round. More than anything else you don't want it to stop, so you're willing to keep "buying tickets." Gifts, nice meals, and vacations are all expensive things that can artificially keep the merry-go-round spinning. In fact, some people reach a point where they start saying things like, "I'd rather be in debt than be alone."

◆ When you open your heart to someone, it's sometimes hard to keep your wallet closed. You become the Bank of Love, which provides overdraft protection for your careless partner. I've seen relationships ruined, not necessarily maliciously, by someone who couldn't stop asking and someone else who couldn't say no.

◆ The moment you truly mix your financial lives, everything changes. If you rent an apartment together, co-sign on a loan, or share a joint bank account, your partner's bad habits can directly affect your financial reputation.

So what does happen to your credit when you get married? Well, until your spouse screws it up, nothing. Your credit scores do not merge, their score does not lower yours, and you do not assume their debts. But any bad choices they make on your account as an authorized user will end up reflecting on you. If one spouse has bad credit, it would be wise to continue to run separate bank and credit card accounts.

When I used to counsel high school kids, we used to laugh about young couples needing to have the "DTR," or the "define the relationship" talk. It's when they officially called themselves a couple, set boundaries, and yaddah yaddah.

When it's clear that a relationship is going to go the distance, you've got to have "the talk." In this talk, you share the gory details of your journey to eliminate your debt problem and how desperately you never want to do that again. You make it clear that though you may love this person, you hate debt. And for your sake, your significant other needs to work on getting rid of his or hers sooner than later.

As part of this discussion, you should talk about how money gets spent on your relationship. If that person is going into debt to try to keep you happy or impressed, do them a favor and release them from it. Be the first to demonstrate that love doesn't have to cost an arm or a leg. Then point them toward the nearest debt counselor, workshop, or copy of this book. In fact, you'd be a great accountability partner if they're looking for one, because you've been down this road!

The Least You Need to Know

- ◆ In the end, if you don't change your money attitudes, any financial change you've managed to accomplish will not likely be permanent.

- ◆ You need to examine your irrational thoughts about borrowing money and replace them with rational beliefs based on your experience.

- ◆ Once out of debt, the only debts you should ever consider having in the future are a mortgage, student loan, and car loan.

- ◆ Your total monthly debt expenditures for a mortgage, student loan, and car loan should be less than 50% of your monthly income.

- ◆ It is important to have a talk about the use of credit and loans when you officially enter into a long-term relationship with someone.

Chapter 24

Tools and Tips for Staying Out of Debt

In This Chapter

- ◆ Sticking with a plan that works
- ◆ Establishing an emergency fund
- ◆ Say no to car loans
- ◆ Making sure you're properly insured
- ◆ Putting a stop to junk mail temptation

You've got to keep reminding yourself: *staying* out of debt is a whole lot easier than getting out of debt! It's the truth and it's your ongoing mission when you're finally to where you want to be.

But staying out of debt, just like getting out of debt, takes more than good intentions. It takes a plan that consists of boundaries, forethought, and spending some money on the right things. Follow the advice in this chapter, and you'll prevent debt from sneaking back into your life overnight and over time.

Sticking with What Works

There's an old Groucho Marx joke that goes something like this: Guy walks into the Doctor, says "Doc, I've got this pain … it only hurts when I laugh." Doctor says "I've got two words for you: Don't laugh." Ba-dump-ching!

I'm a big believer in cause and effect and marvel how we fail to do the things we know will work, and work the things we know will fail. There's something hilarious there in our human nature that I haven't quite figured out yet.

Just like running one marathon won't keep you healthy for the rest of your life, getting out of debt won't automatically translate into financial stability. You've got to keep working at it, month by month and year by year.

At the heart of your battle to get out of debt is your quest to create and protect discretionary income. In other words, creating a situation where you have money left over at the end of each month that you can choose how to spend. This is far more preferable than looking at an empty bank account and wondering where the money went.

> **Dollars and Sense**
>
> Some of the best news about paying off your debts is that your discretionary income will rise. With those funds no longer needed to meet your payment obligations, you can begin spending it on things that bring you a lot more joy!

While I'd encourage you to loosen the belt up and enjoy life a little more once you're out of debt, I would also encourage you to do that within the confines of a budget and spending plan. You can increase the amounts that you spend on your wants (a.k.a. variable expenses), but you still need that barrier in place to protect your other financial goals.

Your Most Immediate Financial Goal

Once you are out of debt, your first major financial goal is the establishment of your emergency fund. This will be your safety net in case of a large unexpected expense, disability, job change, or other unforeseen event. By having it, you won't have to rely on credit cards and loans to make ends meet while you figure out your next steps in a crisis.

But consider yourself warned—having an emergency fund is as tempting as having a credit card. It's money that is begging to be spent. To ensure this doesn't happen, you need to keep it in a separate account, and maybe even a separate institution from your main banking account. A great option to consider is a no-cost money market account at a discount brokerage house such as Fidelity, Schwab, or E*Trade.

Some people feel like a true emergency fund should be stashed somewhere that they can get at it, like under their mattress, if a true emergency were to come along in the middle of the night. Other people like the idea of having a large amount of cash sitting in a safe deposit box, just in case. In this day and age, I would say that those ideas are each risky in their own way. If you stick a few thousand dollars under the mattress, you have no recourse if it disappears. If you stick it in a safe deposit box, you can only get at it during bank hours. Your best option is an FDIC-insured account with a debit card that would allow for emergency charges and withdrawals.

Planning Ahead to Have Fun

Just as you are now setting aside money in an emergency fund, you also need to look down the road and begin planning for the fun expenses in your future. While these should not consume an excessive amount of your discretionary income, you want to plan adequately so that there is no excuse to use a credit card or loans. Again, a discount brokerage house account is a great place to begin stashing a little bit of money each month to plan ahead for these fun goals.

This type of planning for fun should also apply to all your major purchases and expenses going forward. It's what I like to call "layaway" accounting, and it ensures that no one expense derails your financial progress.

Breaking the Auto Loan Cycle

Auto payments can be one of the biggest ongoing drains on your finances if you don't take proactive steps to end what I call the "auto loan cycle." This cycle, which entails a new set of car payments every five years, keeps many people from ever making solid progress.

Think about how much money many people dump into car loans with every passing year. A $350-per-month car payment pencils out to $4,200 every year. On a four-year loan, that's $16,800 bucks. If you repeat that cycle every five years, that's $33,600 per decade, or more than $125,000 over most people's working lives!

Debt in America

Various studies have placed the average length of car ownership at somewhere between five and six years, with the lengths of car ownership slowly climbing.

By breaking the never-ending cycle of borrowing money to buy a slightly newer car, you'll have tens of thousands of dollars to funnel into enjoying life and meeting your other goals.

Breaking the auto loan cycle comes down to three steps:

1. Stretching the useful life of your car

2. Continuing to make payments to yourself

3. Repeating this healthy cycle

Stretching the Useful Life of Your Car

One of the most absurd parts of the auto loan cycle is that we get rid of cars long before their useful life is over. Now, granted, they may be less useful to our social life as the paint begins to chip and the inside takes on the permanent smell of drive-thru burgers. But the mechanical life, especially with proper maintenance, can easily stretch to 7 to 10 years, if not longer.

Making your car stretch is the secret ingredient of the remainder of this process. To help you in that daunting task, here are some pointers:

- **Buy the extended warranty.** When it comes to just about anything else in life, especially electronics, I skip the extended warranty. Oftentimes, the prices are about 25% of the cost of a new item, and I just don't break that much stuff. But the extended warranties on cars can be a steal.

   Consider my wife's last car, which cost us just under $25,000. For another $1,500, which translates into about $30 per month, I added five years to the bumper-to-bumper warranty. As a rule of thumb, if the extended warranty costs less than 10% of the purchase price, and adds more than 25% to the useful life, it's a good deal.

- **Perform regular maintenance.** For a long time, I struggled to bring myself to pay $25 bucks every three months for an oil change. It seemed like a scam, with them putting those little reminder stickers inside your front windshield. Anyway, my cars seemed to last to five years with no problems. That was until I met my father-in-law, who seems to make cars last for decades. His secret? The regular maintenance—especially the oil changes.

- **Get over yourself.** I'm not trying to be mean, but if you hate the way that car "makes you look," you're probably going to trade it in sooner than later. Guess what? No one really notices what kind of car you drive unless it costs more than a house. In fact, my old rickety Honda gets as many looks from the ladies as my neighbor's Mercedes. Then again, my Honda makes some pretty funny noises at 10 years old …

Dollars and Sense

Speeding is a costly event is so many ways. Aside from the increased death rate in accidents for every 5 mph increment over 55 mph, the increased likelihood of a ticket, and the accelerated wear and tear on a car, the gas mileage associated with speeding is horrible. Most cars get their best mileage somewhere between 55 and 60 mph. If you go faster than that, your fuel efficiency begins to decline rapidly. Drive slower, be safer, and save some money on gas to put toward your balances!

Continuing to Make Payments to Yourself

The real magic of this technique has to do with continuing to do what you have financially grown comfortable with. In this case, having made payments for 60 months in a row, there's a good chance that your budget has adjusted and you've learned to live without that monthly payment.

Once your car loan is paid off, you should continue to make payments to yourself. In other words, you should take the same amount you were paying each month—let's say it's $350—and deposit it into a savings account. You'll want to continue to do this until your old car or your ego finally implodes.

But here's where this gets really cool. Let's say that you made this car last an additional two years beyond the end of the loan. During that time, you've made two years worth of payments into a savings account you had earmarked for your next car purchase. That's $8,400 dollars you've managed to save toward your new down payment.

Dollars and Sense

When it comes to down payments on cars, 25% of the purchase price seems to be the magic number. Not only will a down payment of that size make it easier to qualify for your loan, it may help ensure a lower interest rate.

So when you walk into the dealer, you've got an $8,400 down payment, plus a rusted heap that will get you a little bit on trade-in. With that kind of down payment, what do you imagine would happen to your next auto loan? That's right, smaller loan, smaller payment.

Repeat This Healthy Cycle

Now, because you've continued to make the same payment of $350 per month on either your loan or into your savings account, there's no reason to stop now. I'd encourage you to continue making that $350-per-month payment on your new auto loan, which actually has a lower minimum monthly payment.

Do you see where this is going yet? In a matter of a few years, your next car is paid off. And, if you keep making $350-per-month payments into a savings account, now for five or six years more, you will be sitting on a mountain of cash. In fact, I'll promise you that within one to two car purchases, you'll always be buying your cars for cash. And unless you can truly get 0% financing, this will help you accumulate net worth faster than paying someone 8% a year for a good portion of your working life!

Being Properly Insured

Even though I love the concept of the emergency fund, there are just some emergencies that are too rare and too costly to try to prepare for. For example, I could try to prepare for the possibility that I'll need an organ transplant that will cost over $500,000, but that wouldn't leave me a lot of money to play cards with the guys. Instead, I'll opt to buy insurance that covers me for events that are unknown, unlikely, but also unrecoverable if they were to happen to my finances.

Having the proper amount of insurance (which means not too much and not too little) is key. Also, having the right kind of insurance to cover my "exposures" is crucial to keep a traumatic event from ruining me for life.

But before you start stocking up on insurance like it's canned goods, be forewarned. Certain kinds of insurance are the highest-commission financial products sold in the financial services industry. There's a natural conflict of interest there when the person selling you the insurance gets paid more if you buy more. Oftentimes, scare tactics will be used to convince you to max out your coverage, which takes money away from your debt reduction plan and other goals.

Health Insurance

Unplanned medical costs are the single largest avoidable expense for most Americans. A single trip to the hospital for a relatively minor ailment can cost tens of thousands of dollars. That alone is enough to take a financially stable person and turn their world upside down.

I say that they're avoidable, because many Americans have access to some kind of health-care coverage but choose not to sign up for it. Now, I know people choose not to use it because it can be ridiculously expensive. But the bills associated with a medical emergency are typically a lot more expensive.

One of the easiest ways to get coverage is through an employer. If at all possible, you'll want to consider taking or finding a job that offers these benefits to you, your partner, and your dependents. The savings can be enormous.

If you leave or are fired from an employer that you depend on for your health coverage, you have 60 days to elect to "COBRA" your coverage. COBRA stands for the Consolidated Omnibus Budget Reconciliation Act, which was passed in 1986. This election essentially allows you to pay the entire premium yourself and keep your existing coverage for up to 18 months—but be aware the payment may be substantially larger than what was deducted from your paycheck. For more information on COBRA, talk to your company's Human Resources department or visit www.dol.gov and search for COBRA.

Auto Insurance

Considering how much money we pour into our cars in terms of just our monthly payments, it is complete insanity to drive around without adequate coverage. Unlike your home, which I'll talk about in a moment, cars are destroyed or damaged quite often. In fact, you'll probably experience at least one major car accident in your life, even if it is someone else's fault. You probably won't experience your home burning down or being destroyed by a natural disaster.

Being adequately protected against loss doesn't just mean insuring your car for its replacement value. It also means insuring yourself against medical costs caused by you or your family, damage to someone else's property or car, and the cost of renting a car while yours is out of commission.

While it is tempting to skimp on some of the auto insurance coverages offered to you, I'd generally take a medium level of most types of coverage offered. This type of protection will help keep your finances from slipping back into a desperate situation after you've worked hard to eliminate debt.

Disability Insurance

Depending on the source, it's argued that anywhere from one out of every three to five American workers will experience a temporary disability during their working

In the Red

The scariest part of a disability or long-term care need is that standard health insurance covers none or very little of these costs. This is especially true if you elect to enter a long-term care facility as opposed to being told to go by a doctor. You need to thoroughly read your health insurance coverage to see how you are covered in the event of a long-term care need or nonworkplace disability.

career. This means that they'll be out of work for an extended period of time, potentially without a paycheck, depending on the nature of their injury. Of course, many people in this situation again resort to borrowing money to help maintain their lifestyle.

Disability insurance is available through a number of insurance companies, but like other coverage for events with a high probability of occurring, it's very expensive. In fact, to buy a disability policy by itself would force many Americans to skip other important financial goals and important insurance coverages.

Your best bet in preparing for the potential of a short-term disability is to continue to build your emergency fund, as well as take advantage of any low-cost disability policies that might be offered through your employer.

Long-Term Care

With people living longer and longer, the probability that you or your partner will spend some time in a nursing home is skyrocketing. Considering the costs associated with this type of care can exceed $50,000 per year, it is understandable to see why many people are interested in what we call "long-term care" insurance.

However, due to the high probability that most people will someday need this kind of care, insurance policies that specifically cover for it are very expensive. In fact, as I like to explain it to clients, "most people who need it can't afford it. Most people who can afford it don't need it."

If someone tries to sell you or your loved one a personal version of this insurance, be sure to get some outside and unbiased advice. Separately, if it is offered through your employer, it is usually a good deal and should be considered.

Homeowner's Insurance and Renter's Insurance

For many people, their home might be their most valuable asset, worth even more than their retirement accounts at the end of their career. Homeowner's insurance will help assure that a traumatic event will not move you back to square one with probably the single largest debt that you'll ever work to pay off.

As a bonus, many homeowners' policies include, or offer at a low cost, liability insurance in case anyone gets hurt in your home and tries to sue you. This is important coverage that will help protect you from legal debts that take years to repay.

Renter's insurance refers to a cheap policy (usually $100–$200 per year) that tenants renting an apartment, condo, or house can get to cover damage to their personal property and possessions. These policies, as with homeowner's policies, do not cover excessive amounts of things like jewelry or collectibles. If you want that kind of coverage, you will need to apply for additional coverage, also known as a "rider."

Liability Insurance

In the last few decades, we've seen the number of lawsuits between private individuals go through the roof. This has been fueled by increased awareness and access to small claims court for smaller lawsuits.

Keeping in mind the lawsuit-happy environment we now live in, having adequate coverage against potential suits is worth consideration. In addition to the liability coverage that comes with your homeowner's and auto policies, many insurance companies will sell an additional "umbrella" policy. These policies cover nonwork-related lawsuits and will pay judgments into the million-dollar range. They can be purchased for a few hundred dollars per year and should be added to your coverage as the value of your assets becomes significant.

Additionally, anyone in a profession that is prone to lawsuits, such as the medical field, should carry professional liability insurance. This would protect your assets from any lawsuits arising from an accusation (whether it's accurate or false) of failing to do your job correctly.

Life Insurance

I didn't start with life insurance, because I think it is the one people worry about to an unreasonable extent. The other types of insurance we've covered are far more crucial to keeping you from slipping back into debt.

In a nutshell, life insurance should cover a financial loss created because you die. If there is no loss created, then I'd argue that it's a waste of money for most people.

Now, as a young father with school-age children, there's a definite financial loss created if I die. There is no way my wife could immediately recreate the lifestyle my career provides while simultaneously being the mom we want her to be. That makes me a good candidate for insurance.

However, when I'm 65, our kids are through college, and we're living solely off the income of our retirement investments, there is no financial loss created if I die. In fact, our household expenses probably go down because there is one less car, one less mouth to feed, and a lot less junk being bought. It's grim, but true, and means that my wife doesn't need insurance on me at that point.

Term insurance, which is the kind I recommend most people buy, covers you for a specified window of time, usually something like 20 years. If I die after those 20 years, no one gets any money. But then again, we don't need it then. As such, it is fairly inexpensive because my coverage period is limited.

Whole life insurance, which as the name implies, covers you for your whole life, is pretty darn expensive. In fact, if you think about it logically, what will an insurance company charge you for a policy that there's a 100% probability they'll have to pay on? Statistically, they'd have to charge you more than they pay out to stay in business. Sounds like a waste of money to me. As we say in the financial planning business, "Buy term and invest the rest!"

> ### Set a Goal
>
> Grab your calendar and pick a day when you can spend a few hours reviewing your insurance policies, their coverage, and the fine print. Then, if you have questions about the coverage or notice areas where you think you might be exposed to a significant loss, call your agent to ask about changing your policy to include those areas.

Putting an End to Solicitations

Temptation to borrow money and use credit will stalk you for the rest of your life. New, innovative lending products will continue to be offered, which seem to make happiness available through affordable monthly payments. Your mailbox, inbox, and voicemail will continue to fill up with teaser rates and no-money-down offers. Staying out of debt will mean continually saying no to these offers.

But it doesn't have to be that much work. With a little bit of work, you can make sure that financial garbage doesn't stink up your plans.

To put an end to incoming junk mail, visit the Direct Marketing Association's website at www.DMAChoice.org and click on the "Consumers" tab. By registering on this free site, it will stop a large portion of all junk mail that is delivered through the U.S. Postal Service.

To specifically request a halt to new credit card offers, visit another free website, www. OptOutPreScreen.com.

For telephone marketing, federal law requires all telemarketers to not call you if you register with the Federal Do-Not-Call list. This list is also free to register for and can be found on the web at www.DoNotCall.gov.

The Least You Need to Know

◆ Even when you get out of debt, a budget and spending plan will help ensure that controlling your expenses each month is a piece of cake.

◆ You need to establish an emergency fund, as well as a "layaway" account, to which you add money each month to prepare for both expected and unexpected events.

◆ Continue to make payments to yourself when your car is paid off in order to break the auto loan cycle.

◆ It's crucial to be properly insured (especially in the area of health care) to avoid new debt.

◆ Spend a few minutes online and put an end to tempting solicitations and marketing that could lead you back into old habits.

Passing Along Good Money Skills

In This Chapter

- ◆ They're not your kids' debts …

- ◆ Why attitudes toward money are contagious

- ◆ What lessons are you teaching?

- ◆ Helping your kids use credit wisely

For my money (no pun intended), perhaps the greatest quote ever uttered comes from a writer named George Santayana. A citizen of Spain, Santayana lived through watching Europe endure not just one world war, but two. His thoughts on the matter: "Those who do not learn from history are bound to repeat it."

There are so many reasons why your kids (if you have them) need to learn from your mistakes and missteps with debt management. It may be one of the greatest favors you'll ever do for them, even more than paying for college, helping them buy that first car, or leaving them your vast fortune someday.

The two biggest reasons to pass along the wisdom of your lessons are that you love them and you hate debt. If you don't share the knowledge you've acquired through your struggles, your kids may find themselves where you are by their early 20s. This, in turn, may put you back in the middle of something you swore off for life—a state of debt.

Keep Your Debt from Being Traumatic ...

If you desire for your kids to never go where you've been, you've got to keep them open to the discussion and open to learning. The easiest way to prevent open discussion is to make your journey out of debt so stressful that it defines the early portion of their lives.

> **Dollars and Sense**
>
> Pick a time to do your bills when you know your kids will be occupied elsewhere, whether they're at Grandma's house, school, or watching Saturday morning cartoons. Having them asking for your time or assistance in the midst of being focused on or frustrated with your finances doesn't help you or them.

To help ensure your kids don't run from the room screaming and shaking their heads every time you mention money, you need to do your absolute best to insulate them before age 13. They don't need to know that debt and money problems are the bane of your existence. This is especially easy before they hit middle school, and don't really have a concept of whose parents are loaded and whose parents are making the minimum payments.

I know it is so hard for money stress not to ooze out of your pores. But it can be done if you are being proactive in how you talk and react to your kids when your money stress hits.

Your Debt Is Not Their Fault

Scientists have yet to isolate the gene, but I think there is a DNA strand in all of us that causes us to eventually lose control and chastise our kids with "You must think money grows on trees!" This is usually paired with some kind of zinger like, "You have no idea how lucky you are. When I was a kid, we had to make our clothes out of scraps of burlap, candy bar wrappers, and duct tape ..."

The irony for most of us who heard these things as kids is that they did nothing to keep us out of debt. In fact, the constant reminder of how much money was a pain in the rear may have caused a lot of us to act carelessly in some type of subconscious rebellion. What was your experience with money in your household growing up? Do you remember it being tight or easy? Did people fight over it or about it? How did all those things affect you? How do you want your child to perceive you and money?

When it comes to how your children will eventually handle money and debt, as well as for the long-term health of your relationship with them, it is crucial that they don't perceive that your money problems are their fault. This doesn't mean you don't teach lessons about learning to be happy with what you have, learning to be thankful for who gave it to you, or learning that you can't always get what you want. But it means that those lessons need to be completely disconnected in their mind from the stress that you as a parent are exhibiting.

Because of the way kids work developmentally, they will internalize their parents' stress as their own fault at the first indication that they might be to blame. It is why kids of divorced parents so often blame themselves. Mom and Dad get mad at each other, often fighting about parenting issues within earshot of a child, and then get divorced. What else is a child to assume but that if he or she could have been a better kid, Mom and Dad wouldn't have fought, much less split up?

The same occurs with money. If you reprimand your eight-year-old for throwing a tantrum when he doesn't get a new toy, you're normal. If you inform him of how legitimately spoiled he acts sometimes, that makes you even more normal. But when he catches you crying over the bank statements at the dining room table, what else could he possible deduce except that "Mom or Dad is stressed about money and it's all my fault"? If money is stressful, it's going to cause you to crack at times—that's normal, and it makes you like everyone else. But when you do that, it's crucial that you help your child understand that you are stressed about money, not because of anything he did.

Avoid Guilt Trips

One habit that's very easy to slip into, even in adult relationships, is reminding people how much we do for them. Now, psychologically, I think there is a reason we do that. Usually it is because we need to know how much we matter to someone else, and they haven't told us enough lately or they've done something to make us feel just the opposite. So naturally, we remind them of how valuable we are to them in the hopes that they'll agree.

If you feel underappreciated by your kids, tell them straight up what you're feeling. Even a five-year-old can understand that and respond accordingly. But if you beat around the bush and use financial guilt as a reason your children should appreciate you, it's going to make them hate dealing with personal finance stuff later in life. Do you remember what we call that avoidance of a topic? That's right, denial. That's the last attitude you want your kid to have toward dealing with their money!

Don't Use Debt to Say No

I've got two precious boys who are fairly convinced that the four main food groups are candy from the mall, candy from their grandparents, candy from the ice cream truck, and candy at Halloween. Not a day goes by in our household that one of them is not lobbying to have candy for one of their three meals.

Now, on my days where I just can't take it anymore, I'm tempted to (and sometimes do) lie to them and tell them that we're out of candy. Of course, they'll rummage through the drawers until they find a single loose candy corn and then beg to eat that. Now, realistically, I should just tell my kids that all their teeth are going to fall out and I'd be a lousy parent if I allowed them to eat that much candy. By taking the momentarily easy road, though, and lying to them, I've essentially said "I'd let you have candy, but we are out." I've been a good parent in the sense that they're not eating candy, but a lousy parent because I haven't helped them understand why.

The same is true with money and debt. If I use debt, bills, or tight finances as my cop-out reason to say no, I've done nothing to teach my kids about controlling their spending. I haven't done anything to help them learn that fine line between needs and wants. All I've said is, "We can't afford it right now, but if I had money I'd say yes."

This ultimately backfires on you as a parent on a couple of levels. First, your kids will continue to drive you nuts. It'll be the financial version of "Are we there yet?" They'll keep asking and asking and asking. Chances are, that'll frazzle you even more, you'll snap at your kids, and they'll have a growing hate of money and careful spending.

Second, your kids will have a growing false perception that you've failed to provide as their parent. Instead, as I'll discuss in a few pages, you want to work with your kids to create a spending plan just like yours. They'll have ownership of it and will have to learn to choose their purchases carefully. You'll be teaching them exactly how life works, while also shifting the burden and blame off of you.

In the Red

I've said that you should never use debt as your excuse for saying no to your child. I also believe that you should never use it as an excuse to say yes. Even when their budgets are extremely tight or maxed out, many parents will still dip into credit because they don't want their kid to "miss out." The reality is, most kids want quality connection with their parents over a possession, and most possessions are forgotten about within a matter of months. Don't let your guilt talk you into overstretching yourself.

Money Attitudes Are Contagious

I do a lot of work with marriage and family therapists helping couples that are getting married to figure out how they'll jointly handle finances. In the premarital sessions, I have them fill out a short quiz that helps to uncover their "money attitudes." By understanding these underlying attitudes, they have a much easier time understanding why each person acts the way he or she does.

The questions on this quiz are really meant to uncover the source of their money attitudes—what money was like in their household growing up. The reality is, just as with so many other things, we do as we witnessed. If you saw people act responsibly with money, you'll act responsibly. If you saw them be stressed out (even for just a few years while they eliminated debt), you'll probably be stressed out about money your whole life.

If your parents demonstrated bad money habits, poor use of debt, careless and unchecked spending, especially during your formative years, as an adult you'll probably do the same. Likewise, if your parents demonstrated responsibility, even in the sense of realizing they had a problem and took active steps to solve it, you probably learned to do that instead.

So what attitudes would I, as both a Certified Financial Planner and trained family counselor, tell you are the most important attributes to model to your kids? As with all these characteristics you're modeling to them, you should both participate in them and praise them for doing them. Let's look at the three main ones.

Delayed Gratification

Delayed gratification is the idea that you can wait to enjoy something. In fact, waiting might even mean that it is more enjoyable than if you got it immediately when you wanted it. If your kids see you wanting something, but then happily waiting because it is not the best time to buy it, they'll learn to do the same. In fact, in time, they'll come to admire that behavior because it's so out of place in the world.

Look for opportunities to delay gratification, whether it is an ice cream cone, a movie, or a new toy. Then, after they've patiently waited until a better time, praise them for that behavior. Tell them how rare and impressive it is.

Contentment

If there is something that is a true challenge to pass on, it is contentment. That's probably because people confuse what contentment is. Contentment is not necessarily being happy with all of life's circumstances all of the time. Rather, contentment is realizing that all of life's "things" are just that, and what makes people rich is the fact that they have one another.

When it really comes down to it, we need to show our kids that driving in a beat-up old car with the windows down, singing at the top of our lungs with them, is far more special than driving in a brand-new car and being so distracted with our financial stress that we can't have fun.

Contentment is not about getting what you want. Contentment is about wanting what you've got. Chances are, as you've had to buckle down your finances to eliminate debt, you have or will learn that. By making sure your kids see contentment without all the "stuff," there's a good chance they won't try to find contentment by charging their brains out on a credit card.

> ### Debt in America
>
> Over my years as a financial planner, one of the greatest things that I've seen tear apart families is the division of an inheritance. Don't let money be the unspoken "elephant in the room" in your extended family. But don't try bringing up your elderly mom or dad's finances at Thanksgiving dinner. If there are issues that need to be talked about, consider holding a family meeting for the sole purpose of discussing finances.

Prudence

Early in my career as a stockbroker, I would get compliment after compliment about how my financial wisdom was beyond my years. Before you think I'm bragging about being some kind of prodigy, understand that I'm really bragging about my dad letting me watch him work with his clients. Not only that, after he would meet with a client, he'd spend 15 minutes "debriefing" me about why he made different decisions, what he was still wrestling with, and what questions he needed to answer to move forward. I became a good financial planner because I was permitted to look over the shoulder of one.

By letting your kids look over your shoulder when they get into their teen years, talking with them about your financial options, and even asking for their input, you'll teach them to be prudent. They'll learn to make educated decisions that incorporate their personal risk and reward.

There are numerous financial decisions that you can include your children on even if you don't give them a real "vote" in the final decision. Whether it is how much to spend on a vacation or whether or not you should build a pool in the backyard, get their opinion and ask for their input. For example, when you are thinking about buying your next car, spend 15 minutes sitting at the local burger stand talking through the purchase with your kids. "Think out loud" about the size of the payments you're committing to, what the benefits of a new car are versus keeping the old one, and ask for their opinion. In doing so, you're teaching them to think carefully and actually giving them an opportunity to do it. Do it now with them, and they'll do it the rest of their life, especially when it comes to borrowing money or using credit.

Helping Your Kids Manage Debt Wisely

Considering that the world abounds with offers to use credit and borrow money, you need to begin financially educating your kids early on. As with most things in parenting, it's not so much about handing our kids the playbook for life. Truthfully, as much as you want your kids to learn from your mistakes, trust your word completely, and listen to every nugget that falls out of your mouth, they won't. For your child to truly learn healthy financial and debt habits from you, it's going to come down to "teachable moments."

To me, a teachable moment is one of those when your kids are truly tuned in to what's going on and what your input is as a parent. Usually, this happens because you are a key step to them getting what they want. But that's okay—take whatever platform you can get! It's in these moments, when they really want something and are willing to listen to your advice, that you can teach them life lessons.

Teaching Them to Save

This should be one of the first lessons every parent tries to teach their kid about finances. The opportunity arises when they come to you begging for that Mighty Change-O-Bot or that Malibu Betty doll. In this moment, you give them two options:

1. You can wait and see what you get for your birthday or the holidays (which is a fun one if you enjoy seeing your kids roll their eyes at you).

2. You can save up some of your own money and buy it.

Now, I'm not saying that you need to be a no-fun parent who never treats his kid or buys him something once in a while. What I am saying is that if your kids always get what they want, when they want it, at no cost to them, then you're creating the expectation that they should get what they want as soon as they decide they want it.

But by forcing them to either wait and maybe get it, or save up and definitely get it, you are teaching them that you have to plan ahead to get the enjoyable things you want. In other words, you're teaching them to set financial goals and move toward them.

One important aspect of this is to avoid the situation where your kid begs, or even worse, you suggest, that he or she can get it but will have to pay you back. If that isn't setting them up for a repeat of your own struggle to eliminate debt, I don't know what would.

> **Dollars and Sense** _____
>
> The multiple-account spending plans I discussed in Chapter 9 work for children from preschool age through college as well. Give them a certain amount of money to manage each week or month. These funds ideally would be for their entertainment, eating out, etc. For young kids, put it in a jar where they can see and contemplate it. For older kids, set up an account and make an automatic transfer on a regular basis. This will ultimately help all kids to learn to live within their means.

Preparing Them for All That Debt Offers

As soon as your children turn 18, the offers will start showing up in their mailbox. Being the trusting (or naive) sweethearts that they are, they'll also be dropping their names in every contest box at the mall and signing up for every online giveaway. It's just a matter of time before their names are on a bunch of mailing lists.

While you could try to hide every offer from your kids, you're only delaying the inevitable. They're eventually going to figure out that they can put their groceries and gas on a credit card, earn rewards for doing it, and think that you're a fool for not doing the same.

Before you ever get to that point, it's time to go back to the first few chapters of this book and review the basics of how we get into debt, how the math of debt works, and how people's denial causes their problem to snowball. You need to convince your teen that she is not the first one to discover credit cards and that these companies make huge profits off people like her. You need to put the fear of accumulating debt into her, because it is the only thing that may truly keep her from going crazy with it.

All those credit card offers they're getting in the mail also present a great opportunity to talk to your kids about identity theft (see Chapter 21). With the "We're indestructible" attitude of youth, they won't be proactive about thinking how to protect their vital information. A little advice from you will go a long way toward protecting you and them!

The Myth That They Should Build Credit

With that fierce streak of independence that most 18- to 25-year-olds seem to possess, they will be anxious to make their financial mark in the world. Inevitably, one of their know-it-all friends will tell them how they need to begin building credit, or no one will ever give them a loan. It's at this point that you need to talk to them about how income is the most important factor in getting a loan, and how building credit backfires on so many people, yourself included.

If they are still determined to build credit, try to get them to sign up for some type of subscription or membership on the credit card they've signed up for. By just paying that off each month, even though it is a small amount, it'll accomplish virtually the same thing as running wild with a credit card and scrambling to pay it off. An alternative would be to help them open a gas credit card, since they naturally have low limits, provided they are paid off each month.

Co-Signing for Your Child

To me, this is a great alternative to your kids getting a credit card to build credit. By co-signing an auto loan with them for their first car, you'll help them get a loan they couldn't otherwise obtain. By them getting the loan and keeping the payments current on it, they'll build all the credit they need.

But before you do this, make sure you get a firm commitment from your child on a couple of things. If they don't live up to these expectations, you shouldn't hesitate to sell the car.

- **She makes the monthly car and insurance payments.** If you are the one actually writing the checks each month, there's a good chance she'll flake on you at some point. "Dad, you just keep the car …"

- **He proves he's paying the loan.** Because your credit score is on the line as a co-signer, you should have him send you copies of the check or statement verifying that it's getting paid on time. You can stop after a year or so, but this will help you ensure that he's initially following through on his commitment.

- **She agrees to keep the car for the long term.** In Chapter 24, I talked about trying to make your car last longer and making payments to yourself once the loan is paid off. Have your adult child do that with her first real car purchase and it may be a habit that sticks with her the rest of her life.

> **In the Red**
>
> While you should consider co-signing on your child's first car if it helps him to get his feet on the ground, you should be really cautious co-signing on your child's home. The purchase of a home is a large enough decision that your child needs to fully be prepared to take that obligation on. If he hasn't gotten his finances to the point where a lender deems him worthy, you may be setting him up for failure by forcing it.

Get Them Thinking About Retirement

There's an incredibly good chance that your children, who are now young adults, are going to live a heck of a long time. I'd guess that by the time they are 50 years old, living to age 100 will be the norm.

With that in mind, retirement is going to require them to save a whole lot of money. But if you can get them doing it within a few years of turning 18, it will be a lot less costly year to year. That, of course, translates into more leftover cash at the end of each month (discretionary income), which means fewer reasons to use credit.

Take a look at a simple example of how much someone needs to save to accumulate $1,000,000 by age 65 (based on 8% compounded rate of return).

Starting Age	Annual Savings Required	Total Required
18	$2,044	$96,068
28	$4,560	$168,720
38	$10,600	$286,200
48	$27,435	$466,395
58	$103,771	$726,397

Aren't those numbers amazing? An 18-year-old only has to save $96,068 total over their lifetime to be a millionaire, if she starts when she's 18. But if she just waits 10 years, her required annual savings more than doubles, and her total out-of-pocket costs rise by over $70,000.

By getting your kids to care about retirement early, you'll help ensure that they have more discretionary income each month and year. Again, this translates into less need to use credit and borrowing to attain the lifestyle they need or want.

You can actually open a Roth IRA for your children before they turn 18, as long as they have earned income (from a job) of their own. Even if you put the initial money in yourself, it is a great way to help them get involved in planning for their future and educated about investing.

The Least You Need to Know

- ◆ You've got to insulate your kids from your debt stress in their early years.
- ◆ Both good and bad money attitudes are contagious—which are you passing on?
- ◆ To keep your kids out of debt, teach them delayed gratification, contentment, and prudence.
- ◆ Teach your kids the wisdom of saving up for something instead of trying to figure out how to pay it off.
- ◆ Get your kids excited about how "cheap" retirement is if they start saving for it early in their adult life.

Glossary

401(k)   A retirement plan put in place by companies for their employees, which allows employees to save for their retirement by having money subtracted from their paycheck.

actual budget   The budget you create by reviewing and recording what you actually have spent. *See also* compromise budget, ideal budget.

adjustable-rate mortgage (ARM)   A mortgage or loan whose interest rate changes at some preset intervals (monthly, yearly, etc.) based on a preset formula. *Compare with* fixed rate.

alimony   A share of a divorced person's income that is paid to his or her spouse as part of an agreement or court order.

appreciation   When an asset increases in value. *Compare with* depreciation.

APR   Also known as annual percentage rate, this calculation helps a consumer to understand the true cost of a loan's interest on an annual basis.

APY   Also known as annual percentage yield, this calculation helps a consumer to understand the true interest that will be earned on their savings account.

back-end ratio   A ratio used by lenders to calculate a potential borrower's ability to make the monthly payment on a loan. This ratio is calculated by dividing the total of all a borrower's monthly debt payments, including the potential loan, by the borrower's pre-tax monthly income.

balance to limit ratio   *See* utilization.

balance transfer   The process of moving a balance on a credit card to another credit card company to lower your interest rate.

bankruptcy   The legal process in which a borrower asks for court protection and assistance in dealing with their creditors.

biweekly mortgage payment   A payment plan in which you pay half of your mortgage every two weeks, which results in an extra month's payment being made every year, and in turn a shortened overall mortgage term.

budget   Serves as both a historical review of how you've spent your money, as well as a road map for how you'd like to spend it going forward.

bureau   *See* credit agency.

cash   Traditionally refers to physical currency that could be used to purchase something. More frequently, it is being used to refer to money someone has available in a bank account.

CCCS   Stands for Consumer Credit Counseling Services, which is a nonprofit organization offering free and low-cost financial guidance to consumers with debt problems.

cease and desist   A letter sent to a collection agency ordering them to stop all contact with a consumer.

Chapter 7   Refers to bankruptcy proceedings in which an individual's assets are sold and used to pay off debts. Most of the remaining debts after all assets are sold are discharged or erased.

Chapter 11   Refers to bankruptcy proceedings in which an individual is allowed to propose a payment plan to help eliminate their debts.

child support   Money required to be paid by agreement or court order to help support a child; payments usually cease when the child is 18 years old.

collateral   Assets or property used to guarantee that a loan will be paid off. If it is not, the collateral may be seized and sold by the lender.

compound interest   Interest that is calculated on both the remaining principal of the loan, as well as the interest that has been added to the loan since the last payment. *Compare with* simple interest.

compromise budget   The budget you make as your road map moving forward, which integrates both your ideal and actual budgets. *See also* actual budget, ideal budget.

conforming mortgage   A mortgage that must meet certain strict requirements in order to be purchased by either the Fannie Mae or Freddie Mac mortgage corporation. Typically considered one of the hardest, but also one of the best, mortgages for a borrower to get.

conventional mortgage   Most often refers to a mortgage in which part of each monthly payment goes to reduce the principal or amount owed. Sometimes is also used to refer to mortgages issued without sponsorship of the Federal Housing Administration or Veteran's Administration.

credit   Money that is loaned to someone on a short-term basis to finance a purchase, often through the use of a credit card.

credit agency   The organization that tracks an individual's credit history.

credit report   An individual's history of borrowing money, consistency of repayment, employment, and residences.

credit score   An estimate of an individual's likelihood of *not* repaying a loan. The higher the score, the better.

creditor   Someone who is owed money by someone else. *Compare with* debtor.

debt consolidation   The process of transferring multiple loans or balances to one institution, simplifying the repayment process for a borrower.

debt service   The total of all someone's required or minimum payments on all types of debt and credit.

debt settlement   An agreement between a lender and a borrower to accept less than what is owed in exchange for canceling the remaining debt.

debtor   Someone who owes money to someone else. *Compare with* creditor.

default   When a borrower fails to make the required payments on his or her loan.

deferment   The time period during which a college student is not expected to make any payments on their student loans, though interest is still calculated.

delayed gratification   The act of temporarily putting off the enjoyment of something until a later time.

depreciation   When an asset declines in value. *Compare with* appreciation.

discharge   A term for the cancellation of a debt.

discretionary income   The money that is left over at the end of the month after all of your bills are paid.

e-lerts   E-mail reminders sent from your bank or credit card account to notify you of payments, deposits, balances, or limits being reached.

emergency fund   A bank account that a consumer puts money into for emergencies so they can avoid having to use credit or loans.

envelope system   An old-fashioned version of a spending plan, in which money earmarked for certain expenses would be put into separate envelopes.

Equifax   One of the three major credit agencies. *See also* Experian, TransUnion.

Experian   One of the three major credit agencies. *See also* Equifax, TransUnion.

FCBA   The Fair Credit Billing Act, which protects users of open-end credit accounts such as credit cards.

FDCPA   The Fair Debt Collection Practices Act, which entitles consumers to fair and reasonable collection practices by collection agencies hired by their lenders.

FICO   The most widely used credit score, calculated by the Fair Isaac Corporation.

fixed expense   Expenses that do not change too much month to month, and are not tied to our impulsivity. Examples include mortgage or rent, utilities, tuition, and gas. *Compare with* variable expense.

fixed rate   A mortgage or loan whose interest rate remains the same for the life of the loan. *Compare with* adjustable rate mortgage.

forbearance   A temporary suspension of student loan repayments for a former college student based on financial hardship or other circumstances.

foreclosure   The process of a bank or lender taking back a house that is collateral for an unpaid mortgage.

forgiveness   Certain employers, government programs, and nonprofit organizations will pay or forgive a portion of your student loan balance in return for service or employment.

front-end ratio   A ratio used by lenders to calculate a potential borrower's ability to make the monthly payment on a loan. Calculated by dividing the payment on the new loan by the borrower's monthly income.

FTC The Federal Trade Commission, which helps protect consumers from unfair business practices.

garnishment The process of a lender or the government taking a portion of each of a borrower's paychecks to help pay off debts.

HELOC Also known as a home equity line of credit, a HELOC allows consumers to borrow money against the value of their home, above and beyond their current mortgage.

HUD Stands for the Department of Housing and Urban Development, which is a nonprofit government agency that works to protect the interests of homeowners.

ideal budget The budget you create based on what you think you should spend. *See also* actual budget, compromise budget.

income sensitive A federal student loan repayment option under which payments are based on the borrower's income in a given year.

inflation The rate at which the cost of goods and services increase as each year passes.

installment agreement An agreement between a consumer and a business or government agency, usually the IRS, to pay outstanding balances.

interest The cost to a borrower, usually expressed as a percentage and calculated on the balance owed, for borrowing money. Conversely, it may also refer to the amount a depositor or lender earns for letting someone else use its money.

interest-only A mortgage in which the borrower only pays the interest that is calculated each month. The actual loan balance does not decrease over time.

IRA Stands for individual retirement account and is used by individuals to save for retirement. There are two main versions of IRAs: Roth and Traditional.

lease An agreement between two parties for the use of some kind of property or possession for a period of time in exchange for payment. At the end of the lease, the property is returned to its owner.

levy A claim made against a borrower's bank account for unpaid balances.

LIBOR Stands for London Interbank Overnight Rate, and is a rate that is often used as a base rate for calculating the rate customers will be able to borrow at.

lien An official claim filed by a lender against an asset used as collateral, which keeps the asset from being sold or disposed of without the lender's approval.

long-term care   Special insurance policies bought to help cover expenses associated with being placed in a nursing home or similar facility.

long-term debt   Debt that is used to acquire appreciating assets with an expected payoff period greater than 10 years.

modification   A process in which a mortgage lender changes the term or interest rate of an existing loan without making you go through the entire refinancing process.

needs   A term for the basic costs required for you to stay clothed, fed, housed, etc.

NegAm   Also know as a negative amortization mortgage, these loans actually allow you to add your unpaid interest to the loan principal, which causes you to owe more at the end of the month than at the beginning.

offer in compromise   An offer made to the IRS to pay a portion of an outstanding debt in exchange for the remaining debt being erased, similar to a debt settlement.

opportunity cost   The opportunity missed when one choice is made over another.

origination fee   Essentially a commission, paid in part to the person who handles setting up your loan.

payday loan   A very high-interest loan or advance made against your next paycheck.

points   A fee, usually expressed in 1% increments of a loan's total value, paid at the time of lending to obtain a lower interest rate.

pre-approved   When a bank has officially agreed to loan money to a borrower prior to him or her finding a home or auto they wish to purchase.

pre-qualified   When a bank believes that someone has the financial qualifications to receive a loan from the bank, but the loan itself has not been officially approved.

principal   The remaining portion of a loan's original balance that was borrowed.

purchase   To buy something either all at once by paying the entire cost or over time through the use of a loan.

refinance   The process of exchanging an old loan or mortgage for a newer one.

repo   More formally known as a repossession, a repo is the process of a lender seizing a non–real estate asset (usually a car) to pay off a delinquent loan.

reverse mortgage   An agreement between a bank or investor to make monthly payments to a homeowner based on the value of their home. At the end of the reverse mortgage, the bank or investor typically becomes the owner of the home.

roll-down method   The process of applying the payments from your paid-off debts to the remaining debts, which speeds up the remaining elimination of debts.

short-term debt   Debt that is used to acquire depreciating assets and has a payoff period shorter than 10 years.

simple interest   Interest that is calculated only on the remaining balance or principal of the loan. *Compare with* compound interest.

spending plan   A system in which money is actually put into separate accounts to make sure it gets spent as intended.

T-bills   Refers to Treasury bills, which are short-term bonds issued by the U.S. Treasury. Their rate is often used as a base rate in deciding the interest rate for borrowers.

term   The length of time, usually expressed in months or years, until a loan with a fixed payment amount is fully repaid.

TransUnion   One of the three major credit agencies *See also* Equifax, Experian.

TRW   The initials of a former credit agency that is still often used by people to refer to all credit agencies as well as a credit report.

unsecured debt   A loan or debt that was made without any collateral or property to guarantee the repayment of that loan.

usury   The criminal act of charging an abusively high rate of interest on a loan, as determined by state laws.

utilization   A percentage measure of how "maxed out" someone's credit cards are relative to their limits.

variable expense   An expense that can vary widely month to month, depending on your leisure and shopping choices for the month. Examples would include groceries, entertainment, clothing, and gifts. *Compare with* fixed expense.

wants   A term for the costs required to keep us happy above our basic needs.

windfall   A surprise receipt of money or property.

Sample Letters

These letters are just a sample of some of the many communications that you can initiate yourself to get your creditors off your back, lower your balance or interest rate, or begin repairing your credit. In the end, if you feel uncomfortable contacting your creditors yourself, consider enlisting the help of an attorney.

Cease and Desist Letter

Customer Name and Address

Date

Dewey, Cheatum & Howe Collection Agency
1234 Main Street
Anytown, USA 12345

Re: File #1234
ACME Bank Account #987654321

To Whom It May Concern:

This serves as legal notice under the provisions of the Fair Debt Collection Practices Act (FDCPA), to cease and desist from all communication with me concerning the above referenced debt. If you fail to comply with this notice, I will file a formal complaint against your company with the Federal Trade Commission.

I have concluded that I no longer wish to work with a collection agency under any circumstances. I will contact my original creditor directly to resolve this matter.

You are also notified that in the event any negative information is placed on my credit reports in retaliation for this order to cease contact, I will also take immediate and appropriate steps to prosecute your company to the fullest extent of the law.

Thank you in advance,

Your Name

Billing Dispute Letter

Customer Name and Address

Date

RIPUOFF Credit Card Company
Attn: Billing Inquiries
1234 Main Street
Anytown, USA 12345

Re: File #1234
RIPUOFF Credit Card Account #1111222233334444

To Whom It May Concern:

I'm writing to dispute a billing error in the amount of $_____ on my account. I know that this amount is incorrect because _____.

Please correct this error as soon as possible, reverse any finance and/or other charges related to this incorrect amount, and send me an updated and accurate statement.

I've enclosed the following documentation to verify that this charge is erroneous.

Again, please investigate this matter and correct the billing error as soon as possible.

Sincerely,

Your Name

Incorrect Late Fee

Customer Name and Address

Date

Usu-Ry Lending Co.
Attn: Billing Inquiries
1234 Main Street
Anytown, USA 12345

Re: File #1234
Usu-Ry Account #987654321

To Whom It May Concern:

This letter is to formally request that the late fee of $_____ charged to my account on _____'s statement be reversed. Additionally, I would like you to ensure that no adverse mark was made on my credit report.

I did not submit this payment late as verified by _____.

If you have any further questions in this matter, please feel free to contact me at the address listed above or at 555-555-1234.

Thank you for your prompt handling of this matter so no further action is required against your company.

Sincerely,

Your Name

Unauthorized Credit Inquiry

Customer Name and Address

Date

Overage Cellular Communications
Attn: Customer Service
1234 Main Street
Anytown, USA 12345

Re: Account #1234

To Whom It May Concern:

Upon a recent review of my credit report, I noticed a credit inquiry from your company that I did not authorize. I find this to be a very concerning matter as this has a direct effect on my ability to obtain credit.

I need you to immediately contact all three credit bureaus and have this inquiry removed due to lack of authorization.

If this matter is not promptly handled, I will report you to the Federal Trade Commission and sue for damages under the Consumer Credit Protection Act.

If you would like to discuss this inquiry further, please contact me at 555-555-1234.

Thank you in advance,

Your Name

Debt Settlement Offer

Customer Name and Address

Date

MegaBuck Credit Cards
Attn: Collections Department
1234 Main Street
Anytown, USA 12345

Re: MegaBuck Credit Card #1111222233334444

To Whom It May Concern:

I would like to propose a settlement to the above referenced account. I am offering this settlement because this may be my only chance to do so.

I am currently experiencing an extreme financial hardship that makes monthly payments very difficult. However, I have a small reserve of cash that I can use to settle this debt before my financial state declines further, as I expect it to.

I propose to settle the above referenced account for a one-time payment of $_____. In return, you fully agree to discharge this balance once and for all, as well as to refrain from reporting this as a debt settlement to the credit bureaus.

If you accept these terms, please send a signature-ready contract to me, which I will review and return with payment.

If you would like to discuss this settlement further, please feel free to contact me at 555-555-1234.

Thank you in advance,

Your Name

Appendix C

Resources

Here is a list of books, organizations, and websites that might be useful to you in your journey to eliminate debt.

Books

Clason, George. *The Richest Man in Babylon*. CreateSpace, 2008.

Dacyczyn, Amy. *The Complete Tightwad Gazette*. Villard, 1998.

Foster, Richard. *Freedom of Simplicity: Finding Harmony in a Complex World*. HarperOne, 2005.

McKay, Charles. *Extraordinary Popular Delusions and the Madness of Crowds*. Harriman House, 2003.

Stanley, Thomas, and William Danko. *The Millionaire Next Door*. Pocket Books, 1998.

Counseling and Support Services

Bankruptcy Resources

American Bar Association
www.abanet.org

National Association of Consumer Bankruptcy Attorneys
www.nacba.org

NOLO Legal Forms
www.nolo.com

U.S. Court System
www.uscourts.gov/bankruptcycourts/resources.html

Consumer Protection

Better Business Bureau (BBB)
www.bbb.org

Federal Trade Commission (FTC)
Consumer Response Center
600 Pennsylvania Avenue, NW
Washington, D.C. 20580
877-382-4357
www.ftc.gov

Privacy Rights Clearinghouse
www.PrivacyRights.org

Credit Agencies and Scoring

Equifax—Credit Report Disputes
P.O. Box 740241
Atlanta, GA 30374
www.equifax.com

Experian—Credit Report Disputes
P.O. Box 2002
Allen, TX 75013
www.experian.com

Free Annual Credit Report
Annual Credit Report Request Service
P.O. Box 105283
Atlanta, GA 30348
877-322-8228
www.annualcreditreport.com

myFICO Credit Scoring
800-319-4433
www.myFICO.com

TransUnion
P.O. Box 2000
Chester, PA 19022
www.transunion.com

Credit Card Resources

www.bankaholic.com

www.cardratings.com

www.creditcards.com

www.epinions.com/credit_cards

Credit Counseling

National Foundation for Credit Counseling
801 Roeder Road, Suite 900
Silver Spring, MD 20910
301-589-5600
www.nfcc.org

Family and Individual Counseling

American Association of Marriage and Family Therapists
112 South Alfred Street
Alexandria, VA 22314
703-838-9808
www.aamft.org

American Counseling Association
5999 Stevenson Avenue
Alexandria, VA 22304
800-347-6647
www.Counseling.org

Therapist Locator
www.TherapistLocater.net

Financial Calculators

www.bankrate.com

www.fool.com

www.kiplinger.com

www.money.com

Financial Professionals

American Institute of Certified Public Accounts (AICPA)
1211 Avenue of the Americas
New York, NY 10036
www.aicpa.org

Certified Financial Planner Boards of Standards
1425 K Street, NW, Suite 500
Washington, D.C. 20005
800-487-1497
www.cfp.net

Financial Planning Association
1600 K Street, NW, Suite 201
Washington, D.C. 20006
800-322-4237
www.fpanet.org

The Garrett Planning Network—Fee Only Financial Planner Referrals
866-260-8400
www.garrettplanningnetwork.com

Frugal Living and Discount Resources

www.beingfrugal.net

www.couponmom.com

www.flamingoworld.com

www.frugalliving.about.com

www.frugalmom.com

The Grocery Game—Grocery Discounts
www.thegrocerygame.com

Getting Off Marketing Lists

Direct Marketing Association—Stops junk mail
www.dmachoice.org/consumerassistance.php

FTC's Do Not Call List—Stops telephone solicitations
888-382-1222
www.donotcall.gov

OptOutPreScreen—Stops credit card offers
P.O. Box 600344
Jacksonville, FL 32260
888-567-8688
www.OptOutPreScreen.com

Government Assistance Programs

Food and Nutrition Services—Food stamps and other assistance
800-221-5689
www.fns.usda.gov

GovBenefits.Gov—Links to thousands of government programs
www.govbenefits.gov

Medicaid
800-633-4227
www.cms.hhs.gov

Internal Revenue Service Resources

IRS Help Line for Businesses: 800-829-4933

IRS Help Line for Individuals: 800-829-1040

IRS website: www.irs.gov

National Taxpayer Advocates: 877-777-4778

Mortgage Resources

Department of Housing and Urban Development
877-234-2717
www.hud.gov

www.epinions.com/finc-Mortgage-All

Mortgage Bankers Association
1331 L Street, NW
Washington, D.C. 20005
www.mbaa.org

Retirement Planning Resources

American Association of Retired Persons
www.aarp.org/money/financial_planning

Social Security Retirement Planning Page
www.socialsecurity.gov/retire2

Scam and Rip-Off Resources

www.fraud.org

www.infomercialscams.com

www.scambusters.org

www.snopes.com

Spending Problems

Debtors Anonymous
P.O. Box 920888
Needham, MA 02492
800-421-2383
www.debtorsanonymous.org

Student Loan Resources

www.CollegeSavings.About.com

Department of Education
800-433-3243—General
800-621-3115—Defaulted Student Loans
www.studentaid.ed.gov

www.FinAid.org

SallieMae
P.O. Box 3800
Wilkes-Barre, PA 18773
888-272-5543
www.salliemae.com

Student Loan Forgiveness Programs

Student loan forgiveness programs are perhaps one of the greatest opportunities available to eliminate a large amount of personal debt without having to change your lifestyle much, if at all. Many of these programs simply pay off portions of your student loans in return for working in an underserved profession or area. This benefit is usually in addition to the paycheck you'd normally receive from the job.

In this appendix you'll find a directory of volunteer, federal, and state-sponsored programs that help eliminate student loan debt in return for employment.

Human Services

Early Childhood Care Providers—Dept. of Education
Up to 100% of loan value
www.studentaid.ed.gov

Legal Careers

Directory of Law School Loan Forgiveness Programs
www.abanet.org/legalservices/sclaid/lrap/home.html

Major State Loan Forgiveness Programs

Arizona   www.ahela.org/loanforgivenessandrepayment

Arkansas   http://dwe.arkansas.gov/LoanForgiveness/atcslfp.htm

California   www.csac.ca.gov/doc.asp?id=111

Colorado   www.uchsc.edu/ahec/lrp/index.htm

Connecticut   www.ct.gov/dph/cwp/view.asp?a=3137&q=388024

Florida   www.floridastudentfinancialaid.org/SSFAD/home/ProgramsOffered.htm

Idaho   www.boardofed.idaho.gov/scholarships/loan.asp

Indiana   www.in.gov/isdh/20545.htm

Iowa   www.iowacollegeaid.org/commissioncentral/loanforgiveness/teacher.html

Kentucky   www.gohigherky.org/finaid/overview/conversion.asp

Maine   www.famemaine.com/education/loanprograms.asp

Maryland   www.mhec.state.md.us/financialAid/descriptions.asp

Massachusetts   www.mass.gov. Search "loan repayment"

Michigan   www.michigan.gov/mdch/0,1607,7-132-2945_40012-135399--,00.html

Mississippi   www.ihl.state.ms.us/financialaid/complete.html

New Hampshire   www.nh.gov/postsecondary/financial/WIP.html

New Mexico   www.nmstudentloans.org/borrowers/troublepaying.html

New York   www.schools.nyc.gov/teachnyc/default.htm

Ohio   www.odh.ohio.gov/odhprograms/ohs/oral/dshort/loanpgm.aspx

Oklahoma   www.ogslp.org/students/loan-discharge.shtml

Oregon   www.osac.state.or.us/wiseguy_faq.html

Pennsylvania   www.pheaa.org/loanforgiveness/index.shtml

South Dakota   www.sdbor.edu/administration/finance_administration/
EducationLoanForgivenessPrograms.htm

Texas   www.collegefortexans.com/cfbin/tofa.cfm?Kind=LFP

Utah   www.uheaa.org/forms01.html

Virginia   www.vdh.state.va.us/healthpolicy/primarycare/incentives/loanrepayment

Washington   www.hecb.wa.gov/paying/waaidprgm/waaidprgmindex.asp

West Virginia   www.wvochs.org/dr/loans.aspx

Other states   www.aft.org/tools4teachers/loan-forgiveness.htm

Medical Careers

Directory of State Loan Forgiveness Programs for Medical Professionals
http://services.aamc.org/fed_loan_pub/index.cfm

National Health Services
Over $100,000 for licensed medical clinicians
http://nhsc.bhpr.hrsa.gov/applications/lrp

NIH Repayment Program for Medical Researchers
Up to $35,000 per year with two-year commitment from student
www.lrp.nih.gov

Nursing Loan Repayment (National Health Services)
Up to 60% of your loan balance
www.bhpr.hrsa.gov/nursing/loanrepay.htm

Military

Air Force
Up to $10,000 per recruit
www.airforce.com/education/enlisted/moneyForSchool.php

Army Loan Repayment Program
$1,500 per year up to $65,000
www.hrc.army.mil/site/education/LRP.html

National Guard
Up to $20,000 in loan forgiveness for service, with commitment periods from three to
eight years
www.1800goguard.com/education/payingfor.php

Navy Loan Repayment Program
$1,500 per year up to $65,000
www.navy.com/benefits/education/payoff

Teachers and Education Professionals

Directory of State Loan Forgiveness Programs for Teachers
www.aft.org/tools4teachers/loan-forgiveness.htm

Federal FFEL and Direct Loan Forgiveness
Up to $17,500 for qualifying teachers
www.studentaid.ed.gov

Volunteer Organizations

AmeriCorps
$4,725 toward your loan for 12 months service
800-942-2677
www.americorps.org

Peace Corps.
15% to 70% of your student loan balance in return for a one- to five-year commitment
800-424-8580
www.peacecorps.gov

Volunteers in Service to America (VISTA)
$4,725 for 1,700 hours of volunteer service
www.friendsofvista.org

Index

Symbols

401(k) loans
  overview, 24-25
  payment strategies, 122
  risks, 185-186
5/1 mortgages, 16
7/1 mortgages, 16

A

accountability needs (debt
  reduction plan), 48-49
accounts, closing, 125-126
ACORN (Association of
  Community Organizations
  for Reform Now), 214
actual budgets, 78-79
adjustable-rate mortgages
  7/1 or 5/1 mortgages, 16
  balloon mortgages, 16
  overview, 16-17
  refinancing to fixed rate, 147
alimony
  overview, 27
  payment strategies, 121,
    178-179
appreciating assets, 10
assets, appreciating versus
  depreciating assets, 10
Association of Community
  Organizations for Reform
  Now. See ACORN
assumable mortgages, 151
attitude (financial attitude
  adjustments)
  borrowing, 256-257
  budgeting, 257

credit usage, 257-258
future plans, 258-260
future use of credit,
  260-262
handling emergencies, 258
time considerations,
  262-264
auto insurance, staying out of
  debt tips, 273
auto loans. See car loans
automatic stays (bankruptcy
  law), 199-200

B

back-end ratios, 41
bad versus good debts, 8-10
  appreciating versus depreci-
    ating assets, 10
  identifying needs and
    wants, 9
balance reduction plans, credit
  card strategies, 138-140
balloon mortgages, 16,
  145-146
bankruptcy
  Chapter 7, 193
  Chapter 11, 194
  Chapter 12, 194-195
  Chapter 13, 193-194
  Chapter 15, 195
  costs
    credit scores, 201
    reputation, 202
    telling lenders, 201-202
  filing process, 200-201
  laws
    automatic stays, 199-200
    debt counseling, 199

    IRS concerns, 200
    means test, 198-199
  overview, 192-193
  pros and cons, 195-197
Beacon Score, 222
billing dispute letters, 211
bills
  online bill pay option,
    113-114
  organizing paperwork
    filing, 111-112
    opening bills immedi-
      ately, 109-110
    review of details, 110
    shredding tips, 112
    transferring balances to
      Progress Chart, 110
    writing next month's
      payment now, 110-111
  payment strategies
    bad debts, 121-122
    changing, 127
    closing accounts,
      125-126
    credit score consider-
      ations, 125
    good debts, 122-123
    high-interest-rate debts,
      123-124
    large-balance debts, 125
    nondeductible-interest
      debts, 126
    roll-down method,
      118-119
    small-balance debts, 124
    stressful debts, 127
    ugly debts, 120-121
biweekly mortgage payments,
  154

borrowing money
  dealing with unexpected
    expenses, 100-101
  financial attitude adjust-
    ments, 256-257
  risks, 187-188
budgets
  actual budgets, 78-79
  components, 77
  compromise budgets, 79-80
  financial attitude adjust-
    ments, 257
  ideal budgets, 77-78
  limitations, 76
  purpose, 76
  reasons for failure, 86-88
  Three-Budget-System
    Worksheet, 80-83
  tips, 83-84
building credit myth, 287

C

canceling credit cards, 134
car loans
  breaking auto loan cycle,
    269-272
    paying yourself, 271
    stretching life of car,
      270-272
  future use of credit rules,
    262
  payment strategies, 122,
    172
    paying more than mini-
      mum payment, 173
    paying off with home
      equity loans, 174
    refinancing, 173-174
  repossession process,
    215-216
cash, 5
cash flow, controlling
  decreasing fixed expenses,
    70-72

decreasing variable
    expenses, 72-73
  discretionary income, 66-70
CCPA (Consumer Credit
  Protection Act), 209-210
cease and desist letter, 211
chain letter scams, 250-251
Chapter 7 bankruptcy, 193
Chapter 11 bankruptcy, 194
Chapter 12 bankruptcy,
  194-195
Chapter 13 bankruptcy,
  193-194
Chapter 15 bankruptcy, 195
checks, credit card risks, 189
children
    child-support debts
    overview, 27
    payment strategies, 121,
      178-179
  teaching good money skills
    avoiding guilt trips,
      281-282
    building credit myth,
      287
    co-signing loans, 288
    contentment, 284
    credit card offers, 287
    delayed gratification,
      284
    overview, 280-283
    prudence, 285
    retirement consider-
      ations, 288-289
    saving money, 286
closing accounts, 125-126
closing costs, refinancing, 149
co-signing loans, 288
collections
    Consumer Credit
      Protection Act, 209-213
    FCBA (Fair Credit
      Billing Act), 211-212,
      241

FDCPA (Fair Debt
    Collection Practices
    Act), 210
  Restriction on
    Garnishment Act, 212
  TILA (Truth in Lending
    Act), 212-213
  payment strategies, 120
college costs, 58-59
compound interest, 31-32
compromise budgets, 79-80
consolidation of debt
  credit cards, 140-141
  risks, 186-187
  student loans, 163-164
Consumer Credit Protection
  Act. See CCPA
controlling cash flow
  decreasing fixed expenses,
    70-72
  decreasing variable
    expenses, 72-73
  discretionary income
    fixed versus variable
      expenses, 67
    formula, 66-67
    increasing, 68-70
costs
  bankruptcy
    credit scores, 201
    reputation, 202
    telling lenders, 201-202
  college, 58-59
  identity theft, 233
counseling, debt, 199
credit cards, 22
  building credit myth, 287
  check risks, 189
  debt reduction plans
    balance reduction and
      debt settlement plans,
      138-140
    canceling cards, 134

consolidation of credit
cards, 140-141
lower rate negotiations,
135-136
stop using, 132-133
transferring balances to
another card, 136-137
using credit insurance,
141
using home equity to
pay off, 137-138
fees, 33-34
financial attitude adjustments, 257-258
fine print warnings, 34-35
installment purchases, 23
interest rate calculations
compound interest,
31-32
simple interest, 30-31
major companies, 22
minimum payment traps,
32-33
payment strategies, 120
retail credit cards, 22-23
rules for future use of,
260-262
car loans, 262
mortgages, 261
student loans, 261-262
teaching children good
money skills, 287
credit protection plans, risks,
246-247
credit repair scams, 247
credit reports
checking, 240
free credit reports, 246
credit scores
Beacon Score, 222
credit inquiries, 225
credit utilization, 224
debts affecting, 125
discussing, 45-46

Empirica Score, 222
Experian Plus, 221
FICO score, 220-221
formulas, 222-227
credit inquiries, 225
credit utilization, 224
length of credit history
category, 224-225
payment history, 223
types of credit used,
226-227
impact of bankruptcy on,
201
increasing, 229-230
monthly payments, 44-45
overview, 43-44, 220
Plus Score, 222
VantageScore, 221
warnings, 227-228
credit unions, 171
creditors
Consumer Credit
Protection Act, 209-213
FCBA (Fair Credit
Billing Act), 211-212
FDCPA (Fair Debt
Collection Practices
Act), 210
Restriction on
Garnishment Act, 212
TILA (Truth in Lending
Act), 212-213
e-mail warnings, 115-116
understanding, 208-209
currency transactions, get-rich
schemes, 249

D

day-trading, get-rich schemes,
249
debts
avoiding the unavoidable,
10-11

counseling, 199
credit card debts
fees, 33-34
fine print warnings,
34-35
interest rate calculations,
30-32
minimum payment traps,
32-33
denial signs, 38-39
elimination programs, 245
good versus bad debts, 8-10
appreciating versus
depreciating assets, 10
identifying needs and
wants, 9
long-term debts
mortgages, 14-18
risks, 14
student loans, 18-20
love-related debt issues,
264-265
negotiators, 246
organizing paperwork,
108-114
direct deposit options,
112-113
filing, 111-112
opening bills immedi-
ately, 109-110
paying bills online,
113-114
personal accounting
software, 114
review of details, 110
shredding tips, 112
transferring balances to
Progress Chart, 110
writing next month's
now, 110-111
reduction plans
accountability needs,
48-49
budgets, 76-88
car loans, 172-174

changing spending habits, 46-47

child support and alimony, 178-179

controlling cash flow, 66-73

credit card strategies, 132-141

credit score numbers, 43-46

dealing with unexpected expenses, 96-101

evaluation phase, 39-41

hiring professionals, 50-51

IRS debts, 180-181

legal debts, 178

medical debts, 176-177

mortgages, 144-149

opportunity costs, 54-60

payday loans, 170-172

payment strategies, 118-127

reward systems, 47

risks, 184-190

setting goals, 48

spending plans, 88-93

student loans, 158-167

tracking progress, 42-43

windfall strategy, 103

setting goals, 11-12

short-term debts

401(k) loans, 24-25

auto loans, 24

child support and alimony, 27

credit cards, 22-23

IRS, 27-28

legal debts, 26-27

medical bills, 25-26

payday loans, 25

sources, 7

statistics, 6-7

stories, 4-6

teaching children good money skills

avoiding guilt trips, 281-282

building credit myth, 287

co-signing loans, 288

contentment, 284

credit card offers, 287

delayed gratification, 284

overview, 280-283

prudence, 285

retirement consider-ations, 288-289

saving money, 286

tips for staying out of debt

breaking auto loan cycle, 269-272

emergency funds, 268-269

insurance considerations, 272-276

planning ahead, 269

stopping solicitations, 276-277

decreasing fixed expenses, 70-72

decreasing variable expenses, 72-73

defaulted loans, student loans, 166-167

consolidation, 167

loan rehabilitation, 167

deferment options, student loans, 164

delayed gratification, 47, 284

denial, signs of, 38-39

depreciating assets, 10

direct deposit options, 112-113

Direct Marketing Associations website, 276

disability insurance, 273-274

discretionary income

fixed versus variable expenses, 67

formula, 66-67

increasing, 68-70

E

e-mailing creditors, warnings, 115-116

Eliminate ASAP, 123

emergency funds

financial attitude adjust-ments, 258

tips for staying out of debt, 268-269

Empirica Score, 222

envelope system, spending plan, 90

evaluation phase, debt reduc-tion plan, 39-41

loan qualifications, 40-41

monthly debt service, 40

eviction process, 216-217

expenses

dealing with unexpected expenses

borrowing, 100-101

learning from experi-ence, 101

overview, 96-98

paying in full, 99

payment plan requests, 99-100

fixed expenses

decreasing, 70-72

versus variable expenses, 67

variable expenses, decreas-ing, 72-73

Experian Plus, 221

F

FACTA (Fair and Accurate Credit Transaction Act), 242
failed budgets, 86-88
Fair and Accurate Credit Transaction Act. *See* FACTA
Fair Credit Billing Act. *See* FCBA
Fair Debt Collection Practices Act. *See* FDCPA
FCBA (Fair Credit Billing Act), 211-212, 241
FDCPA (Fair Debt Collection Practices Act), 210
Federal Do-Not-Call list, 277
Federal Trade Commission, 218
fees
  nonsufficient fund fees, 66
  overview, 33-34
FICO score, 220-221
filing paperwork, 111-112
filing process, bankruptcy, 200-201
financial attitude adjustments
  borrowing, 256-257
  budgeting, 257
  credit usage, 257-258
  future plans, 258-260
  future use of credit, 260-262
    car loans, 262
    mortgages, 261
    student loans, 261-262
  handling emergencies, 258
  time considerations, 262-264
fine print warnings, 34-35
fixed expenses
  decreasing, 70-72
  versus variable expenses, 67

fixed-rate mortgages
  overview, 15-16
  refinancing options, 147
food costs, getting help with, 172
forbearances, student loans, 164
foreclosures, 152-153
forgiveness programs, student loans, 165-166
formulas
  credit scores, 222-227
    credit inquiries, 225
    credit utilization, 224
    length of credit history category, 224-225
    payment history, 223
    types of credit used, 226-227
  discretionary income, 66-67
free credit reports, 246
front-end ratios, 41
future goals
  college costs, 58-59
  retirement
    overview, 55-56
    strategies, 57
future use of credit rules, 260-262
  car loans, 262
  mortgages, 261
  student loans, 261-262

G

generating revenue from home, 152
get-rich schemes
  day-trading and currency transactions, 249
  multilevel marketing, 248
  real estate, 248-249

goals
  future goals
    college costs, 58-59
    retirement, 55-57
  setting, 11-12, 48
good versus bad debts, 8-10
  appreciating versus depreciating assets, 10
  identifying needs and wants, 9
government student loan programs, 19
GuideStar website, 252

H

health and sanity, opportunity costs, 60
health insurance, staying out of debt tips, 272-273
high-interest-rate debts, payment strategies, 123-124
hiring professionals, 50-51
home equity line of credit
  car loans and, 174
  payment strategies, 122
  using to pay off credit card debts, 137-138
homeowner's insurance, staying out of debt tips, 274-275
homes
  eviction process, 216-217
  selling
    mortgage strategies, 151
    short sales, 151
HUD (U.S. Department of Housing and Urban Development), 152

I-J-K

ideal budgets, 77-78
identity theft
  costs, 233
  process, 234-235

protection tips, 235-240
  monitoring your iden-
    tity, 239-240
  phishing, 237-239
  spoofing, 239
  risks, 232-233
  victim steps, 241-242
impulsive spending habits,
  87-88
income
  discretionary income
    fixed versus variable
      expenses, 67
    formula, 66-67
    increasing, 68-70
  generating revenue from
    home, 152
inquiries, credit, 225
installment debts
  credit cards, 23
  IRS debts, 181
  payment strategies, 121
insurance
  PMI (Primary Mortgage
    Insurance), 154-155
  staying out of debt tips
    auto insurance, 273
    disability insurance,
      273-274
    health insurance,
      272-273
    homeowner's insurance,
      274-275
    liability insurance, 275
    life insurance, 275-276
    long-term care insur-
      ance, 274
  using credit insurance, 141
interest
  nondeductible-interest
    debts, 126
  paying less interest, 59-60
  usury laws, 214
interest-only loans, 17

interest rate calculations
  compound interest, 31-32
  simple interest, 30-31
interest rates
  high-interest-rate debts,
    123-124
  lowering on credit cards,
    135-136
  mortgage adjustments, 145
IRS debts
  bankruptcy laws, 200
  overview, 27-28
  payment strategies, 120
    installment agreement,
      181
    offers in compromise,
      181
    penalty systems, 180-181

L

large-balance debts, 125
laws
  bankruptcy
    automatic stays, 199-200
    debt counseling, 199
    IRS concerns, 200
    means test, 198-199
  Consumer Credit
    Protection Act
    FCBA (Fair Credit
      Billing Act), 211-212,
      241
    FDCPA (Fair Debt
      Collection Practices
      Act), 210
    Restriction on
      Garnishment Act, 212
    TILA (Truth in Lending
      Act), 212, 213
  predatory lending laws,
    213-214
  reporting violations, 218
  usury laws, 214

legal debts
  overview, 26-27
  payment strategies, 178
lenders
  choosing, 150
  predatory lending laws,
    213-214
liability insurance, 275
life insurance, 275-276
loans
  401(k) loans, 24-25
  car loans
    breaking auto loan cycle,
      269-272
    future use of credit rules,
      262
    overview, 24
  co-signing, 288
  compound interest loans,
    31-32
  fees, 33-34
  fine print warnings, 34-35
  minimum payment traps,
    32-33
  mortgages, 14-18
    adjustable-rate mort-
      gages, 16-17
    fixed-rate mortgages, 15-16
    interest-only loans, 17
    payment-optional loans,
      17-18
  pawnshop loans, 189-190
  payday loans, 25
  payment strategies
    car loans, 172-174
    payday loans, 170-172
  pre-approved, 40-41
  pre-qualified, 40-41
  retirement plan loans,
    185-186
  simple interest loans, 30-31
  student loans, 18
    defaulted loans, 166-167
    future use of credit rules,
      261-262

government programs, 19
Perkins Loans, 159
PLUS Loans, 159-160
private loans, 19-20, 160
reducing loan payments, 162-166
repayment options, 161-162
Stafford loans, 158-159
tax refund loans, 189
long-term care insurance, 274
long-term debts
mortgages, 14-18
adjustable-rate mortgages, 16-17
fixed-rate mortgages, 15-16
interest-only loans, 17
payment-optional loans, 17-18
risks, 14
student loans, 18-20
government programs, 19
private loans, 19-20
long-term mortgages, refinancing options, 147
love-related debt issues, 264-265

M

major credit card companies, 22
means test, bankruptcy law, 198-199
Medicaid, 177
medical debts
overview, 25-26
payment strategies, 121, 176-177
Medicare, 177
Microsoft Money, 114

minimum payments
car loans, 173
traps, 32-33
money skills, teaching to children
avoiding guilt trips, 281-282
building credit myth, 287
co-signing loans, 288
contentment, 284
credit card offers, 287
delayed gratification, 284
overview, 280-283
prudence, 285
retirement considerations, 288-289
saving money, 286
monitoring your identity, 239-240
checking credit reports, 240
credit monitoring services, 240
reviewing statements, 240
monthly debt services, 40
monthly payments, credit scores, 44-45
mortgages, 14
adjustable-rate mortgages, 16-17
7/1 or 5/1 mortgages, 16
balloon mortgages, 16
debt reduction plans
assumable mortgages, 151
balloon payments, 145-146
biweekly payments, 154
foreclosing, 152-153
generating revenue from home, 152
interest rate adjustments, 145
overview, 144-145
PMI (Primary Mortgage Insurance), 154-155

principal considerations, 146
refinancing, 146-150
selling home, 151
short sales, 151
talking with lenders, 151
fixed-rate mortgages, 15-16
future use of credit rules, 261
interest-only loans, 17
payment-optional loans, 17-18
payment strategies, 123
multilevel marketing (get-rich scheme), 248

N

negative amortization loans, 17-18
negotiators (debt negotiators), 246
Nigerian 419 scam, 250
nondeductible-interest debts, payment strategies, 126
nonsufficient fund fees, 66

O

offers in compromise (IRS debts), 181
online bill pay options, 113-114
opportunity costs
future goals
college costs, 58-59
retirement, 55-57
health and sanity, 60
overview, 54
paying less interest, 59-60
organizing debt
direct deposit options, 112-113
paperwork, 108-112

filing, 111-112
opening bills immediately, 109-110
review of details, 110
shredding tips, 112
transferring balances to Progress Chart, 110
writing next month's payment now, 110-111
paying bills online, 113-114
personal accounting software, 114
origination fees, refinancing, 149

P

paperwork, organizing, 108-112
filing, 111-112
opening bills immediately, 109-110
review of details, 110
shredding tips, 112
transferring balances to Progress Chart, 110
writing next month's payment now, 110-111
pawnshop loans, 189-190
paychecks, direct deposit options, 112-113
payday loans
overview, 25
payment strategies, 120, 170
breaking the cycle, 170-171
getting help with food costs, 172
paying bills online, 113-114
payment history, credit scores, 223

payment plan requests, dealing with unexpected expenses, 99-100
payment strategies
bad debts, 121-122
car loans, 172-174
paying more than minimum payment, 173
paying off with home equity loans, 174
refinancing, 173-174
changing, 127
child support and alimony, 178-179
closing accounts, 125-126
credit card strategies
balance reduction and debt settlement plans, 138-140
canceling cards, 134
consolidation of credit cards, 140-141
lower rate negotiations, 135-136
stop using, 132-133
transferring balances to another card, 136-137
using credit insurance, 141
using home equity to pay off, 137-138
credit score considerations, 125
good debts, 122-123
high-interest-rate debts, 123-124
IRS debts
installment agreement, 181
offers in compromise, 181
penalty systems, 180-181
large-balance debts, 125
legal debts, 178
medical debts, 176-177

mortgage strategies
assumable mortgages, 151
balloon payments, 145-146
biweekly payments, 154
foreclosures, 152-153
generating revenue from home, 152
interest rate adjustments, 145
overview, 144-145
PMI (Primary Mortgage Insurance), 154-155
principal considerations, 146
refinancing, 146-150
selling home, 151
short sales, 151
talking with lenders, 151
nondeductible-interest debts, 126
payday loans
breaking the cycle, 170-171
getting help with food costs, 172
risks
borrowing money, 187-188
credit card checks, 189
debt consolidation, 186-187
important questions, 184
pawnshop loans, 189-190
retirement plan loans, 185-186
tax refund loans, 189
under the table payments, 190
roll-down method, 118-119
small-balance debts, 124
stressful debts, 127

student loans
  defaulted loans, 166-167
  Perkins Loans, 159
  PLUS Loans, 159-160
  private loans, 160
  reducing loan payments,
    162-166
  repayment options,
    161-162
  Stafford Loans, 158-159
  ugly debts, 120-121
payment-optional loans, 17-18
penalty systems, IRS debts,
  180-181
Perkins Loans, 159
personal accounting software,
  114
phishing, identity theft,
  237-239
plans, debt reduction plans
  accountability needs, 48-49
  budgets
    actual budgets, 78-79
    components, 77
    compromise budgets,
      79-80
    ideal budgets, 77-78
    limitations, 76
    purpose, 76
    reasons for failure, 86-88
    Three-Budget-System
      Worksheet, 80-83
    tips, 83-84
  car loans, 172-174
    paying more than mini-
      mum payment, 173
    paying off with home
      equity loans, 174
    refinancing, 173-174
  changing spending habits,
    46-47
  child support and alimony,
    178-179
  controlling cash flow
    decreasing fixed
      expenses, 70-72

decreasing variable
    expenses, 72-73
  discretionary income,
    66-70
credit card strategies
  balance reduction and
    debt settlement plans,
    138-140
  canceling cards, 134
  consolidation of credit
    cards, 140-141
  lower rate negotiations,
    135-136
  stop using, 132-133
  transferring balances to
    another card, 136-137
  using credit insurance,
    141
  using home equity to
    pay off, 137-138
credit score numbers
  discussing, 45-46
  monthly payments,
    44-45
  overview, 43-44
dealing with unexpected
  expenses
  borrowing, 100-101
  learning from experi-
    ence, 101
  overview, 96-98
  paying in full, 99
  payment plan requests,
    99-100
evaluation phase, 39-41
  loan qualifications,
    40-41
  monthly debt service, 40
hiring professionals, 50-51
IRS debts
  installment agreement,
    181
  offers in compromise,
    181
  penalty systems, 180-181

legal debts, 178
medical debts, 176-177
mortgage strategies
  assumable mortgages,
    151
  balloon payments,
    145-146
  biweekly payments, 154
  foreclosures, 152-153
  generating revenue from
    home, 152
  interest rate adjustments,
    145
  overview, 144-145
  PMI (Primary Mortgage
    Insurance), 154-155
  principal considerations,
    146
  refinancing, 146-150
  selling home, 151
  short sales, 151
  talking with lenders, 151
opportunity costs, 54-60
  future goals, 55-59
  health and sanity, 60
  paying less interest,
    59-60
payday loans
  breaking the cycle,
    170-171
  getting help with food
    costs, 172
payment strategies
  bad debts, 121-122
  changing, 127
  closing accounts,
    125-126
  credit score consider-
    ations, 125
  good debts, 122-123
  high-interest-rate debts,
    123-124
  large-balance debts, 125
  nondeductible-interest
    debts, 126

roll-down method, 118-119
small-balance debts, 124
stressful debts, 127
ugly debts, 120-121
reward systems, 47
risks
  borrowing money, 187-188
  credit card checks, 189
  debt consolidation, 186-187
  important questions, 184
  pawnshop loans, 189-190
  retirement plan loans, 185-186
  tax refund loans, 189
  under-the-table payments, 190
setting goals, 48
spending plans, 88-93
  adjustments, 93
  creating, 89-90
  envelope system, 90
  three-account system, 92-93
  two-account system, 90
student loans
  defaulted loans, 166-167
  Perkins Loans, 159
  PLUS Loans, 159-160
  private loans, 160
  reducing loan payments, 162-166
  repayment options, 161-162
  Stafford Loans, 158-159
tips for staying out of debt
  breaking auto loan cycle, 269-272
  emergency funds, 268-269

insurance considerations, 272-276
planning ahead, 269
stopping solicitations, 276-277
tracking progress, 42-43
windfall strategy, 103
PLUS Loans, 159-160
Plus Score, 222
PMI (Primary Mortgage Insurance), 154-155
points (refinancing), 149
pre-approved loans, 40-41
pre-qualified loans, 40-41
predatory lending laws, 213-214
Primary Mortgage Insurance. *See* PMI
principal, mortgage strategies, 146
private student loans, 19-20, 160
professionals, hiring, 50-51
progress, tracking, 42-43
Progress Charts, transferring balances to, 110
protection tips
  identity theft, 235-240
    monitoring your identity, 239-240
    phishing, 237-239
    spoofing, 239
  scams, 251-252

Q-R

Quicken, 114

real estate, 14
  adjustable-rate mortgages, 16-17
    7/1 or 5/1 mortgages, 16
    balloon mortgages, 16

fixed-rate mortgages, 15-16
get-rich schemes, 248-249
interest-only loans, 17
payment-optional loans, 17-18
reducing loan payments, student loans, 162-166
  consolidation, 163-164
  deferment options, 164
  forbearances, 164
  forgiveness programs, 165-166
reduction plans, debt reduction
  accountability needs, 48-49
  budgets
    actual budgets, 78-79
    components, 77
    compromise budgets, 79-80
    ideal budgets, 77-78
    limitations, 76
    purpose, 76
    reasons for failure, 86-88
    Three-Budget-System Worksheet, 80-83
    tips, 83-84
  car loans, 172-174
    paying more than minimum payment, 173
    paying off with home equity loans, 174
    refinancing, 173-174
  changing spending habits, 46-47
  child support and alimony, 178-179
  controlling cash flow
    decreasing fixed expenses, 70-72
    decreasing variable expenses, 72-73
    discretionary income, 66-70

credit card strategies
  balance reduction and debt settlement plans, 138-140
  canceling cards, 134
  consolidation of credit cards, 140-141
  lower rate negotiations, 135-136
  stop using, 132-133
  transferring balances to another card, 136-137
  using credit insurance, 141
  using home equity to pay off, 137-138
credit score numbers
  discussing, 45-46
  monthly payments, 44-45
  overview, 43-44
dealing with unexpected expenses
  borrowing, 100-101
  learning from experience, 101
  overview, 96-98
  paying in full, 99
  payment plan requests, 99-100
evaluation phase, 39-41
  loan qualifications, 40-41
  monthly debt service, 40
hiring professionals, 50-51
IRS debts
  installment agreement, 181
  offers in compromise, 181
  penalty systems, 180-181
legal debts, 178
medical debts, 176-177

mortgage strategies
  assumable mortgages, 151
  balloon payments, 145-146
  biweekly payments, 154
  foreclosures, 152-153
  generating revenue from home, 152
  interest rate adjustments, 145
  overview, 144-145
  PMI (Primary Mortgage Insurance), 154-155
  principal considerations, 146
  refinancing, 146-150
  selling home, 151
  short sales, 151
  talking with lenders, 151
opportunity costs, 54-60
  future goals, 55-59
  health and sanity, 60
  paying less interest, 59-60
payday loans
  breaking the cycle, 170-171
  getting help with food costs, 172
payment strategies
  bad debts, 121-122
  changing, 127
  closing accounts, 125-126
  credit score considerations, 125
  good debts, 122-123
  high-interest-rate debts, 123-124
  large-balance debts, 125
  nondeductible-interest debts, 126
  roll-down method, 118-119

small-balance debts, 124
stressful debts, 127
ugly debts, 120-121
reward systems, 47
risks
  borrowing money, 187-188
  credit card checks, 189
  debt consolidation, 186-187
  important questions, 184
  pawnshop loans, 189-190
  retirement plan loans, 185-186
  tax refund loans, 189
  under-the-table payments, 190
setting goals, 48
spending plans, 88-93
  adjustments, 93
  creating, 89-90
  envelope system, 90
  three-account system, 92-93
  two-account system, 90
student loans
  defaulted loans, 166-167
  Perkins Loans, 159
  PLUS Loans, 159-160
  private loans, 160
  reducing loan payments, 162-166
  repayment options, 161-162
  Stafford Loans, 158-159
tips for staying out of debt
  breaking auto loan cycle, 269-272
  emergency funds, 268-269
  insurance considerations, 272-276
  planning ahead, 269

stopping solicitations, 276-277
tracking progress, 42-43
windfall strategy, 103
refinancing
car loans, 173-174
mortgages, 146-150
adjustable rate to fixed rate, 147
choosing a lender, 150
closing costs, 149
origination fees, 149
points, 149
short-term to long-term, 147
timing, 148-149
rehabilitation, loan rehabilitation, 167
repayment options, student loans, 161-162
repossession process, 215-216
Restriction on Garnishment Act, 212
retail credit cards, 22-23
retirement
goals
overview, 55-56
strategies, 57
loan risks, 185-186
teaching children good money skills, 288-289
reviewing statements, identity theft, 240
reward systems, debt reduction plan, 47
risks
debt reduction strategy
borrowing money, 187-188
credit card checks, 189
debt consolidation, 186-187
important questions, 184
pawnshop loans, 189-190

retirement plan loans, 185-186
tax refund loans, 189
under-the-table payments, 190
identity theft, 232-233
long-term debts, 14
scams
chain letters, 250-251
credit protection, 246-247
credit repair, 247
debt elimination programs, 245
debt negotiators, 246
free credit reports, 246
get-rich schemes, 248-249
Nigerian 419 scam, 250
overview, 244
seminars and workshops, 247-248
roll-down method, payment strategy, 118-119
rules for future use of credit, 260-262
car loans, 262
mortgages, 261
student loans, 261-262

S

saving money
teaching children good money skills, 286
windfall strategies, 102-103
scams
chain letters, 250-251
credit protection, 246-247
credit repair, 247
debt elimination programs, 245
debt negotiators, 246
free credit reports, 246

get-rich schemes
day-trading and currency transactions, 249
multilevel marketing, 248
real estate, 248-249
Nigerian 419 scam, 250
overview, 244
seminars and workshops, 247-248
taking action against, 251-252
scores, credit scores
Beacon Score, 222
Empirica Score, 222
Experian Plus, 221
FICO score, 220-221
formulas, 222-227
credit inquiries, 225
credit utilization, 224
length of credit history category, 224-225
payment history, 223
types of credit used, 226-227
increasing, 229-230
overview, 220
Plus Score, 222
VantageScore, 221
warnings, 227-228
SCRA (Servicemembers' Civil Relief Act), 200
selling homes
mortgage strategies, 151
short sales, 151
seminars and workshops, scams to avoid, 247-248
Servicemembers' Civil Relief Act. *See* SCRA
services, credit monitoring services, 240
setting goals, 11-12, 48
settlement plans, credit card strategies, 138-140

shopping online, warnings, 116
short sales, 151
short-term debts
  401(k) loans, 24-25
  child support and alimony, 27
  credit cards
    auto loans, 24
    installment purchases, 23
    major companies, 22
    retail credit cards, 22-23
  IRS, 27-28
  legal debts, 26-27
  medical bills, 25-26
  payday loans, 25
shredding tips, 112
signs of denial, 38-39
simple interest loans, 30-31
small-balance debts, payment strategies, 124
software, personal accounting software, 114
solicitations, staying out of debt tips, 276-277
sources
  debts, 7
  windfalls, 97
spending
  changing habits, 46-47
  creating spending plans, 88-90
  impulsive spending habits, 87-88
spoofing, identity theft, 239
Stafford loans, 158-159
statements, reviewing, 240
statistics, 6-7
staying out of debt tips
  breaking auto loan cycle, 269-272
    paying yourself, 271
    stretching life of car, 270-272

emergency funds, 268-269
insurance considerations
  auto insurance, 273
  disability insurance, 273-274
  health insurance, 272-273
  homeowner's insurance, 274-275
  liability insurance, 275
  life insurance, 275-276
  long-term care insurance, 274
planning ahead, 269
stopping solicitations, 276-277
stories of debt, 4-6
strategies
  dealing with unexpected expenses
    borrowing, 100-101
    learning from experience, 101
    overview, 96-98
    paying in full, 99
    payment plan requests, 99-100
  payment strategies
    bad debts, 121-122
    car loans, 172-174
    changing, 127
    child support and alimony, 178-179
    closing accounts, 125-126
    credit score considerations, 125
    good debts, 122-123
    high-interest-rate debts, 123-124
    IRS debts, 180-181
    large-balance debts, 125
    legal debts, 178
    medical debts, 176-177

    nondeductible-interest debts, 126
    payday loans, 170-172
    risks, 184-190
    roll-down method, 118-119
    small-balance debts, 124
    stressful debts, 127
    ugly debts, 120-121
  retirement plans, 57
  windfall strategies
    debt reduction, 103
    developing a formula, 104
    saving money, 102
    seeking assistance, 105
stressful debts, payment strategies, 127
student loans, 18
  defaulted loans, 166-167
  future use of credit rules, 261-262
  government programs, 19
  payment strategies, 122
  Perkins Loans, 159-160
  private loans, 19-20, 160
  reducing loan payments, 162-166
    consolidation, 163-164
    deferment options, 164
    forbearances, 164
    forgiveness programs, 165-166
  repayment options, 161-162
  Stafford Loans, 158-159

T

tax refund loans, risks, 189
teaching children good money skills
  avoiding guilt trips, 281-282

building credit myth, 287
co-signing loans, 288
contentment, 284
credit card offers, 287
delayed gratification, 284
overview, 280-283
prudence, 285
retirement considerations, 288-289
saving money, 286
technology warnings
e-mailing creditors, 115-116
online shopping, 116
online statements, 115
three-account system, spending plan, 92-93
Three-Budget-System Worksheet, 80-83
TILA (Truth in Lending Act), 212-213
timing refinancing, 148-149
tips
budgets, 83-84
eviction process, 216-217
financial attitude adjustments, 258-260
keeping utilities on, 217-218
repossession process, 215-216
rules for future use of credit, 260-262
car loans, 262
mortgages, 261
student loans, 261-262
scams to avoid, 244-252
chain letters, 250-251
credit protection, 246-247
credit repair, 247
debt elimination programs, 245
debt negotiators, 246

free credit reports, 246
get-rich schemes, 248-249
Nigerian 419 scam, 250
seminars and workshops, 247-248
taking action against, 251-252
staying out of debt
breaking auto loan cycle, 269-272
emergency funds, 268-269
insurance considerations, 272-276
planning ahead, 269
stopping solicitations, 276-277
tracking progress, 42-43
transferring balances, credit card strategies, 136-137
Truth in Lending Act. *See* TILA
two-account system (spending plan), 90

U

U.S. Department of Housing and Urban Development. *See* HUD
ugly debts, payment strategy, 120-121
under-the-table payments, risks, 190
unexpected expenses, dealing with
borrowing, 100-101
learning from experience, 101
overview, 96-98
paying in full, 99
payment plan requests, 99-100

usury laws, 214
utilities, tips for keeping on, 217-218

V

VantageScore, 221
variable expenses
decreasing, 72-73
versus fixed expenses, 67
violations, reporting, 218

W-X-Y-Z

warnings
credit reports, 227-228
technology
e-mailing creditors, 115-116
online shopping, 116
online statements, 115
websites
Direct Marketing Association, 276
GuideStar, 252
windfalls
common sources, 97
strategies
debt reduction, 103
developing a formula, 104
saving money, 102
seeking assistance, 105
worksheets, Three-Budget-System Worksheet, 80-83